iPhone® For Seniors

9th Edition

by Dwight Spivey

for
dummies®
A Wiley Brand

iPhone® For Seniors For Dummies®, 9th Edition

Published by: John Wiley & Sons, Inc., 111 River Street, Hoboken, NJ 07030-5774, www.wiley.com

Copyright © 2020 by John Wiley & Sons, Inc., Hoboken, New Jersey

Published simultaneously in Canada

For general information on our other products and services, please contact our Customer Care Department within the U.S. at 877-762-2974, outside the U.S. at 317-572-3993, or fax 317-572-4002. For technical support, please visit https://hub.wiley.com/community/support/dummies.

Wiley publishes in a variety of print and electronic formats and by print-on-demand. Some material included with standard print versions of this book may not be included in e-books or in print-on-demand. If this book refers to media such as a CD or DVD that is not included in the version you purchased, you may download this material at http://booksupport.wiley.com. For more information about Wiley products, visit www.wiley.com.

Library of Congress Control Number: 2019952063

ISBN 978-1-119-60761-8 (pbk); ISBN 978-1-119-60767-0 (ebk); ISBN 978-1-119-60771-7

Manufactured in the United States of America

V10015331_110219

Contents at a Glance

Table of Contents

Introduction

I f you bought this book (or are even thinking about buying it), you've probably already made the decision to buy an iPhone. The iPhone is designed to be easy to use, but you can still spend hours exploring the preinstalled apps, finding out how to change settings, and figuring out how to sync the device to your computer or through iCloud. I've invested those hours so that you don't have to — and I've added advice and tips for getting the most out of your iPhone.

This book helps you get going with your iPhone quickly and painlessly so that you can move directly to the fun part.

About This Book

This book is specifically written for mature people like you, folks who may be relatively new to using a smartphone and want to discover the basics of buying an iPhone, making and receiving phone calls, working with its preinstalled apps, and getting on the Internet. In writing this book, I've tried to consider the types of activities that might interest someone who is 50 years old or older and picking up an iPhone for the first time.

Foolish Assumptions

This book is organized by sets of tasks. These tasks start from the beginning, assuming that you've never laid your hands on an iPhone, and guide you through basic steps using nontechnical language.

This book covers going online using either a Wi-Fi or cellular connection, browsing the web (Chapter 12), and checking email (Chapter 13). I'm also assuming that you'll want to use the Apple Books e-reader app, so I cover its features in Chapter 17. Not to mention covering other great things you can do with your iPhone, such as monitoring use of your iPhone and its apps (Chapter 5), discovering new apps (Chapter 14), taking and sharing your photos and videos (Chapters 19 and 20, respectively), tracking your health (Chapter 24), and much more!

Icons Used in This Book

Icons are tiny pictures in the margin of pages that call your attention to special advice or information, such as:

TIP

These brief pieces of advice help you to take a skill further or provide alternate ways of getting things done.

WARNING

Heads up! This may be difficult or expensive to undo.

REMEMBER

This is information that's so useful, it's worth keeping in your head, not just on your bookshelf.

TECHNICAL STUFF

Maybe this isn't essential information, but it's neat to know.

Beyond the Book

There's even more iPhone information on www.dummies.com. This book's Cheat Sheet offers a list of General settings, Mail, Contacts, and Calendar settings to be aware of, and the settings you can control for browsing in Safari. To get to the cheat sheet, go to www.dummies. com, then type *iPhone For Seniors For Dummies Cheat Sheet* in the Search box. This is also where you'll find any significant updates or changes that occur between editions of this book.

Where to Go from Here

You can work through this book from beginning to end or simply open a chapter to solve a problem or acquire a specific new skill whenever you need it. The steps in every task quickly get you to where you want to go, without a lot of technical explanation.

At the time I wrote this book, all the information it contained was accurate for the iPhone SE, 6s and 6s Plus, 7 and 7 Plus, 8 and 8 Plus, X (the Roman numeral for ten), XR, XS, XS Max, 11, 11 Pro, and 11 Pro Max along with version 13 of iOS (the operating system used by the iPhone). Apple is likely to introduce new iPhone models and versions of iOS between book editions. If you've bought a new iPhone and found that its hardware, user interface, or other software on your computer mentioned in this book looks a little different, be sure to check out what Apple has to say at www.apple.com/iphone. You'll no doubt find updates there on the company's latest releases.

1

Getting to Know Your iPhone

IN THIS PART . . .

Meeting your new iPhone

Navigating iPhone's interface

Customizing your settings

Activating special features

Monitoring how your iPhone is being used

IN THIS CHAPTER

» Discover what's new in
  iPhones and iOS 13

» Choose the right iPhone for
  you and find where to buy it

» Understand what you need to
  use your iPhone

» Explore what's in the box

» Take a look at the gadget

Chapter **1**

Buying Your iPhone

Y ou've read about it. You've seen the lines at Apple Stores on the day a new version of the iPhone is released. You're so intrigued that you've decided to get your own iPhone to have a smartphone that offers much more than the ability to make and receive calls. iPhone also offers lots of fun apps, such as games and exercise trackers; allows you to explore the online world; lets you read e-books, magazines, and other periodicals; allows you to take and organize photos and videos; plays music and movies, and a lot more.

Trust me: You've made a good decision, because the iPhone redefines the mobile phone experience in an exciting way. It's also an absolutely perfect fit for seniors.

In this chapter, you learn about the advantages of the iPhone, as well as where to buy this little gem and associated data plans from providers. After you have one in your hands, I help you explore what's in the box and get an overview of the little buttons and slots you'll encounter — luckily, the iPhone has very few of them.

Discover the Newest iPhones and iOS 13

Apple's iPhone gets its features from a combination of hardware and its software operating system (called iOS, which is short for iPhone operating system). The most current version of the operating system is iOS 13. It's helpful to understand which new features the latest models and iOS 13 bring to the table (all of which are covered in more detail in this book).

Apple's latest additions to the iPhone family are the iPhone 11, 11 Pro, and 11 Pro Max. Like their predecessors, they are highly advanced smartphones that leave competitors in the dust. They also signal that Apple has no plans to include the Home button in future models, which is something seasoned iPhone X and newer model users have come to embrace. Here are some of the key features of the latest iPhone models:

» **An A13 chip:** Each of the three new iPhone models includes the new A13 chip. The truly innovative tech in these models demands a processor that can handle some heavy lifting while still being able to answer calls and retrieve email.

» **Dual SIM technology (nano-SIMs and eSIMs):** These newest iPhone models support the use of both nano-SIMs and eSIMS. Every cellphone uses a chip called a SIM that allows it to work with cellular networks. Traditionally, SIMs (which are nano-SIMs in the iPhone 11, 11 Pro, and 11 Pro Max) are small cards installed in your iPhone by you or your cellular provider. The use of SIMs makes switching providers a bit of an ordeal because each SIM is wired for only a specific network. However, eSIMs are chips embedded into your iPhone that will never need to be changed out and are compatible with any provider, allowing you to easily switch cellular providers by scanning a code or using an app from your cellular provider. You'll want to discuss this option with your cellular provider when your purchase a new iPhone model. Other benefits of dual SIMS are that you can have more than one number on your iPhone (perhaps one could be personal and the other for work); you're able to more easily add local plans when you travel; and you can even have separate voice and data plans.

- » **Splash, water, and dust resistance:** Your new iPhone 11, 11 Pro, or 11 Pro Max is resistant to damage caused by water splashing onto it or from dust collecting within it.

  You might consider acquiring AppleCare+, which is Apple's extended warranty, currently priced at $149 for iPhone 11, or $199 for iPhone 11 Pro and 11 Pro Max. AppleCare+ does cover up to two incidents of accidental damage, which could more than cover the cost of repairing your iPhone without it. You can also get AppleCare+ with Theft and Loss coverage for $100 more, regardless of the model.

  Now, you don't want to take your iPhone 11 Pro or 11 Pro Max deep-sea diving, but it's likely to survive submersion in about 4 meters of water for up to 30 minutes. The iPhone 11 is rated at about 2 meters of water for up to 30 minutes. Mind you, these numbers have been tested in labs and aren't based on real-world conditions. In other words, if your iPhone 11 model gets wet, it's much more likely to survive the ordeal than older iPhone iterations, but it still isn't something you'd like to see happen to your expensive investment.

- » **Glass body and wireless charging:** iPhone 11 models are comprised of an all-glass body (with a tiny sliver of stainless steel around the edges to hold it all together), allowing a beautiful appearance and wireless charging. The glass is also the most durable of that used in any smartphone ever, according to Apple.

  Don't read that as unbreakable. Cases are still a good — no, make that a great — idea. As a matter of fact, Apple has a line of cases that not only protect your iPhone but also allow for wireless charging.

- » **Edge-to-Edge display:** iPhone 11 models sport edge-to-edge displays, meaning there's nothing else on the front of your iPhone but screen. Which brings me to my next point.

- » **No Home button:** As I previously mentioned, the method you've used for a decade now to return to the Home screen is now a thing of the past with iPhone X and newer models. You simply swipe up from the bottom of the screen to provide the same effect as pressing the Home button. This also means that Touch ID as an unlocking method is now relegated to older iPhones.

» **Facial Recognition:** Touch ID is replaced on iPhone X models and newer with Face ID. Using Face ID and the front-facing camera, your iPhone 11 model unlocks when it recognizes your face.

Any iPhone model from the iPhone SE forward can use most features of iOS 13 if you update the operating system (discussed in detail in Chapter 3); this book is based on version 13 of iOS. This update to the operating system adds many features, including (but definitely not limited to)

» **Performance enhancements:** Apple promises that iOS 13 will increase the speed and performance of your iPhone, going all the way back as far as iPhone SE. From apps to keyboards to taking pictures — everything gets a speed upgrade.

» **Siri improvements:** Siri just keeps getting better. Siri can now speak in more natural tones and cadence, thanks to new software rendering capabilities. Siri can also give you more personalized information, including being able to find event information and reminders in other apps. And Siri can now play audio files from third-party app providers.

» **Dark Mode has arrived:** With iOS 13, you have the option of using Dark Mode, which gives the iOS color scheme from light to dark. Dark Mode is especially helpful in low-light situations, or when you don't want to disturb others with the bright light from your iPhone's screen.

» **Accessibility enhancements:** Voice Control allows you to control your iPhone entirely with your voice; dictation is much more accurate; processing of voice commands happens right on your iPhone (as opposed to being transmitted to an online location and then returned to your iPhone); Numbers and Grids help to make more accurate selections; and the list goes on.

» **Upgrades to Photos:** The Photos app receives some love in iOS 13, allowing for faster and more accurate searches of your Photos Library, better organization, better filters, enhanced and non-destructive video editing, and other features make this a great addition.

» **All new Maps:** iOS 13 introduces the new Maps app, which has been completely reconstructed and comes loaded with amazing features and awesome attention to landmark details. Junction View helps make sure you're in the right lane for turns, but the Look Around feature is worth the price of admission alone. Look Around lets you see a 360-degree three-dimensional view of locations, enabling you to know your way around before you even get there.

TIP

Don't need or use all the built-in apps? You can remove them from your Home screen. When you remove a built-in app from your Home screen, you aren't deleting it — you're hiding it. This is due to security reasons that are beyond the scope of this book. However, the built-in apps take up very little of your iPhone's storage space, and they can easily be added back to your Home screen by searching for them in the App Store and tapping the Get button.

These are but a very few of the improvements made to the latest version of iOS. I suggest visiting www.apple.com/ios/ios-13 to find out more.

Choose the Right iPhone for You

The sizes of the latest iPhone 11 models vary:

» iPhone 11 measures 2.98″ by 5.94″ (6.1″ diagonally) with a depth of .33 inch (see **Figure 1-1**).

» iPhone 11 Pro measures 2.81″ by 5.67″ (5.8″ diagonally) with a depth of .32 inch (see **Figure 1-2**).

» iPhone 11 Pro Max measures 3.06″ by 6.22″ (6.5″ diagonally) with a depth of .32 inch (also shown in **Figure 1-2**).

You can get iPhone 11 in white, black, yellow, purple, green, and a beautiful PRODUCT RED version. iPhone 11 Pro and 11 Pro Max both come in gold, silver, midnight green, or space gray.

Other differences between iPhone X models come primarily from the current operating system, iOS 13.

Image courtesy of Apple, Inc.

FIGURE 1-1

Not sure whether to get an iPhone 11 model? Here are a few more key differences:

» The battery life of the iPhone 11 Pro Max is longer than the 11 or 11 Pro. For example, audio playback time on the 11 Pro Max is rated at 80 hours versus 65 hours on the 11 and 11 Pro.

» iPhone 11 Pro and 11 Pro Max have triple rear-facing cameras, providing amazing optical zoom, Portrait mode, and other features. The 11 has dual rear-facing cameras.

» Screen resolution: The higher the resolution, the crisper the phone display. The iPhone 11 provides 1792 x 828 resolution; 11 Pro provides 2436 x 1125; and 11 Pro Max provides a stunning 2688 x 1242.

Image courtesy of Apple, Inc.

FIGURE 1-2

Table 1-1 gives you a quick comparison of iPhone 8, 8 Plus, XR, 11, 11 Pro, and 11 Pro Max (models currently sold by Apple). All costs are as of the time this book was written. (Some carriers may introduce non-contract terms.)

TIP

One exciting pricing option is the iPhone Upgrade Program. You choose your carrier, get an unlocked phone so you can change carriers, and receive Apple Care + to cover you in case your phone has problems, all starting at a cost of $37.41 a month (depending on the iPhone model you select). Data usage from your carrier will come on top of that. Check out `www.apple.com/shop/iphone/iphone-upgrade-program` for more information.

TABLE 1-1   **iPhone Model Comparison**

Model	Storage	Cost (may vary by carrier)	Carriers
8	64 and 128GB	from $449	AT&T, Verizon, Sprint, T-Mobile
8 Plus	64 and 128GB	from $549	AT&T, Verizon, Sprint, T-Mobile
XR	64 and 128GB	from $599	AT&T, Verizon, Sprint, T-Mobile
11	64, 128, and 256GB	from $699	AT&T, Verizon, Sprint, T-Mobile
11 Pro	64, 256GB, and 512GB	from $999	AT&T, Verizon, Sprint, T-Mobile
11 Pro Max	64, 256GB, and 512GB	from $1099	AT&T, Verizon, Sprint, T-Mobile

Decide How Much Storage Is Enough

Storage is a measure of how much information — for example, mov-ies, photos, and software applications (apps) — you can store on a computing device. Storage can also affect your iPhone's performance when handling such tasks as streaming favorite TV shows from the World Wide Web or downloading music.

TIP

Streaming refers to playing video or music content from the web (or from other devices) rather than playing a file stored on your iPhone. You can enjoy a lot of material online without ever down-loading its full content to your phone — and given that the most storage endowed iPhone model has a relatively small amount of storage, that isn't a bad idea. See Chapters 18 and 20 for more about getting your music and movies online.

Your storage options with an iPhone 11 are 64, 128, and 256 gigabytes (GB), while 11 Pro and 11 Pro Max are 64, 256, and 512 gigabytes.

You must choose the right amount of storage because you can't open the unit and add more as you usually can with a desktop computer. However, Apple has thoughtfully provided iCloud, a service you can use to back up content to the Internet (you can read more about that in Chapter 4).

How much storage is enough for your iPhone? Here's a guideline:

» If you like lots of media, such as movies or TV shows, you might need 256GB.

» For most people who manage a reasonable number of photos, download some music, and watch heavy-duty media such as movies online, 64GB may be sufficient. But if there's any possibility you may take things up a notch in the future regarding media consumption and creation (such as the newest grandchild being on the way soon), you should probably seriously consider 256GB.

» If you simply want to check email, browse the web, and write short notes to yourself, 64GB likely is plenty.

TECHNICAL STUFF

Do you know how big a *gigabyte* (GB) is? Consider this: Just about any computer you buy today comes with a minimum of 256GB of storage. Computers have to tackle larger tasks than iPhones, so that number makes sense. The iPhone, which uses a technology called *flash storage* for storing data, is meant (to a great extent) to help you experience online media and email; it doesn't have to store much since it pulls lots of content from the Internet. In the world of storage, 32GB for any kind of storage is puny if you keep lots of content (such as audio, video, and photos) on the device.

What's the price for larger storage? For the iPhone 11, a 64GB unit costs $699; 128GB is $749; and 256GB will set you back $849. iPhone 11 Pro with 64GB is $999; 256GB is $1149; and the model tops out at $1349 for 512GB. Not to be outdone, iPhone 11 Pro Max is the priciest: $1099 for 64GB; $1249 for 256GB; and $1,449 for 512GB. Note that prices may vary by carrier and where you buy your phone.

Understand What You Need to Use Your iPhone

Before you head off to buy your iPhone, you should know what other connections and accounts you'll need to work with it optimally.

At a bare minimum, to make standard cellular phone calls, you need to have a service plan with a cellular carrier (such as AT&T or Verizon), as well as a data plan that supports iPhone. The data plan allows you to exchange information over the Internet (such as emails and text messages) and download content (such as movies and music). Try to verify the strength of coverage in your area, as well as how much data your plan provides each month, before you sign up.

You also need to be able to update the iPhone operating system (iOS) and share media (such as music) among Apple devices. Though these functions can be utilized without a phone carrier service plan, you have to plug your phone into your computer to update the operating system or you may also update wirelessly over a network. You need to use a local Wi-Fi network to go online and make calls using an Internet service, such as Skype.

TIP

Given the cost and high-tech nature of the iPhone, having to jury-rig these basic functions doesn't make much sense. Trust me: Get an account and data plan with your phone service provider.

You should open a free iCloud account, Apple's online storage and syncing service, to store and share content online among your Apple devices. For example, you can set up iCloud in such a way that photos you take on your iPhone will appear on your iPad. You can also use a computer to download photos, music, or applications from non-Apple online sources (such as stores or sharing sites like your local library) and transfer them to your iPhone through a process called syncing.

Apple has set up its software and the iCloud service to give you two ways to manage content for your iPhone — including apps, music, or photos you've downloaded — and specify how to sync your calendar and contact information.

There are a lot of tech terms to absorb here (iCloud, syncing, and so on). Don't worry. Chapters 3 and 4 cover those settings in more detail.

Where to Buy Your iPhone

You can't buy an iPhone from just any retail store. You can buy an iPhone at the brick-and-mortar or online Apple Store and from mobile phone providers, such as AT&T, Sprint, T-Mobile, and Verizon. You can also find an iPhone at major retailers, such as Best Buy and Walmart, through which you have to buy a service contract for the phone carrier of your choice. You can also find iPhones at several online retailers (such as Amazon.com and Newegg.com) and through smaller, local service providers, which you can find by visiting https://support.apple.com/en-us/HT204039.

TIP

Apple offers unlocked iPhones. Essentially, these phones aren't tied into a particular provider, so you can use them with any of the four iPhone cellular service providers. Though you may save a lot by avoiding a service commitment, these phones without accompanying phone plans can be pricey. But there's a trend for providers offering cheaper plans and installment payments on the hardware.

What's in the Box

When you fork over your hard-earned money for your iPhone, you'll be left holding one box about the size of a deck of tarot cards.

Here's what you'll find when you take off the shrink wrap and open the box:

» **iPhone:** Your iPhone is covered in a thick, plastic-sleeve thingy. Take it off and toss it back in the box.

Save all the packaging until you're certain you won't return the phone. Apple's standard return period is 14 days.

» **Apple EarPods with Lightning connector:** Plug the EarPods into your iPhone for a free headset experience.

» **Documentation (and I use the term loosely):** This typically includes a small pamphlet, a sheet of Apple logo stickers, and a few more bits of information.

» **Lightning to USB Cable (iPhone 11):** Use this cable to connect the iPhone to your computer, or use it with the last item in the box, the USB power adapter.

» **Lightning to USB-C Cable (iPhone 11 Pro and 11 Pro Max):** Use this cable to connect the iPhone to your computer (if your computer has a USB-C port), or use it with the last item in the box, the USB-C power adapter.

» **Apple USB (iPhone 11) or USB-C (iPhone 11 Pro and 11 Pro Max) power adapter:** The power adapter attaches to the Lightning to USB Cable (iPhone 11) or Lighting to USB-C Cable (iPhone 11 Pro and 11 Pro Max) so that you can plug it into the wall and charge the battery.

That's all there is in the box. It's kind of a study in Zen–like simplicity.

Search for iPhone accessories online. You'll find iPhone covers and cases (from leather to silicone), car chargers, and screen guards to protect your phone's screen.

Take a First Look at the Gadget

In this section, I give you a bit more information about the buttons and other physical features of the newest iPhone models. **Figure 1-3** shows you where each of these items is located on the iPhone 11, 11 Pro, and 11 Pro Max.

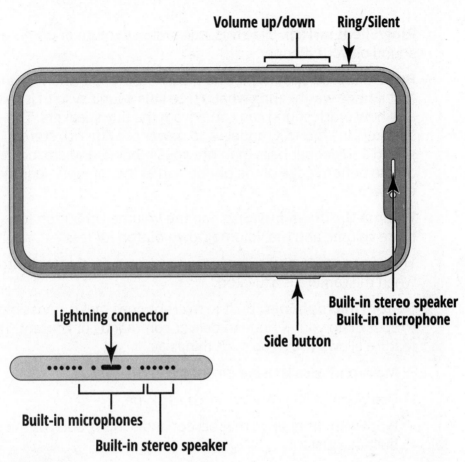

FIGURE 1-3

Here's the rundown on what the various hardware features for iPhone X models and newer are and what they do:

» **Side button:** You can use this button to power up your iPhone X model, put it in Sleep mode, wake it up, lock it, force a restart, power it down, and much more.

» **Lightning connector:** Plug in the Lightning connector at one end of the Lightning to USB Cable (iPhone 11) or Lightning to USB-C Cable (iPhone 11 Pro and 11 Pro Max) that came with your iPhone to charge your battery, listen to audio with your EarPods, or sync your iPhone with your computer (which you find out more about in Chapter 4).

» **Ring/Silent switch:** Slide this little switch to mute or unmute the sound on your iPhone.

» **Built-in stereo speakers:** One pleasant surprise when I got my first iPhone was hearing what a nice little sound system it has and how much sound can come from the tiny speakers. The speakers in iPhone X models and newer provide rich stereo sound and deeper bass than previous models, and are located on the bottom edge of the phone and at the top part near the earpiece.

» **Volume Up/Down buttons:** Tap the Volume Up button for more volume and the Volume Down button for less.

You can use the Volume Up button as a camera shutter button when the camera is activated.

» **Built-in microphones:** Built-in microphones make it possible to speak into your iPhone to deliver commands or content. This feature allows you to do such things as

- Make phone calls using the Internet.

- Use video calling services, such as Skype.

- Work with other apps that accept audio input, such as the Siri built-in assistant.

If you have an iPhone model prior to the X series, read your iPhone's documentation or visit `https://support.apple.com/iphone` to discover the hardware features specific to your device.

IN THIS CHAPTER

» See what you need to use iPhone

» Turn on iPhone for the first time

» Meet the multi-touch screen

» Say hello to tap and swipe

» Display and use the onscreen keyboard

» Flick to search

Chapter **2**

Exploring the Home Screen

won't kid you: You're about to encounter a slight learning curve if you're coming from a more basic cellphone (but if you own another smartphone, you've got a good head start). For example, your previous phone might not have had a Multi-Touch screen and onscreen keyboard.

The good news is that getting anything done on the iPhone is simple, once you know the ropes. In fact, using your fingers to do things is a very intuitive way to communicate with your computing device, which is just what iPhone is.

In this chapter, you turn on your iPhone, register it, and then take your first look at the Home screen. You also practice using the onscreen keyboard, see how to interact with the touchscreen in various ways, get pointers on working with cameras, and get an overview of built-in applications (more commonly referred to as "apps").

TIP

Although the iPhone's screen has been treated to repel oils, you're about to deposit a ton of fingerprints on your iPhone — one downside of a touchscreen device. So you'll need to clean the screen. A soft cloth, like the microfiber cloth you might use to clean your eyeglasses, is usually all you'll need to clean things up. There's no need to use harsh chemicals.

What You Need to Use iPhone

You need to be able, at a minimum, to connect to the Internet to take advantage of most iPhone features, which you can do using a Wi-Fi network (a network that you set up in your own home through an Internet service provider or access in a public place such as a library) or a cellular data connection from your cellular provider. You might want to have a computer so that you can connect your iPhone to it to download photos, videos, music, or applications and transfer them to or from your iPhone through a process called *syncing*. (See Chapter 4 for more about syncing.) An Apple service called iCloud syncs content from all your Apple iOS devices (such as the iPhone or iPad), so anything you buy on your iPad that can be run on an iPhone, for example, will automatically be pushed (in other words, downloaded and installed) to your iPhone. In addition, you can sync without connecting a cable to a computer using a wireless Wi-Fi connection to your computer.

Your iPhone will probably arrive registered and activated, or if you buy it in a store, the person helping you can usually handle that procedure.

For an iPhone 7, 7 Plus, 8, 8 Plus, X, XR, XS, XS Max, 11, 11 Pro, and 11 Pro Max, Apple recommends that you have

» A Mac or PC with a USB 2.0 or 3.0 port and one of these operating systems:

- macOS version 10.11.6 (El Capitan) or newer
- Windows 7 or newer

» iTunes 12.8 or newer on a Mac running macOS El Capitan (10.11.6) through macOS Mojave (10.14.6), the Finder on Macs running macOS Catalina (10.15), and iTunes 12.9 or newer on a PC, available at www.itunes.com/download

» An Apple ID

» Internet access

Turn On iPhone for the First Time

The first time you turn on your iPhone, it will probably have been activated and registered by your phone carrier or Apple, depending on whom you've bought it from. Follow these steps:

1. **Press and hold the Side button (found a little bit below the top of the upper-right side of newer iPhone models) or the Top button (for iPhone SE and earlier models) until the Apple logo appears.** In another moment, a series of screens appears, asking you to enter your Apple ID username and password.

2. **Enter your Apple ID.** If you don't have an Apple ID, you can follow the instructions to create one.

3. **Follow the series of prompts to set up initial options for your iPhone.** You can make choices about your language and location, using iCloud (Apple's online sharing service), whether to use a passcode, connecting with a network, and so on.

TIP

You can choose to have personal items transferred to your iPhone from your computer when you sync the two devices using iTunes, including music, videos, downloaded apps, audiobooks, e-books, podcasts, and browser bookmarks. Contacts and Calendars are downloaded via iCloud, or (if you're moving to iPhone from an Android phone) you can download an app from the Google Play Store called Move to iOS (developed by Apple) to copy your current Android settings to your iPhone (Apple provides more information about migrating from Android to iOS at https://support.apple. com/en-us/HT201196). You can also transfer to your computer any content you download directly to your iPhone by using iTunes, the App Store, or non-Apple stores. See Chapters 14 and 16 for more about these features.

Meet the Multi-Touch Screen

When the iPhone Home screen appears (see **Figure 2-1**), you see a pretty background and two sets of icons.

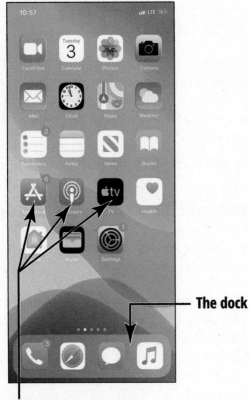

The dock

Examples of app icons

FIGURE 2-1

One set of icons appears in the Dock, along the bottom of the screen. The *Dock* contains the Phone, Safari, Messages, and Music app icons by default, though you can swap out one app for another. You can add new apps to populate as many as 14 additional Home screens for a total of 15 Home screens. The Dock appears on every Home screen.

Other icons appear above the Dock and are closer to the top of the screen. (I cover all these icons in the "Take Inventory of Preinstalled Apps" task, in Chapter 3.) Different icons appear in this area on each Home screen. You can also nest apps in folders, which almost gives you the possibility of storing limitless apps on your iPhone. You are, in fact, limited — but only by your phone's memory.

Treat the iPhone screen carefully. It's made of glass and it will break if an unreasonable amount of force is applied.

The iPhone uses *touchscreen technology:* When you swipe your finger across the screen or tap it, you're providing input to the device just as you do to a computer using a mouse or keyboard. You hear more about the touchscreen in the next task, but for now, go ahead and play with it for a few minutes — really, you can't hurt anything. Use the pads of your fingertips (not your fingernails) and try these tasks:

» **Tap the Settings icon.** The various settings (which you read more about throughout this book) appear, as shown in **Figure 2-2.**

To return to the Home screen, press the Home button for most iPhone models. If you have any iPhone X model or newer, swipe up from the very bottom edge of your screen.

» **Swipe a finger from right to left on the Home screen.** This action moves you to the next Home screen.

The little white dots at the bottom of the screen, above the Dock icons, indicate which Home screen is displayed.

» **To experience the screen rotation feature, hold the iPhone firmly while turning it sideways.** The screen flips to the horizontal orientation, if the app you're in supports it.

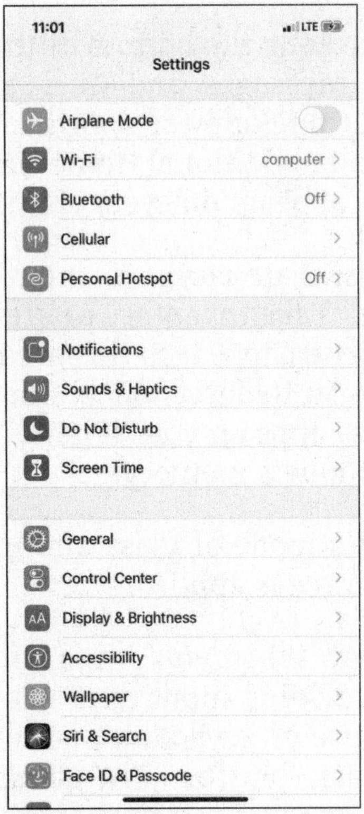

FIGURE 2-2

To flip the screen back, just turn the device so that it's oriented like a piece of paper again. (Some apps force iPhone to stay in one orientation or the other.)

» **Drag your finger down from the very top edge of the screen to reveal such items as notifications, reminders, and calendar entries.** Drag up from the very bottom edge of the Home screen to hide these items, and then drag up on all iPhone models except the X to display Control Center (containing commonly used controls and tools and discussed later in this chapter). With X models and newer, swipe down from the right corner of the screen towards the center to open Control Center.

DISCOVER 3D TOUCH AND QUICK ACTIONS

3D Touch allows you to get different results depending on the amount of pressure you apply to the screen, and get feedback on your actions with taps from the screen. For example, if you open the Photos app, you can tap lightly to select a photo, or press a bit harder to see a preview of that photo, and press even harder to open the photo full screen. The ability to preview such items as emails, websites, maps, and photos before opening them can save you time. The medium press is called a Peek and the hard press is called a Pop.

Quick Actions involve pressing an icon on the screen to see items you're likely to want to select. For example, if you press (rather than tap) the Phone icon, you'll get a shortcut list of commonly called contacts and several other call-related options, as shown in Figure 2-3. If you press the Maps app, you see a list of places you often go, such as your home, to quickly display a map of that location. Quick Actions provide a shortcut menu to your most frequently used items, saving you time and effort.

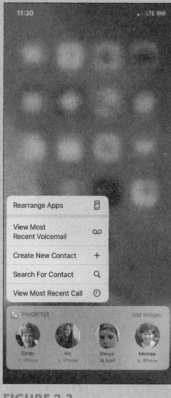

FIGURE 2-3

Say Hello to Tap and Swipe

You can use several methods for getting around and getting things done in iPhone using its multi-touch screen, including

» **Tap once.** To open an application on the Home screen, choose a field, such as a search box, choose an item in a list, use an arrow to move back or forward one screen, or follow an online link, tap the item once with your finger.

» **Tap twice.** Use this method to enlarge or reduce the display of a web page (see Chapter 12 for more about using the *Safari* web browser) or to zoom in or out in the Maps app.

» **Pinch.** As an alternative to the tap-twice method, you can pinch your fingers together or move them apart on the screen (see **Figure 2-4**) when you're looking at photos, maps, web pages, or email messages to quickly reduce or enlarge them, respectively. This method allows you to grow or contract the screen to a variety of sizes rather than a fixed size, as with the double-tap method.

TIP

You can use the three-finger tap to zoom your screen to be even larger or use multitasking gestures to swipe with four or five fingers. This method is handy if you have vision challenges. Go to Chapter 10 to discover how to turn on this feature using Accessibility settings.

» **Drag to scroll (known as *swiping*).** When you touch your finger to the screen and drag to the right or left, the screen moves (see **Figure 2-5**). Swiping to the left on the Home screen, for example, moves you to the next Home screen. Swiping down while reading an online newspaper moves you down the page; swiping up moves you back up the page.

» **Flick.** To scroll more quickly on a page, quickly flick your finger on the screen in the direction you want to move.

» **Tap the Status bar.** To move quickly to the top of a list, web page, or email message, tap the Status bar at the top of the iPhone screen. (For some sites, you have to tap twice to get this to work.)

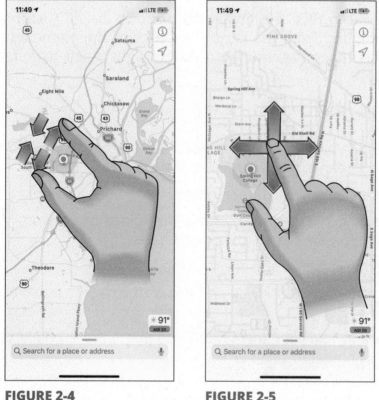

FIGURE 2-4

FIGURE 2-5

> » **Press and hold.** If you're using Notes or Mail or any other application that lets you select text, or if you're on a web page, pressing and holding text selects a word and displays editing tools that you can use to select, cut, or copy and paste the text.

TIP

When you rock your phone backward or forward, the background moves as well (a feature called *parallax*). You can disable this feature if it makes you seasick. From the Home screen, tap Settings ⇨ Accessibility ⇨ Motion and then tap and turn on the Reduce Motion setting by tapping the toggle switch (it turns green when the option is enabled).

Your iPhone offers the ability to perform bezel gestures, which involves sliding from the very outer edge of the phone left to right on the glass to go backward and sliding right to left to go forward in certain apps.

You can try these methods now:

» Tap the Safari button in the Dock at the bottom of any iPhone Home screen to display the web browser.

» Tap a link to move to another page.

» Double-tap the page to enlarge it; then pinch your fingers together on the screen to reduce its size.

» Drag one finger up and down the page to scroll.

» Flick your finger quickly up or down on the page to scroll more quickly.

» Press and hold your finger on a word that isn't a link (links take you to another location on the web).

The word is selected, and the Copy/Look Up/Speak/Share/Spell tool is displayed, as shown in **Figure 2-6**. (You can use this tool to either get a definition of a word or copy it.)

» Press and hold your finger on a link or an image.

A menu appears (shown in **Figure 2-7**) with commands that you select to open the link or picture, open it in a new tab, add it to your Reading List (see Chapter 12), or copy it. If you press and hold an image, the menu also offers the Save Image command.

Tap outside the menu to close it without making a selection.

» Position your fingers slightly apart on the screen and then pinch your fingers together to reduce the page; with your fingers already pinched together on the screen, move them apart to enlarge the page.

» Press the Home button or swipe up from the bottom of the screen (iPhone X models and newer) to go back to the Home screen.

The Copy/Lookup... tool

FIGURE 2-6

FIGURE 2-7

Display and Use the Onscreen Keyboard

The built-in iPhone keyboard appears whenever you're in a text-entry location, such as a search field or a text message. Follow these steps to display and use the keyboard:

1. Tap the Notes icon on the Home screen to open the Notes app.

2. Open a note to work in:

  - Tap the note page.

  - If you've already created some notes, tap one to display the page, and then tap anywhere on the note.

3. Type a few words using the keyboard, as shown in **Figure 2-8.**

FIGURE 2-8

To make the keyboard display as wide as possible, rotate your iPhone to landscape (horizontal) orientation. (If you've locked the screen orientation in Control Center, you have to unlock the screen to do this.)

QuickType provides suggestions above the keyboard as you type. You can turn this feature off or on by tapping and holding either the emoji (the smiley face) or International icon (looks like a globe) on the keyboard to display a menu. Tap Keyboard Settings and then toggle the Predictive switch to turn the feature Off or On (green). To quickly return to Notes from Keyboard Settings, tap the word "Notes" in the upper-left of your screen.

Keyboard shortcuts

After you open the keyboard, you're ready to use it for editing text.

You'll find a number of shortcuts for editing text:

» If you make a mistake while using the keyboard — and you will, especially when you first use it — tap the Delete key (it's near the bottom corner, with the little *x* on it) to delete text to the left of the insertion point.

To type a period and space, just double-tap the spacebar.

» To create a new paragraph, tap the Return button (just like the keyboard on a Mac, or the Enter key on a PC's keyboard).

» To type numbers and symbols, tap the number key (labeled 123) on the left side of the spacebar (refer to **Figure 2-8**). The characters on the keyboard change (see **Figure 2-9**).

FIGURE 2-9

If you type a number and then tap the spacebar, the keyboard returns to the letter keyboard automatically. To return to the letter keyboard at any time, simply tap the key labeled ABC on the left side of the spacebar.

» Press the Home button or swipe up from the bottom of the screen (X models and newer) to return to the Home screen.

» If you own an iPhone 6s Plus, 7 Plus, 8 Plus, XS Max, XR, 11, 11 Pro, or 11 Pro Max, you can use a wide screen. Turn the phone to horizontal orientation. Tap Notes and then tap in a note to display the onscreen keyboard, which now takes advantage of the wider screen and includes some extra keys, such as Cut, Copy, and Paste.

The Shift key

Use the Shift button (it's a wide, upward-facing arrow in the lower-left corner of the keyboard) to type capital letters:

» Tapping the Shift button once causes only the next letter you type to be capitalized.

» Double-tap (rapidly tap twice) the Shift key to turn on the Caps Lock feature so that all letters you type are capitalized until you turn the feature off.

» Tap the Shift key once to turn off Caps Lock.

You can control whether Caps Lock is enabled by opening the Settings app, tapping General and then Keyboard, and toggling the switch called Enable Caps Lock.

» To type a variation on a symbol or letter (for example, to see alternative presentations for the letter *A* when you press the A button on the keyboard), hold down the key; a set of alternative letters/symbols appears (see **Figure 2-10**).

FIGURE 2-10

Emojis

Tap the smiley-faced emoji button to display the emoji keyboard containing symbols that you can insert, including numerical, symbol, and arrow keys, as well as a row of symbol sets along the bottom of the screen. Tapping one of these displays a portfolio of icons from smiley faces and hearts to pumpkins, cats, and more. Tap the ABC button to close the emoji keyboard and return to the letter keyboard.

TIP

A small globe symbol will appear instead of the emoji button on the keyboard if you've enabled multilanguage functionality in iPhone settings.

QuickPath

QuickPath allows you to quickly zip your finger from key to key to quickly spell words without ever lifting it from the screen. For example, as shown in Figure 2-11, spell the word "path" by touching "p" on the keyboard, and then quickly move to "a" then "t" then "h." Tada! You've spelled "path" without leaving the screen.

FIGURE 2-11

Flick to Search

The Search feature in iPhone helps you find suggestions from the web, Music, iTunes, and the App Store as well as suggestions for nearby locations and more. Here's how to use Search:

1. Swipe down on any Home screen (but not from the very top or bottom of the screen) to reveal the Search feature (see **Figure 2-12**).

2. Begin entering a search term.

   In the example in **Figure 2-13,** after I typed the word "restaurants," the Search feature displayed maps and other search results. As you continue to type a search term or phrase, the results narrow to match it.

FIGURE 2-12　　　　**FIGURE 2-13**

3. Scroll down to view more results.

4. Tap an item in the search results to open it in its appropriate app or player.

Chapter **3**

Getting Going

N ow, it's time to get into even more aspects of using the iPhone and its interface (how you interact with your device).

In this chapter, you look at updating your iOS version (the operating system that your iPhone uses), multitasking, checking out the cameras, discovering the apps that come preinstalled on your iPhone, and more.

Update the Operating System to iOS 13

This book is based on the latest version of the iPhone operating system at the time: iOS 13. To be sure that you have the latest and greatest features, update your iPhone to the latest iOS now (and do so periodically to receive minor upgrades to iOS 13 or future versions of the iOS). If you've set up an iCloud account on your iPhone, you'll receive an alert and can choose to install the update or not, or you can update manually:

1. Tap Settings. (Be sure you have Wi-Fi enabled and that you're connected to a Wi-Fi network to perform these steps.)

2. Tap General.

3. Tap Software Update (see **Figure 3-1**).

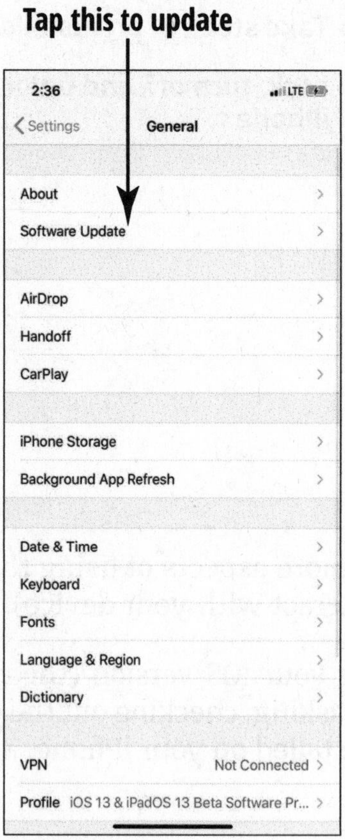

Tap this to update

2:36	..ıl LTE 🔋
‹ Settings	**General**
About	›
Software Update	›
AirDrop	›
Handoff	›
CarPlay	›
iPhone Storage	›
Background App Refresh	›
Date & Time	›
Keyboard	›
Fonts	›
Language & Region	›
Dictionary	›
VPN	Not Connected ›
Profile iOS 13 & iPadOS 13 Beta Software Pr...	›

FIGURE 3-1

Your iPhone checks to find the latest iOS version and walks you through the updating procedure if an update is available.

You can also allow your iPhone to perform automatic updates overnight. Go to Settings ⇨ General ⇨ Software Update ⇨ Automatic Updates and toggle the switch to On (green). Your iPhone must be connected to Wi-Fi and its charger to automatically update.

Learn App Switcher Basics

iOS 13's App Switcher lets you easily switch from one app to another without closing the first one and returning to the Home screen. This is accomplished by previewing all open apps and jumping from one to another; you can completely quit an app by simply swiping it upward. To learn the ropes of the App Switcher, follow these steps:

1. Open an app.

2. Press the Home button twice, or for X models or newer, drag up from the bottom of the screen and pause a moment. The App Switcher appears and displays a list of open apps (see **Figure 3-2**).

3. To locate another app that you want to switch to, flick to scroll to the left or right.

4. Tap an app to switch to it.

Press the Home button once to close the App Switcher and return to the app that you were working in. If you have an iPhone X model or newer, tap an app in the list to exit the App Switcher.

FIGURE 3-2

Examine the iPhone Cameras

iPhones have front- and back-facing cameras. You can use the cameras to take still photos (covered in more detail in Chapter 19) or shoot videos (covered in Chapter 20).

For now, take a quick look at your camera by tapping the Camera app icon on the Home screen. The app opens, as shown in **Figure 3-3.**

You can use the controls on the screen to

» Switch between the front and rear cameras.

» Change from still-camera to video-camera operation by using the slider at the bottom of the screen.

» Take a picture or start recording a video.

FIGURE 3-3

» Choose a 3- or 10-second delay with the Timed Photos button.

» Turn HDR (high dynamic range for better contrast) on or off.

» Tap the Flash button to set flash to On, Off, or Auto.

» Use color filters when taking photos or videos.

» Take a "burst" of photos by tapping-and-holding the Camera's button. A small photo count will display above the button to show how many photos you've taken.

» Open previously captured images or videos.

When you view a photo or video, you can use an iPhone sharing feature to send the image by AirDrop (iPhone 5 and later only), Message, Notes, Mail, and other options (depending on which apps you've installed). You can also share through iCloud Photo Sharing, a tweet, Facebook, Instagram, and other apps.

More things that you can do with images are to print them, use a still photo as wallpaper (that is, as your Home or lock screen background image) or assign it to represent a contact, and run a slideshow. See Chapters 19 and 20 for more detail about using the iPhone cameras.

Take a Look at Face ID

iPhone X and newer models don't have a Home button, so Touch ID isn't available. However, they do utilize a different — and very cool — method of authenticating a user: Face ID. Face ID uses your iPhone's built-in cameras and scanners to scan your face and save a profile of it. It then remembers the information and compares it to whoever is facing the iPhone. If the face doesn't match the profile, the person can't access the iPhone (unless they know and use your passcode, which you have to set up to use Face ID). Face ID is so advanced that it can even work in total darkness.

To set up Face ID:

1. Go to Settings and tap Face ID & Passcode.

2. Tap Set Up Face ID.

3. Hold the iPhone in front of your face (in portrait mode, not landscape).

4. Tap the Get Started button and then follow the prompts to slowly move your head in a complete circle. If you have difficulty moving your head, tap the Accessibility Options button at the bottom of the screen and follow the prompts from there.

5. Tap Continue and follow the prompts to perform the circle step again.

6. Tap Done when finished.

The next time you want to use your iPhone, simply hold it up in front of you, swipe up from the bottom of the screen when the lock icon unlocks (see **Figure 3-4**), and you'll jump right into the Home screen or whatever app you were last using.

FIGURE 3-4

For more information on using Face ID and its capabilities, visit https://support.apple.com/en-us/HT208109.

Discover Control Center

Control Center is a one-stop screen for common features and settings, such as connecting to a network, increasing screen brightness or volume, and even turning the built-in flashlight on or off. Here's how to use it:

1. To display Control Center with many iPhone models, swipe up from the very bottom of the screen. Access Control Center with an iPhone X or newer by swiping from the right corner of the screen to the center. The Control Center screen appears.

2. In the Control Center screen, tap a button or tap and drag a slider to access or adjust a setting (see **Figure 3-5**).

FIGURE 3-5

3. After you make a change, swipe the top of Control Center down to hide the screen.

Some options in Control Center are hidden from initial view, but may be accessed by pressing-and-holding (using slightly more force than a typical tap) a button in Control Center. For example, use press-and-hold on any of the Communications buttons (Airplane Mode, Cellular Data, Wi-Fi, and Bluetooth) to reveal two more options: AirDrop and Personal Hotspot (as shown in **Figure 3-6**).

FIGURE 3-6

Other press-and-hold options in Control Center include

» Adjust the Flashlight brightness level.

» Select a device for AirPlay.

» Set a quick timer.

» Instantly start recording video or take a selfie.

TIP

Try pressing-and-holding other buttons in Control Center to see what other options are waiting for you to discover. If you press-and-hold an item and its icon just bounces, there are no further options available for the item.

Did you notice the large amount of empty space in Control Center when you opened it? That's because iOS 13 allows you to customize Control Center (a feature I love). All that extra space is waiting to be filled by you:

1. Tap Settings.

2. Tap Control Center and then tap Customize Controls to open the Customize screen (shown in **Figure 3-7**).

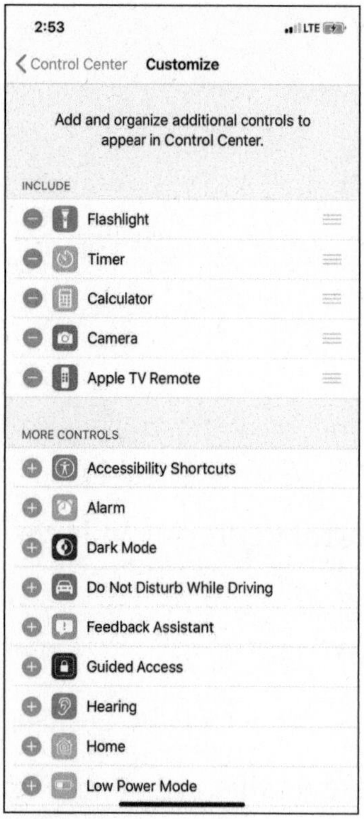

FIGURE 3-7

3. Add or remove items from Control Center:

- To remove an item, tap the "-" to the left, and then tap the Remove button that appears to the right.

- To add an item, tap the "+" to the left. You'll see the item in Control Center the next time you visit it.

TIP

Remember to use press-and-hold to find any extras for the item. If the item just bounces when you press-and-hold, there are no further options.

Lock Screen Rotation

Sometimes you don't want your screen orientation to flip when you move your phone around. Use these steps to lock the iPhone into portrait orientation (narrow and tall, not low and wide):

1. Open Control Center.

2. Tap the Lock Screen button. (It's the button that looks like a padlock with a circular arrow around it.) When locked, the button appears white.

3. Swipe down from the top of Control Center to hide it.

Explore the Status Bar

Across the top of the iPhone screen is the Status bar (see **Figure 3-8**). Tiny icons in this area can provide useful information, such as the time, battery level, and wireless-connection status. Table 3-1 lists some of the most common items you find on the Status bar.

Status bar

FIGURE 3-8

TABLE 3-1 ## Common Status Bar Icons

Icon	Name	What It Indicates
	Wi-Fi	You're connected to a Wi-Fi network.
	Activity	A task is in progress — a web page is loading, for example.
2:30 PM	Time	You guessed it: You see the time.
	Screen Rotation Lock	The screen is locked in portrait orientation and doesn't rotate when you turn the iPhone.
	Battery Life	This shows the charge percentage remaining in the battery. The indicator changes to a lightning bolt when the battery is charging.

TIP

If you have GPS, cellular, Bluetooth service, or a connection to a virtual private network (VPN), a corresponding symbol appears on the Status bar whenever a feature is active. (If you don't already know what a virtual private network is, there's no need to worry about it.)

Apple supplies a full list of Status bar icons at `https://support.apple.com/en-us/HT207354`. Keep in mind that icons may not be in the same location on an iPhone X model's Status bar as they are on those of other iPhone models.

Take Inventory of Preinstalled Apps

The iPhone comes with certain functionality and applications — or apps, for short — built in. When you look at the Home screen, you see icons for each app. This task gives you an overview of what each app does.

By default, the following icons appear in the Dock at the bottom of every Home screen (refer to **Figure 3-1**), from left to right:

» **Phone:** Use this app to make and receive phone calls, view a log of recent calls, create a list of favorite contacts, access your voice mail, and view contacts.

» **Safari:** You use the Safari web browser to navigate on the Internet, create and save bookmarks of favorite sites, and add web clips to your Home screen so that you can quickly visit favorite sites from there. You may have used this web browser (or another, such as Google Chrome) on your desktop computer.

» **Messages:** If you love to instant message, the Messages app comes to the rescue. The Messages app has been in iPhone for quite some time. Now you can engage in live text- and image-based conversations with others on their phones or other devices that use email. You can also send video or audio messages.

» **Music:** Music is the name of your media player. Though its main function is to play music, you can use it to play audio podcasts and audiobooks as well.

Apps with icons above the Dock on the Home screen include

» **FaceTime:** Use FaceTime to place phone calls using video of the sender and receiver to have a more personal conversation.

» **Calendar:** Use this handy onscreen daybook to set up appointments and send alerts to remind you about them.

» **Photos:** The Photos app in iPhone helps you organize pictures in folders, send photos in email, use a photo as your iPhone wallpaper, and assign pictures to contact records. You can also run slideshows of your photos, open albums, pinch or unpinch to shrink or expand photos, and scroll photos with a simple swipe.

Your iPhone can use the Photo Sharing feature to share photos among your friends. Since iOS 7, Photos displays images by collections, including Years and Moments.

» **Camera:** As you may have read earlier in this chapter, the Camera app is Control Center for the still and video cameras built into the iPhone.

» **Mail:** You use this application to access email accounts that you have set up in iPhone. Your email is then displayed without you having to browse to the site or sign in. You can use tools to move among a few preset mail folders, read and reply to email, and download attached photos to your iPhone. Read more about email accounts in Chapter 13.

» **Clock:** This app allows you to display clocks from around the world, set alarms, and use timer and stopwatch features.

» **Maps:** With this iPhone mapping app, you can view classic maps or aerial views of addresses and find directions from one place to another whether traveling by car, foot, or public transportation. You can even get your directions read aloud by a spoken narration feature.

» **Weather:** Get the latest weather for your location and others instantly with this handy app. You can easily add other locations to check for weather where you're going or where you've been.

» **Reminders:** This useful app centralizes all your calendar entries and alerts to keep you on schedule and allows you to create to-do lists.

» **Notes:** Enter text, format text, or cut and paste text and objects (such as images) from a website into this simple notepad app.

» **News:** News is a customizable aggregator for stories from your favorite news sources.

» **Apple Books:** The Apple Books app is bundled with the iPhone out of the box. Because the iPhone has been touted as being a good small screen e-reader — a device that enables you to read books on an electronic device, similar to the Amazon Kindle Fire HD — you should definitely check this one out. (To work with the Books e-reader application itself, go to Chapter 17.)

» **App Store:** Here you can buy and download applications that do everything from enabling you to play games to building business presentations. Many of these apps and games are free!

» **Podcasts:** Before iOS 8, you had to download the free Podcast app, but now it's built into your iOS iPhone. Use this app to listen to recorded informational programs. Chapter 18 provides the scoop on using the Podcasts app.

» **TV:** This media player is similar to Music but specializes in playing videos and offers a few features specific to this type of media, such as chapter breakdowns and information about a movie's plot and cast.

» **Health:** This is exciting very useful app that you can use to record various health and exercise statistics and even send them to your doctor. See Chapter 24 for details.

» **Home:** Home helps you control most (if not all) of your home automation devices in one convenient app. See Chapters 9 and 25 for more information.

» **Wallet:** This Apple Pay feature lets you store a virtual wallet of plane or concert tickets, coupons, and more and use them with a swipe of your iPhone across a point of purchase device.

» **Settings:** Settings is the central location on the iPhone where you can specify settings for various functions and do administrative tasks, such as set up email accounts or create a password.

There are also some preinstalled apps located on the second Home screen by default, including some in a Utilities folder. Wrapped up in the Utilities folder are some other handy tools: Compass, Calculator, and Voice Memos.

Additionally, on the second Home screen, you'll find

» **Files:** This app allows you to browse files that are stored not only on your iPhone but also files you may have stored on other services, such as iCloud Drive, Google Drive, Dropbox, and the like.

» **Find My:** The Find My app combines the Find iPhone and Find Friends apps to help you locate Apple devices that you own (see Chapter 25 for more info) and track down friends who also own an Apple device.

» **Shortcuts:** This new app helps you string together multiple iPhone actions into single Siri commands.

» **iTunes Store:** Tapping this icon takes you to the iTunes Store, where you can shop 'til you drop (or until your iPhone battery runs out of juice) for music, movies, TV shows, and audiobooks and then download them directly to your iPhone. (See Chapter 16 for more about how the iTunes Store works.)

» **Contacts:** Use this simple app to add, edit, and remove contacts and their information. See Chapter 7 for more details on using the Contacts app.

TIP

Several useful apps are free for you to download from the App Store. These include iMovie and iPhoto, as well as the Pages, Keynote, and Numbers apps of the iWork suite.

Lock iPhone, Turn It Off, or Unlock It

Earlier in this chapter, I mentioned how simple it is to turn on the power to your iPhone. Now it's time to put it to sleep (a state in which the screen goes black, though you can quickly wake up the iPhone) or turn off the power to give your new toy a rest.

Here are the procedures you use to put your iPhone to sleep or turn it off:

TIP

» **Sleep:** Press the Side button just below the top of the right side of the phone. The iPhone goes to sleep. The screen goes black and is locked.

The iPhone automatically enters Sleep mode after a brief period of inactivity. You can change the time interval at which it sleeps by adjusting the Auto-Lock feature in Settings ⇨ Display & Brightness.

» **Power Off:** From any app or Home screen press and hold the Side button until the Slide to Power Off bar appears at the top of the screen, and then swipe the bar from left to right. You've just turned off your iPhone.

» **Force Off:** If the iPhone becomes unresponsive, for many models hold the Power and Home buttons simultaneously until the phone shuts itself off. For iPhone X models or newer, press and hold both the Side and Volume Down buttons to achieve the same result.

To wake most iPhone models up from Sleep mode, simply pick up your iPhone (this feature was introduced in iOS 10 and only works on models from the iPhone 6s and newer) or press the Home button once. Notice at the bottom of the screen the iPhone tells you to press the Home button again. Do so and the iPhone unlocks. If you have an iPhone X model or newer, simply tap the screen to wake from sleep, or press the Side button once.

TIP

If you have the Passcode feature enabled, you'll need to enter your Passcode before proceeding to unlock your screen after rais-ing your iPhone or pressing the Home button. However, if you have Touch ID enabled, you only need press the Home button once and rest your finger on it for it to scan your fingerprints; the iPhone will automatically unlock. iPhone X model (or newer) users who have Face ID enabled simply need to look at their iPhone to unlock it.

TIP

Want a way to shut down your iPhone without having to press buttons? Go to Settings⇨General and then scroll all the way to the bottom of the screen. Tap the Shut Down button, slide the Power Off slider, and your iPhone will go off.

Chapter **4**

Beyond the Basics

Your first step in getting to work with the iPhone is to make sure that its battery is charged. Next, if you want to find free or paid content for your iPhone from Apple, from movies to music to e-books to audiobooks, you'll need to have an iTunes account.

You can also use the wireless sync feature to exchange content between your computer and iPhone over a wireless network.

Another feature you might take advantage of is the iCloud service from Apple to store and push all kinds of content and data to all your Apple devices — wirelessly. You can pick up where you left off from one device to another through iCloud Drive, an online storage service that enables sharing content among devices so that edits you make to documents in iCloud are reflected in all iOS devices, iPadOS devices, and Macs running OS X Yosemite (version 10.10) or later.

TECHNICAL
STUFF

The operating system for Apple's Mac computers used to be called OS X. These days it's referred to as macOS. The Mac operating system is mentioned a few times throughout this book, and you should know that OS X and macOS are different names for the same thing.

Charge the Battery

My iPhone showed up in the box fully charged, and let's hope yours did, too. Because all batteries run down eventually, one of your first priorities is to know how to recharge your iPhone battery.

Gather your iPhone and its Lightning to USB Cable and the Apple USB power adapter.

Connector cables from earlier versions of iPhone or other Apple devices (such as iPad or iPod) don't work with your iPhone 5 or newer. However, adapters are available from Apple.

TIP

Here's how to charge your iPhone:

1. Gently plug the Lightning connector end (the smaller of the two connectors) of the Lightning to USB Cable into the iPhone.

If you have a hard case for your iPhone, you should remove the phone from it if you're charging it over several hours because these cases retain heat, which is bad for the iPhone and the case.

TIP

2. Plug the USB end of the Lightning to USB Cable into the Apple USB power adapter (see **Figure 4-1**).

3. Plug the adapter into an electric outlet.

If you're moving from an Android phone to an iPhone, consider downloading the Move to iOS app (which was developed by Apple). This app allows you to wirelessly transfer key content, such as contacts, message history, videos, mail accounts, photos, and more from your old phone to your new one. If you had free apps on your Android device, iPhone will suggest you download them from the App Store. Any paid apps will be added to your iTunes Wish List. By the way, when you download the app from the Google Play Store you'll be well-served not to bother reading some of the viciously negative comments made by some Android users who harbor a true hatred of all things Apple. Jealousy is an ugly thing.

TIP

FIGURE 4-1

Sign into an iTunes Account for Music, Movies, and More

The terms iTunes Account and Apple ID are interchangeable: Your Apple ID *is* your iTunes Account, but you'll need to be signed into iTunes with your Apple ID to download items from the iTunes Store.

TIP

If you've never set up an Apple ID or iTunes Account, please visit https://support.apple.com/en-us/HT204316 on your computer, iPhone, or iPad for help in doing so.

To be able to download free or paid items from the iTunes Store or the App Store on your iPhone, you must open an iTunes account. Here's how to sign in to an account once you've created it:

1. Tap Settings on your iPhone.

2. Scroll down and tap iTunes & App Stores; the screen shown in **Figure 4-2** appears.

3. Tap Sign In, enter your Apple ID and password (see **Figure 4-3**), and then tap the Sign In button.

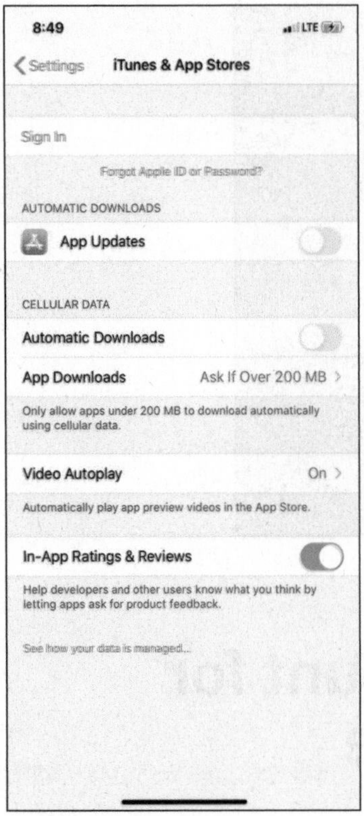

FIGURE 4-2

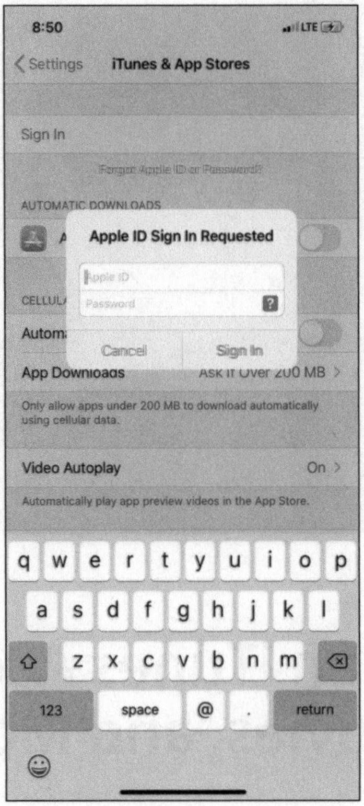

FIGURE 4-3

4. Tap Password Settings in the iTunes & App screen to bring up the screen shown in **Figure 4-4.**

5. Select whether you'd like your password to be requested every time a download is attempted (recommended) or to allow downloads for up to 15 minutes after the password has been entered without having to reenter it. Also, toggle the switch to On or Off (depending on whether you require your password to be entered when downloading free items). I recommend setting it to On; even if an app is free, there may be some items that you just don't want loaded onto your iPhone without your permission.

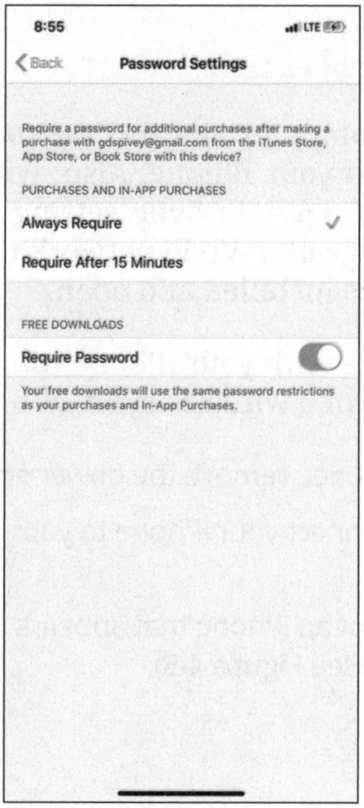

FIGURE 4-4

TIP If you prefer not to leave your credit card info with Apple, one option is to buy an iTunes gift card and provide that as your payment information. You can replenish the card periodically through the Apple Store.

SIGN IN WITH APPLE

Sign in with Apple is new privacy feature in iOS 13 that allows you to use your Apple ID to sign in to any social media account or website. This service provides a simple and secure way to sign in to accounts without having to remember a unique password for each one. Think of it as Apple's more secure replacement for Sign in with Google or Sign in with Facebook, both of which you've probably seen online. The Sign in with Apple button will show up in apps and websites when an account log-in is required.

Sync Wirelessly

You can connect your iPhone to a computer and use the tools there to sync content on your computer to your iPhone. Also, with Wi-Fi turned on in Settings, use the iTunes Wi-Fi Sync setting to allow cordless syncing if you're within range of a Wi-Fi network that has a computer connected to it with iTunes installed and open.

There are a few steps you have to take with your iPhone connected to your computer before you can perform a wireless sync with iTunes:

1. If you're charging with an electrical outlet, remove the power adapter.

2. Use the Lightning to USB Cable to connect your iPhone to your computer.

3. Open iTunes and then click the icon of an iPhone that appears in the tools in the left corner of the screen (see **Figure 4-5**).

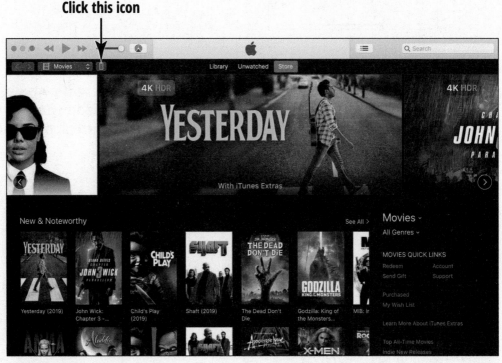

FIGURE 4-5

4. Click the check box labeled Sync with this iPhone over Wi-Fi (as seen in **Figure 4-6**).

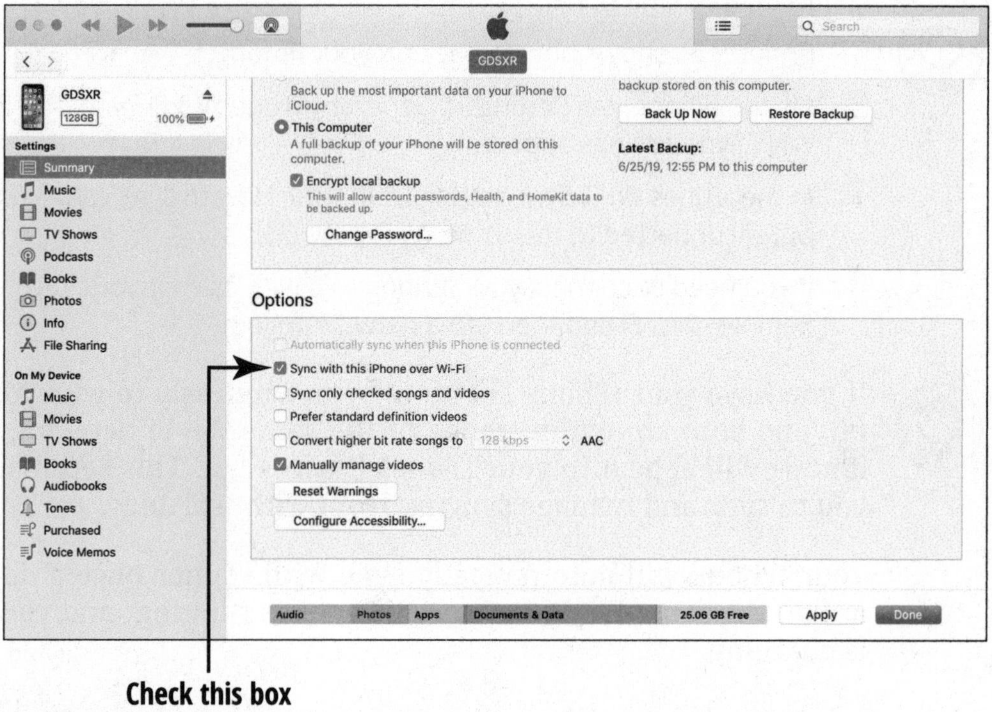

Check this box

FIGURE 4-6

TIP

You may need to scroll down a bit to see the Sync with this iPhone over Wi-Fi option.

5. Click Apply in the lower-right corner of the iTunes window.

6. Disconnect your iPhone from your computer.

TIP

You can click any item on the left side of the screen shown in **Figure 4-6** to handle settings for syncing such items as Movies, Music, and Apps. In the Apps category, you can also choose to remove certain apps from your Home screens. You can also tap the list of items in the On My Device section on the left side to view and even play contents directly from your iPhone.

After you complete the preceding steps, you'll be able to wirelessly sync your iPhone with your computer. Follow these steps:

TIP

1. Back up your iPhone.

   Chapter 25 shows how to back up your iPhone.

2. On the iPhone, tap Settings ⇨ General ⇨ iTunes Wi-Fi Sync. The iTunes Wi-Fi Sync settings appear.

3. In the iTunes Wi-Fi Sync settings, tap Sync Now to sync with a computer connected to the same Wi-Fi network.

4. If you need to connect your iPhone to a wireless network, tap Settings ⇨ Wi-Fi and then tap a network to join.

TIP

If you have your iPhone set up to sync wirelessly to your Mac or PC, and both are within range of the same Wi-Fi network, your iPhone will appear in your iTunes Devices list. This setup allows you to sync and manage syncing from within iTunes.

Your iPhone will automatically sync with iTunes once a day if both are on the same Wi-Fi network, iTunes is running, and your iPhone is charging.

Understand iCloud

There's an alternative to syncing content by using iTunes. iCloud is a service offered by Apple that allows you to back up most of your content to online storage. That content is then pushed automatically to all your Apple devices wirelessly. All you need to do is get an iCloud account, which is free (again, this is simply using your Apple ID), and make settings on your devices and in iTunes for which types of content you want pushed to each device. After you've done that, content that you create or purchase on one device — such as music, apps, and TV shows, as well as documents created in Apple's iWork apps (Pages, Keynote, and Numbers), photos, and so on — is synced among your devices automatically.

TIP

See Chapter 16 for more about using the Family Sharing feature to share content that you buy online and more with family members through iCloud.

You can stick with iCloud's default storage capacity, or you can increase it if you need more capacity:

>> Your iCloud account includes 5GB of free storage. You may be fine with the free 5GB of storage.

Content that you purchase from Apple (such as apps, books, music, iTunes Match content, Photo Sharing contents, and TV shows) isn't counted against your storage.

The following section shows how to enable iCloud.

>> If you want additional storage, you can buy an upgrade. Currently, 50GB costs only $0.99 per month, 200GB is $2.99 per month, and 2TB (which is an enormous amount of storage) is $9.99 per month. (All prices are in U.S. dollars.) Most likely, 50GB will satisfy the needs of folks who just like to take and share pictures, but if videos are your thing, you may eventually want to consider the larger capacities.

To upgrade your storage, go to Settings, tap your Apple ID at the top of the screen, go to iCloud⇨Manage Storage, and then tap Change Storage Plan. On the next screen, tap the amount you need and then tap Buy (in the upper-right corner), as shown in **Figure 4-7.**

TIP

If you change your mind, you can get in touch with Apple within 15 days to cancel your upgrade.

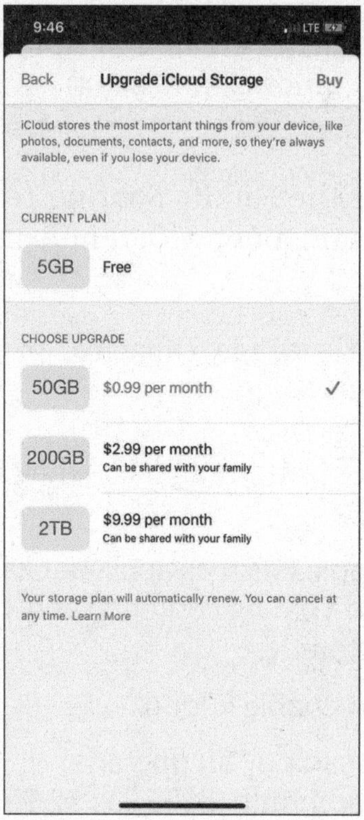

FIGURE 4-7

Turn on iCloud Drive

iCloud Drive is the online storage space that comes free with iCloud (as covered in the preceding section).

Before you can use iCloud Drive, you need to be sure that iCloud Drive is turned on. Here's how to turn on iCloud Drive:

1. Tap Settings and then tap your Apple ID at the top of the screen.

2. Tap iCloud to open the iCloud screen.

3. Scroll down in the iCloud screen until you see iCloud Drive.

4. Tap the On/Off switch to turn on (green) iCloud Drive (see **Figure 4-8**).

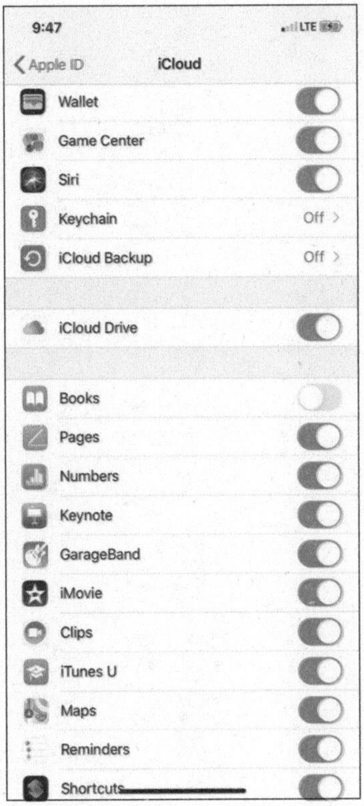

FIGURE 4-8

Set Up iCloud Sync Settings

When you have an iCloud account up and running, you have to specify which type of content should be synced with your iPhone by iCloud. Follow these steps:

1. Tap Settings, tap your Apple ID at the top of the screen, and then tap iCloud.

2. In the iCloud settings shown in **Figure 4-9,** tap the On/Off switch for any item that's turned off that you want to turn on (or vice versa). You can sync Photos, Mail, Contacts, Calendars, Reminders, Safari, Notes, News, Wallet, Keychain (an app that stores all your passwords and even credit card numbers across all Apple devices), and more. The listing of apps on this screen isn't alphabetical, so scroll down if you don't see what you're looking for at first.

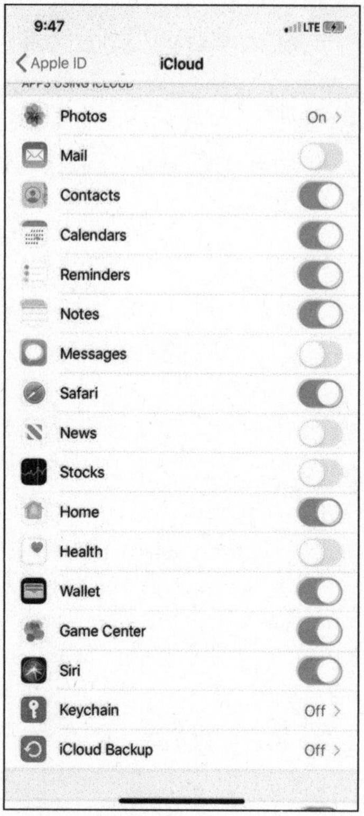

FIGURE 4-9

If you want to allow iCloud to provide a service for locating a lost or stolen iPhone, toggle the On/Off switch in the Find My iPhone field to On (green) to activate it. This service helps you locate, send a message to, or delete content from your iPhone if it falls into other hands. See Chapter 25 for more information.

3. To enable automatic downloads of iTunes-purchased music, apps, and books, return to the main Settings screen by tapping the Apple ID button in the top-left corner of the screen (refer to **Figure 4-9**), and then tap iTunes & App Stores.

4. Tap the On/Off switch for Music, Apps, Books & Audiobooks, or Updates to set up automatic downloads of any of this content to your iPhone by iCloud.

TIP

Consider turning off the Cellular Data option, which you find in the Cellular section of Settings, to avoid having these downloads occur over your cellular connection, which can use up your data allowance. Wait until you're on a Wi-Fi connection to have iPhone perform the updates.

Browse Your iPhones Files

Long-time iPhone users have pined for a way to browse files stored on our devices, as opposed to being limited to finding documents and other files only within the apps they're intended for or created by. Finally, iOS 11 introduced us to a new app called Files, which allows us to browse not only for files stored on our iPhone, but also see our stuff that we've stored on other online (cloud) services such as Google Drive, Dropbox, and others.

You'll find the Files app on the second home screen, by default.

1. Tap the Files icon to open the app.

2. On the Browse screen (shown in **Figure 4-10**):

- Tap the Search field to search for items by title or content.

- Tap a source in the Locations section to browse a particular service or your iPhone.

- Tap colors under Tags to search for files you've tagged according to categories.

3. Once in a source, illustrated in **Figure 4-11,** you may tap files to open or preview them, and you may tap folders to open them and view their contents.

4. Tap Select in the upper-right corner of the screen and then tap items to select them for an action. Available actions, found at the bottom of the screen, include

- **Duplicating files:** Make copies of selected items.

- **Moving files:** Move files to other sources.

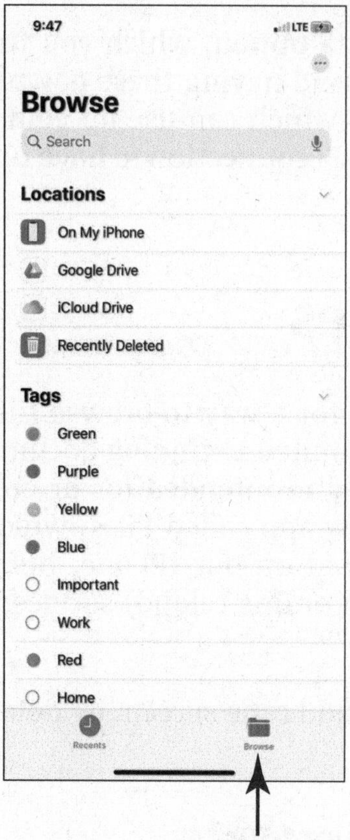

FIGURE 4-10

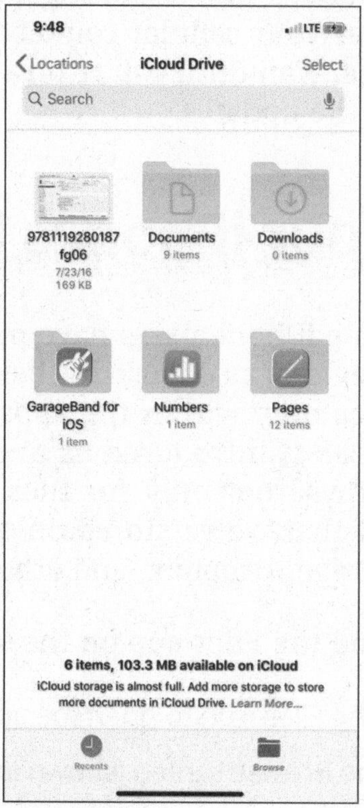

Browse button

FIGURE 4-11

- **Sharing files:** Share files with other people in a variety of ways (Messages and Mail, for example). You can even invite them to make edits, if you like.

- **Deleting files:** Trash files you no longer need.

Should you like to retrieve a file you've deleted, go to the Browse screen (tap Browse at the bottom of the screen if you're not already there) and tap Recently Deleted. Tap Select in the upper-right corner, tap the file you'd like to retrieve, and tap the Recover button at the bottom of the screen. The file will be placed back in the location it was originally deleted from.

IN THIS CHAPTER

» **Understand Screen Time features**

» **Monitor how apps are used**

» **Create Downtime during your day**

» **Limit how long apps may be used**

» **Restrict access to certain websites**

» **Control privacy settings**

Chapter **5**

Managing and Monitoring iPhone Usage

The iPhone you have will quickly become like an additional limb for you, if it hasn't become so already. And put one of these things down near a kid and you may likely not see it (or them) for a long time. Your iPhone may well become one of the most important tools you own, but your use of it really can get out of hand if you're not careful.

Apple understands this concern and has been one of the more active tech companies in helping resolve this problem. One of the most important additions to iOS in a while is Apple's response to the issue of spending too much time on our devices: Screen Time.

Screen Time is a feature that not only helps you monitor how much time you're spending on your iPhone but also keep track of which apps are consuming your days (and nights). It also can set time limits for app use, lock down your iPhone after certain times, and even set content filters to help you or others in your sphere stay away from certain websites or apps.

Meet Screen Time

Screen Time isn't an app unto itself, but it is part of the Settings app. To find Screen Time:

1. On the Home screen, tap the Settings app icon to open it.

2. Swipe until you find the Screen Time options, shown in **Figure 5-1,** and tap to open it. If the Screen Time switch is Off (white), tap to turn it On (green).

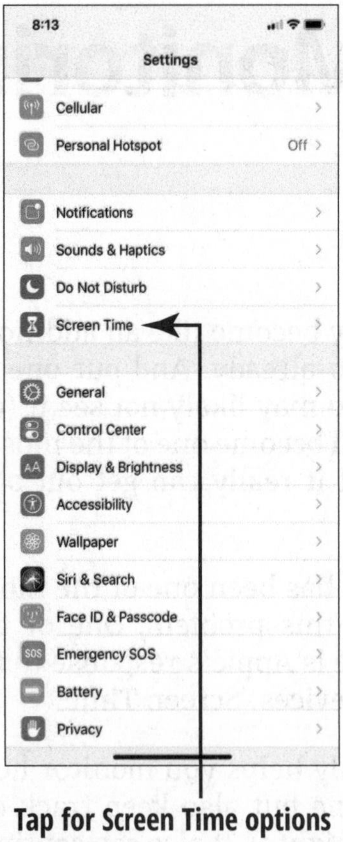

Tap for Screen Time options

FIGURE 5-1

REMEMBER

You won't see much information in Screen Time if you've just enabled it for the first time, or if you've only had your iPhone for a very short while.

3. You're greeted with a bird's-eye view of your iPhone usage, illustrated in **Figure 5-2.** You'll see your iPhone's name as well as a quick glance at total usage time and a graph displaying the length of time you spent using apps of various categories.

4. Tap See All Activity to view the Screen Time details screen, which is a more detailed listing (see **Figure 5-3**) of your iPhone activities, including a breakdown of how you used your apps throughout the day, which apps you used the most, and so on. In the Most Used section, tap Show Categories to see apps listed by category (such as Social Networking, Entertainment, Productivity, and more); tap Show Apps & Websites to return to the previous view.

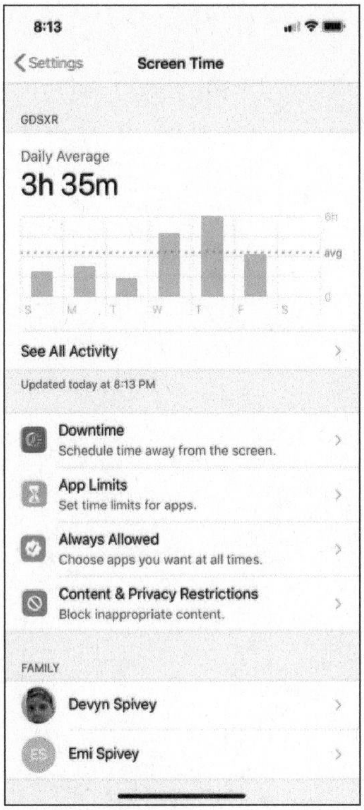

FIGURE 5-2

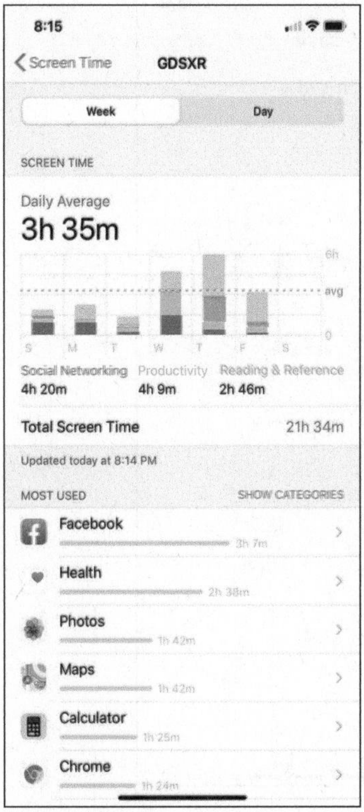

FIGURE 5-3

TIP

Tap a bar graph for a particular day (designated by S for Sunday, M for Monday, and so forth) to see even more detailed information about an activity for that day. Tap the same bar graph to return to the weekly information breakdown.

TIP

There are two tabs at the top of the page: one called Day and another called Week (see **Figure 5-3**). Tap the one you'd like to see displayed.

5. Tap an app under the Most Used section to see app-specific information, and then tap the back arrow in the upper-left corner to return to the previous screen.

6. Scroll down the page to see how many times you've picked up your iPhone and when (see to **Figure 5-4**), get an overview of how many notifications you've received, and which apps generated them.

FIGURE 5-4

TIP

Tap an app's name in the Notifications section to open the Notification settings for that app, should you want to make adjustments based on the activity reported for it.

7. Tap the Screen Time button in the upper-left corner to return to the main Screen Time settings.

8. Scroll down to Use Screen Time Passcode. If you'd like to use a passcode to keep your Screen Time settings secure (I recommend it), tap the option and provide a 4-digit passcode. This will prevent anyone else from changing your settings and also lets you allow users more time with apps when time limits have been set for them (more on that later in this chapter). If you prefer not to use a passcode, skip to the next step.

9. Toggle the Share Across Devices switch On or Off, depending on whether you'd like to view your Screen Time for this device on other iOS or iPadOS devices you may own.

10. Finally, Tap the Turn Off Screen Time button at the bottom of the options if you want to disable this awesome feature. Can you tell I very much like this new addition to iOS and can't imagine why you'd want to disable it?

Create Some Downtime

Screen Time's Downtime option lets you set aside some time during your day when you least use your iPhone (or should use it the least). This feature would seem to be best used in the evening and during sleeping hours, but it could also be set up to discourage iPhone use during other times, such as meals or while at work. When Downtime is on, the only apps that will be available are the Phone app and those others you choose to allow (more on that in the next section).

To create some iPhone downtime in your day:

1. Open the Screen Time options in the Settings app.

2. Tap Downtime and then toggle the Downtime switch to On (green) by tapping it, as shown in **Figure 5-5.**

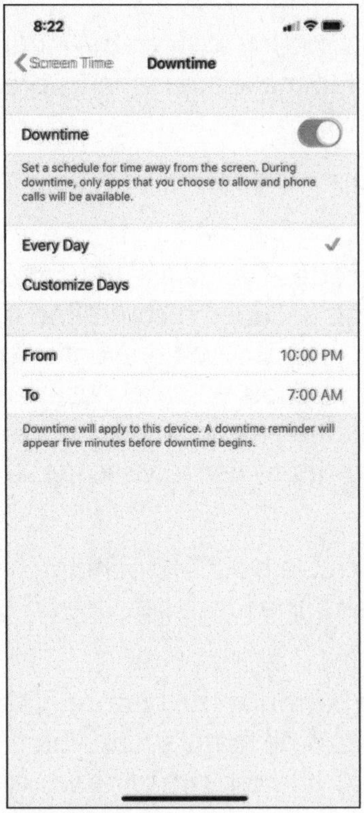

FIGURE 5-5

3. Tap From to select a time of day to begin your downtime, and then tap To to choose a time for downtime to stop.

> If you have other iOS or iPadOS devices and are signed into iCloud using the same Apple ID as your iPhone, the Downtime settings will apply for all those devices (assuming iOS 13 is installed on them).

TIP

Allow Certain Apps during Downtime

If you've decided to use Downtime, you may want certain apps to always be available, even during the Downtime period. The Phone app is always available, but you may allow others as you please.

1. Open Screen Time options in the Settings app.

2. Tap the Always Allowed option.

3. In the Allowed Apps section, you'll see a list of apps that are already enabled for use during Downtime by Apple (shown in **Figure 5-6**). These include Phone, Messages, FaceTime, and Maps. Note that Phone cannot be disabled.

Tap to remove apps

Tap to add apps
FIGURE 5-6

4. To allow other apps, scroll through the list in the Choose Apps section and tap the green plus sign (+) to the left of the app's name to add it to the Allowed Apps list.

5. To remove apps from the Allowed Apps list, tap the red minus sign (–) to the left of its name, and then tap the red Remove button that appears to its right.

If you're wondering which apps to allow, consider starting with those that may be used for contacting friends and family as well as those that are used for medical monitoring and other health-related needs.

Set App Limits

App Limits is an ingenious feature of Screen Time that acts to help you curtail excessive use of apps that tend to consume most of your time. Let's face it: Sometimes we just get so engrossed in checking out social media and browsing the web that we end up wondering where half the day went. App Limits helps remind you when the time limit is up, but it does allow you to have a bit of extra time or completely ignore the limit for the day if need be.

To create app limits:

1. Open the Screen Time options in the Settings app.

2. Tap App Limits, and then tap the Add Limit button.

3. Tap the circle to the left of a category to select all apps in the category, as shown in **Figure 5-7,** or tap a category name and tap a circle next to a particular app to only select it (as opposed to selecting all apps in the category).

Tap All Apps & Categories to set limits for everything in one fell swoop.

4. Tap Next in the upper-right corner of the screen.

5. Use the scroll wheel to set time limits in terms of hours and minutes, seen in **Figure 5-8.** Tap Customize Days under the scroll wheel to set specific times for particular days.

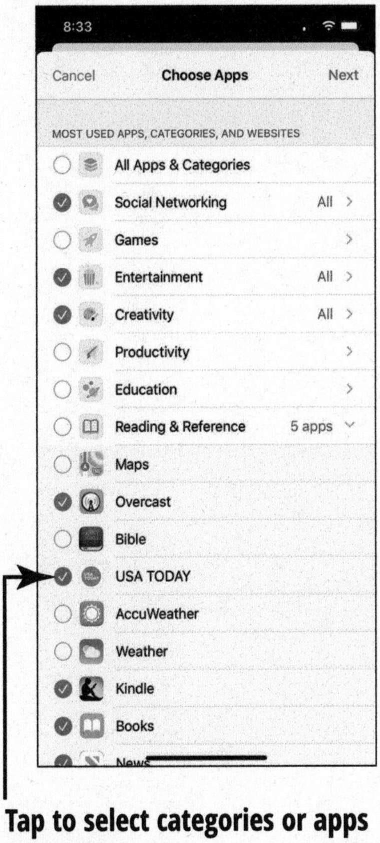

Tap to select categories or apps

FIGURE 5-7

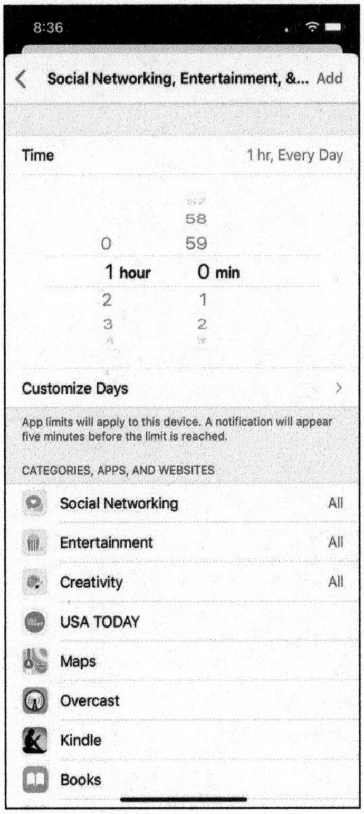

FIGURE 5-8

6. Tap Add in the upper-right corner and the new limit appears in the App Limits list, as shown in **Figure 5-9.** Tap it to make changes to the allotted time or to delete it by tapping the red Delete Limit button at the bottom of the screen, and then tap Delete Limit again to confirm.

7. Tap Add Limit button on the App Limits screen to add more limits, or tap the Screen Time button in the upper-left corner to exit the App Limits screen.

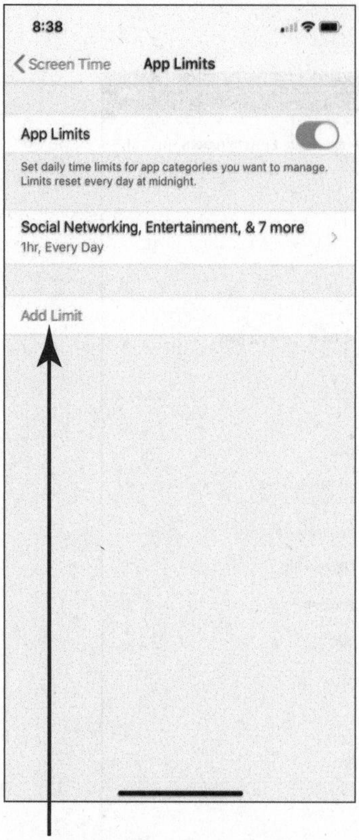

Tap to add another limit

FIGURE 5-9

Your iPhone will notify you when you've reached an app's limit: The screen will become gray, displaying an hourglass, and the app's icon is also grayed out on the Home screen where it resides. If you'd like more time, tap the blue Ignore Limit button at the bottom of the screen, and then tap One More Minute, Remind Me in 15 Minutes, or Ignore Limit For Today (see **Figure 5-10**). Tap Cancel if you'd like to adhere to the limit you've set for the app.

TIP If you enabled a passcode for Screen Time, you must enter it before overriding the app's time limit.

FIGURE 5-10

Set Content and Privacy Restrictions

Screen Time helps you prevent access to content that you don't want to be accessed on your iPhone, and you can also use it to set privacy limits. Content to be restricted could be apps, websites, media (movies, music, and so on), books, and more.

WARNING If you're going to restrict content and set privacy restrictions, it's advisable to enable the Screen Time passcode. That way, only someone knowledgeable of the passcode can alter the settings you're about to make. This is highly recommended, especially if your original intent is to provide safety for any children who may use your iPhone.

To set content and privacy options:

1. Open Screen Time options in the Settings app.

2. Tap Content & Privacy Restrictions and then toggle the Content & Privacy Restrictions switch to On (green), as shown in **Figure 5-11**.

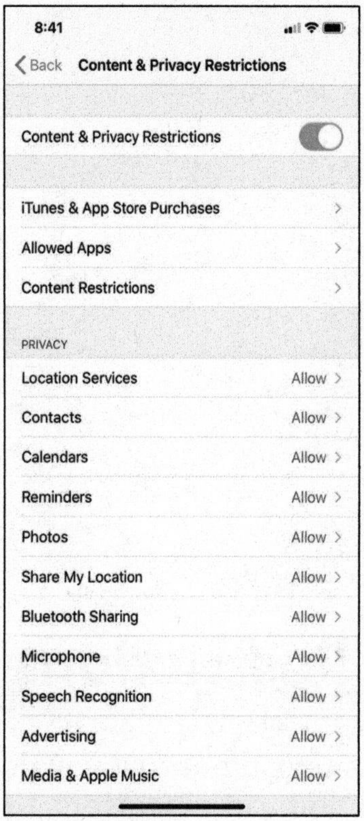

FIGURE 5-11

3. Tap iTunes & App Store Purchases to allow or block installation of apps, deletion of apps, or in-app purchases (purchases that may occur within an app, such as buying upgrades for characters in games). Also decide whether users always require a password when making purchases in the iTunes Store or App Store. (I very much recommend using this option if other people use your iPhone.)

4. Tap the Back button in the upper-left to return to the Content & Privacy Restrictions screen, and then tap Allowed Apps. This feature allows you to enable or disable apps that are created by Apple and are installed on your iPhone by default. As you can see in **Figure 5-12,** all of them are enabled to start. If you'd like to disable any of them, simply tap the switch to turn it Off (white). This will completely remove the app from the Home Screen; reenabling the app will place it back on the Home Screen.

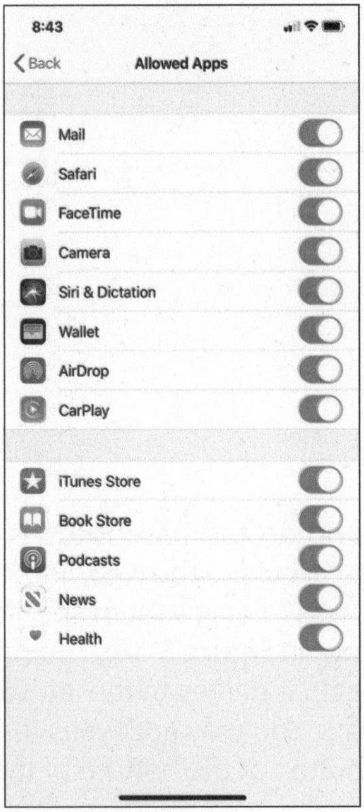

FIGURE 5-12

5. Tap the Back button in the upper-left to return to the Content & Privacy Restrictions screen, and then tap Content Restrictions.

6. In the Allowed Store Content section, you can make restrictions based on certain criteria. For example, you can limit which movies are available for purchase or rent in the iTunes Store based on their ratings, as shown in **Figure 5-13.**

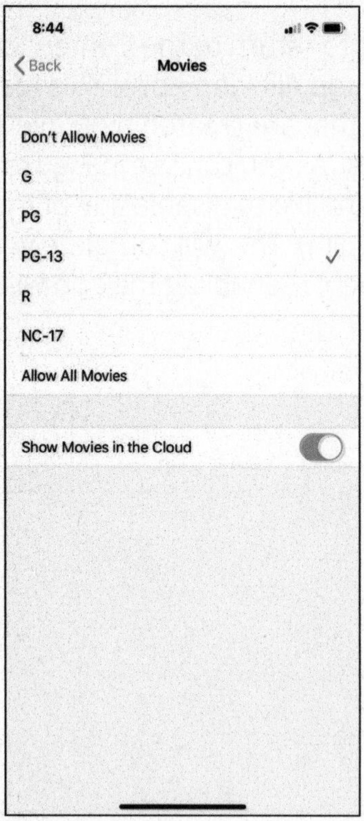

FIGURE 5-13

7. The Web Content section lets you restrict access to websites. From there, you're able to allow unrestricted access to the web, limit access to adult websites, and further limit access to only a list of specific websites that you can customize (shown in **Figure 5-14**). You may remove sites from the list by dragging their names to the left and tapping the red Delete button that appears. You may add websites to the list by tapping the blue Add Website button at the bottom of the list.

8. Options in the Siri and Game Center sections let you prevent access to untoward content or language, as well as disabling multiplayer games, adding friends to games, and turning off the ability to record your iPhone's screen.

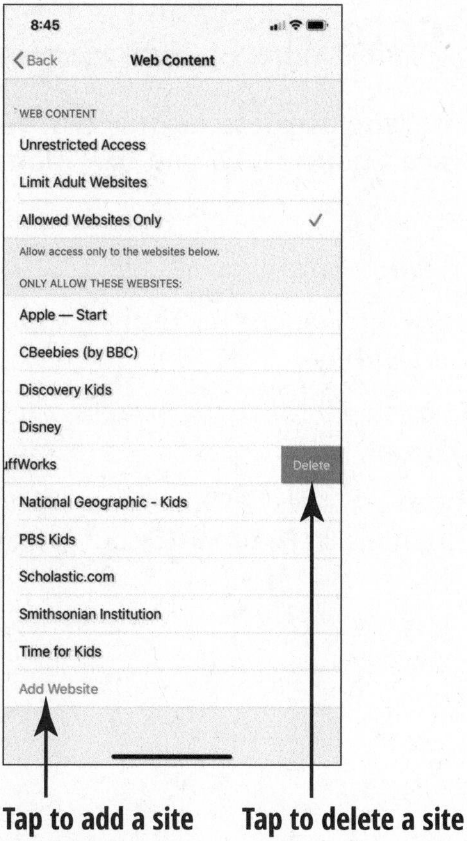

Tap to add a site   **Tap to delete a site**

FIGURE 5-14

9. Tap the Back button in the upper-left to return to the Content & Privacy Restrictions screen, and then view the items listed in the Privacy section. This area lists features and functions built-in to your iPhone. Tapping one shows you which apps are accessing the feature or function, enabling you to limit access to specific apps or to turn off access altogether (by selecting Don't Allow Changes).

10. Finally, the Allow Changes section of the Content & Privacy Restrictions screen lets you determine whether changes may be made to such features of your iPhone such as Volume Limit settings, Cellular Data options, and more.

Manage Children's Accounts

If you have children in your life who use devices linked to your Apple ID through Family Sharing (see Chapter 16), you can manage their activities using Screen Time.

1. Open Screen Time options in the Settings app.

2. Scroll down to the Family section and tap the name of a child's account. Then tap Turn On Screen Time.

3. Tap Continue and move step by step through the process of enabling Screen Time for the child's account.

4. Tap the Start and End options to set times for Downtime, and then tap the Set Downtime button (shown in **Figure 5-15**), or tap Not Now to skip.

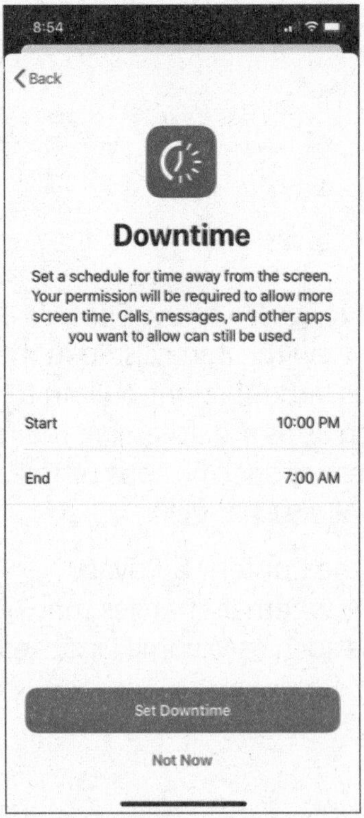

FIGURE 5-15

5. Tap the circles next to app categories, or just tap All Apps & Categories, to set App Limits for the child's account. Tap Set next to Time Amount to set a time limit, and then tap the Set App Limit button at the bottom of the screen. Of course, you can also tap Not Now to skip.

6. In the Content & Privacy screen, tap the Continue button, shown in **Figure 5-16.**

FIGURE 5-16

7. Set a Screen Time Passcode to prevent changes from being made to the settings for this account, if prompted.

Don't forget the Screen Time Passcodes you use for Screen Time accounts! Write them down somewhere safe if you need help remembering.

8. Screen Time is now activated for the child's account. You may make changes to the account's Screen Time settings at any time.

2

Beginning to Use Your iPhone

IN THIS PART . . .

Phoning your friends and family

Managing contacts

Messaging and video calls

Discovering utilities

Customizing accessibility

Getting to know Siri, your personal iPhone assistant

IN THIS CHAPTER

» Place and end calls

» Place calls using Contacts

» Receive and return calls

» Use Favorites

» Use tools during calls

» Enable Do Not Disturb

» Reply to calls via text and set reminders to call back

Chapter **6**

Making and Receiving Calls

I f you're someone who only wants a cellphone to make and receive calls, you probably didn't buy an iPhone. Still, making and receiving calls is one of the primary functions of any phone, smart or otherwise.

In this chapter, you discover all the basics of placing calls, receiving calls, and using available tools during a call to mute sound, turn on the speakerphone, and more. You also explore features that help you manage how to respond to a call that you can't take at the moment, how to receive calls when in your car, and how to change your ringtone.

Use the Keypad to Place a Call

Dialing a call with a keypad is an obvious first skill for you to acquire, and it's super-simple.

TIP

CarPlay is a feature that provides the ability to interact with your car and place calls using Siri voice commands and your iPhone. Apps designed for CarPlay allow you to interact with controls while keeping your attention on the road. Visit www.apple.com/ios/carplay/available-models to see which auto manufacturers are currently utilizing CarPlay in their products. To date there are over 500 models supporting CarPlay.

To manually dial a call, follow these steps:

1. On any Home screen, tap Phone in the Dock, and the app opens; tap the keypad button at the bottom of the screen, and the keypad appears (see **Figure 6-1**).

TIP

   If anything other than the keypad appears, you can just tap the Keypad button at the bottom of the screen to display the keypad.

2. Enter the number you want to call by tapping the number buttons; as you do, the number appears above the keypad.

   When you enter a phone number, before you place the call, you can tap Add Number (blue text found directly underneath the phone number) to add the person to your Contacts app. You can create a new contact or add the phone number to an existing contact using this feature.

3. If you enter a number incorrectly, use the Delete button that appears on the keypad after you've begun to enter a number (a left-pointing arrow with an X in it) to clear numbers one at a time.

4. Tap the Call button shaped like a telephone headset. The call is placed and tools appear, as shown in **Figure 6-2.**

Keypad button

FIGURE 6-1

FIGURE 6-2

TIP

If you're on a call that requires you to punch in numbers or symbols (such as a pound sign), tap the Keypad button on the tools that appear during a call to display the keypad. See more about using calling tools in the "Use Tools During a Call" task, later in this chapter.

End a Call

In the following tasks, I show you several other ways to place calls; however, I don't want to leave you on your first call without a way out. When you're on a phone call, the green Call button (refer to **Figure 6-1**) changes to a red End Call button (see **Figure 6-3**). Tap End, and the call is disconnected.

End call button

FIGURE 6-3

Place a Call Using Contacts

If you've created a contact (see Chapter 7) and included a phone number in that contact record, you can use the Contacts app to place a call.

1. Tap the Phone icon in any Home screen dock.

2. Tap the Contacts button at the bottom of the screen.

3. In the Contacts list that appears, scroll up or down to locate the contact you need or tap a letter along the right side to jump to that section of the list. You can also search for a contact by tapping the Search field and entering part of the contact's name, as shown in **Figure 6-4.**

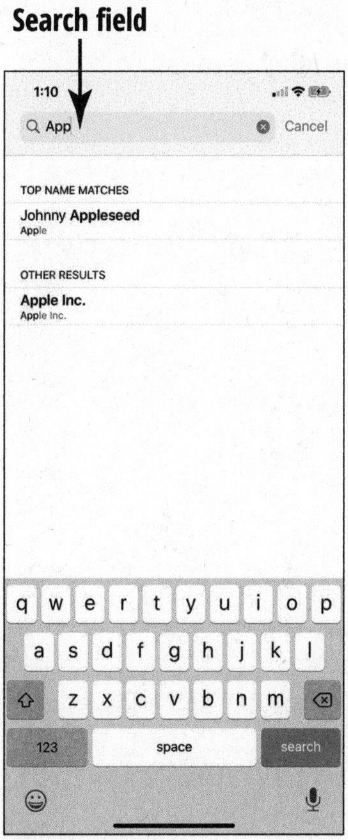

Search field

1:10

Q App   ⊗ Cancel

TOP NAME MATCHES

Johnny **Appleseed**
Apple

OTHER RESULTS

Apple Inc.
Apple Inc.

q w e r t y u i o p
a s d f g h j k l
⇧ z x c v b n m ⌫
123   space   search

FIGURE 6-4

4. Tap the contact to display their record. In the record that appears (see **Figure 6-5**), tap the phone number field. The call is placed.

TIP If you locate a contact and the record doesn't include a phone number, you can add it at this point by tapping the Edit button, entering the number, and then tapping Done. Place your call following Step 4 in the preceding steps.

main
1 (800) MYAPPLE ← ——————— **Tap the phone number to call**

FIGURE 6-5

Return a Recent Call

If you want to dial a number from a call you've recently made or received, you can use the Recents call list.

1. Tap Phone in the Dock on any Home screen.

2. Tap the Recents button at the bottom of the screen. A list of recent calls that you've both made and received appears (see **Figure 6-6**).

REMEMBER

Missed calls appear in red.

3. If you want to view only the calls you've missed, tap the Missed tab at the top of the screen.

Recents button

FIGURE 6-6

4. Tap the Info icon (a tiny i within a small circle) to the right of any item to view information about calls to or from this person or establishment (see **Figure 6-7**). The information displayed here might differ depending on the other phone and connection.

5. Tap the Recents button in the upper-left corner to return to the Recents list, and then tap any call record to place a call to that number.

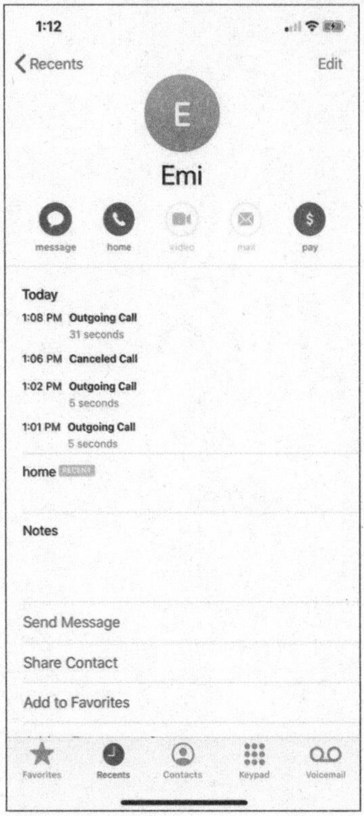

FIGURE 6-7

Use Favorites

You can save up to 50 contacts to Favorites in the Phone app so that you can quickly make calls to your A-list folks or businesses.

1. Tap Phone on any Home screen.

2. Tap the Favorites button at the bottom of the screen.

3. In the Favorites screen that displays (see **Figure 6-8**), tap the Add button.

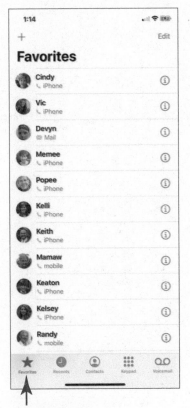

Favorites button

FIGURE 6-8

4. Your Contacts list appears and contact records that contain a phone number are bolded. Locate a contact that you want to make a Favorite and tap it. Next, in the menu that appears, tap Call or Video, depending on which type of call you prefer to make to this person most of the time (see **Figure 6-9**). Tap the arrows to the right of Call or Video to choose other options for the contact, such as alternate phone numbers. The Favorites list reappears with your new favorite contact on it.

5. To place a call to a Favorite, display the Phone app, tap Favorites, and then tap a person on the list to place a call.

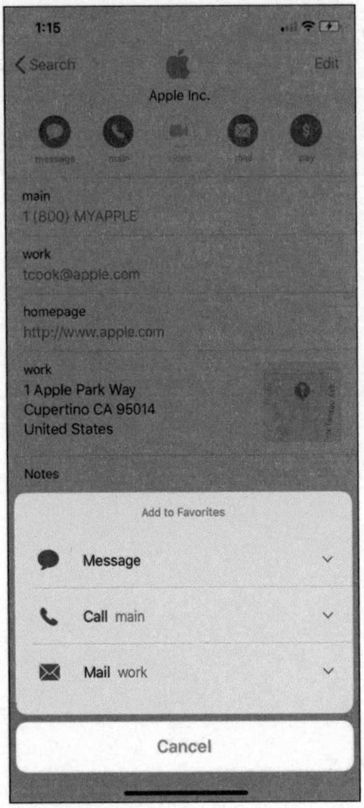

FIGURE 6-9

TIP

If you decide to place a FaceTime call to a Favorite that you've created using the Voice Call setting, just tap the Information icon that appears to the right of the favorite's listing and tap the Face-Time call button in the contact record that appears. You can also create two contacts for the same person, one with a cellphone and one with a land-line phone, for instance, and place one or both in Favorites. See Chapter 8 for more about making FaceTime calls.

Receive a Call

There's one step to receiving a call. When a call comes in to you, the screen shown in **Figure 6-10** appears:

» Tap Accept to pick up the call.

» Tap Message to send a preset text message without picking up. Select the message in Settings under Phone ➪ Respond with Text.

» Tap Remind Me to have iPhone send you a reminder to return the call without answering it.

» If you tap Decline or don't tap either of the other buttons after a few rings, the call goes to your voice mail.

FIGURE 6-10

TIP

There's another quick way to send a call to voice mail or decline it: Press the Sleep/Wake button on the top or side of your phone once to send a call to voice mail or press the same button twice to decline the call. You can also press the Volume button once to perform the same task, if it's more convenient.

BLOCKING AND SILENCING UNSOLICITED CALLERS

Are you receiving calls from people and companies that you'd rather not get? Are telemarketers constantly bothering you? Never fear, Apple is here! You can easily block unwanted or unsolicited callers. Open the Phone app, tap the Recents button at the bottom of the screen, and then tap the number of the caller you want to block. Swipe to the bottom of the screen, tap the Block this Caller button, and then tap Block Contact to confirm. Simply follow the same steps to unblock the caller if you'd like to resume reception of their calls.

iOS 13 introduced a feature that goes one step further. If you're getting inundated with telemarking calls, your iPhone can now *silence* unknown calls automatically and send them directly to voicemail. In other words, if you get a call from someone who isn't listed in your contacts, the call will go directly to voicemail, and your iPhone won't bother you with a ring or vibrate. You'll simply see a notification that an incoming call was received, and the caller will appear in your list of recent calls. If the caller leaves a voicemail, you'll receive a notification for that as well.

If you want to turn on the silencing feature, open the Settings app, scroll down to Phone, and turn on the Silence Unknown Callers option. For many people, this feature is a godsend. Just make sure that all the important people in your life — including not just family and friends but also doctors, insurance agents, pharmacists, school principals, and so forth — are in your contacts. That way they won't be silenced when they try to reach you. If a silenced caller is someone you want to hear from in the future, add that person's number to your contacts, and your phone will ring or vibrate when they call.

With the Handoff feature, if your iPhone is near an iPad or Mac computer (2012 model or later) and a call comes in, you can connect to the call via Bluetooth from any of the three devices by clicking or swiping the call notification. All devices have to be signed into the same iCloud account and have enabled Bluetooth and Handoff under Settings.

Use Tools During a Call

When you're on a call, whether you initiated it or received it, a set of tools, shown in **Figure 6-11,** is displayed.

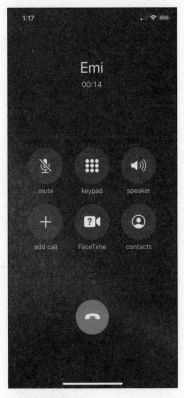

FIGURE 6-11

Here's what these six buttons allow you to do, starting with the top-left corner:

» **Mute:** Silences the phone call so that the caller can't hear you, though you can hear the caller. The Mute button background turns white, as shown in **Figure 6-12**, when a call is muted. Tap again to unmute the call.

» **Keypad:** Displays the numeric keypad.

FIGURE 6-12

» **Speaker:** Turns the speakerphone feature on and off.

If you are near a Bluetooth device and have Bluetooth turned on in your iPhone Settings, you will see a list of sources (such as a car Bluetooth connection for hands-free calls) and you can choose the one you want to use.

» **Add Call:** Displays Contacts so that you can add a caller to a conference call.

» **FaceTime:** Begins a video call with somebody who has an iPhone 4 or more recent model, iPod touch (4th generation or later), iPad 2 or third-generation or later, an iPad mini, or a Mac running macOS 10.7 or later.

» **Contacts:** Displays a list of contacts.

You can pair your Apple Watch with your iPhone to make and receive calls using it. For more information, visit Apple's Support site at `https://support.apple.com/watch`.

Turn On Do Not Disturb

Do Not Disturb is a feature that causes your iPhone to silence incoming calls when it's locked, displaying only a moon-shaped icon to let you know that a call is coming in.

1. To access the feature, tap Settings.

2. To enable the feature, find and tap Do Not Disturb, and then toggle the Do Not Disturb switch to On (green).

When you turn on the Do Not Disturb feature, calls from Favorites are automatically allowed through by default. You can change that setting by tapping the Allow Calls From option in Settings ⇨ Do Not Disturb.

Way back in iOS 11, Apple introduced an important addition to the Do Not Disturb feature: Do Not Disturb While Driving (shown in **Figure 6-13**). This option is near the bottom of the Settings ⇨ Do Not Disturb screen. You can block incoming calls, notifications, and texts while you're driving to prevent distractions and accidents. There are three ways to activate Do Not Disturb While Driving:

» **Manually (default):** You activate the feature through Control Center (see Chapter 3 for more information).

» **When Connected to Car Bluetooth:** The feature activates automatically only when your iPhone connects to your vehicle's Bluetooth.

» **Automatically:** The feature is enabled whenever your iPhone detects that you're in an accelerating vehicle. Yes, it's that smart! This could be inconvenient when you're simply a passenger. In this case, disable the feature for the duration of the ride.

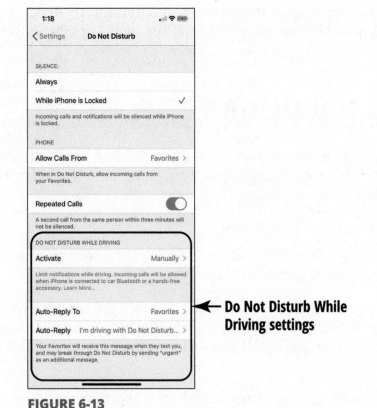

FIGURE 6-13

Phone calls can come through when you're connected to your vehicle's Bluetooth or a hands-free accessory, but not texts or notifications.

You can set up an Auto-Reply feature to send a text to certain people who are texting you (your Favorites are enabled by default). This option is in the Do Not Disturb While Driving section of Settings ⇨ Do Not Disturb.

If your car is equipped with CarPlay, you can have your iPhone automatically activate Do Not Disturb when you connect it to your car via Bluetooth or USB. Go to Settings ⇨ Do Not Disturb ⇨ Activate, and then toggle the Activate With CarPlay switch to On (green).

Set Up Exceptions for Do Not Disturb

If there are people whose calls you want to receive even when the Do Not Disturb feature is turned on, you can set up that capability. You can also set up a feature that allows a second call from the same number made within 3 minutes of the first to ring through. The theory with this feature is that two calls within a few minutes of each other might suggest an emergency situation that you'll want to respond to.

1. With the Do Not Disturb feature turned on (see the previous task), tap Settings.

2. Tap Do Not Disturb, and on the Do Not Disturb screen, toggle the Repeated Calls On/Off switch to On (refer to **Figure 6-13**).

If you want to schedule Do Not Disturb to be active only during a certain time period, such as your lunch hour, toggle the Scheduled switch to On (green), and then set a time range.

Reply to a Call via Text or Set a Reminder to Call Back

You can reply with a text message to callers whose calls you can't answer. You can also set up a reminder to call the person back later.

1. When a call comes in that you want to send a preset message to, tap Message.

2. Tap on a preset reply, or tap Custom, and then enter your own message.

3. To set up a reminder, tap Remind Me when the call comes in, and then tap In One Hour or When I Leave to be reminded when you leave your current location.

Change Your Ringtone

The music or sound that plays when a call is coming in is called a ringtone. Your phone is set up with a default ringtone, but you can choose among a large number of Apple-provided choices.

1. Tap the Settings icon.

2. Tap Sounds and then tap Ringtone.

3. Scroll down the list of ringtones and tap on one to preview it (see **Figure 6-14**).

4. When you have selected the ringtone that you want in the list of ringtones, tap Sounds to return to the Sounds settings with your new ringtone in effect.

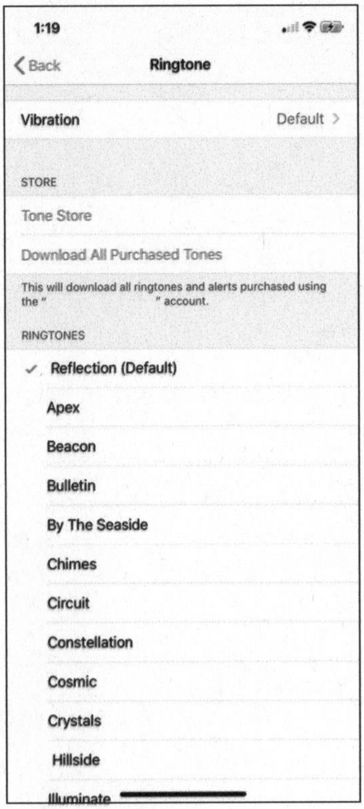

FIGURE 6-14

TIP

You can also set custom ringtones for contacts using the Contacts app to give that person's calls a unique sound. Open a contact's record, tap Edit, and then tap the Ringtone setting to display a list of ringtones. Tap one and then tap Done to save it.

IN THIS CHAPTER

» Add, share, and delete
  contacts

» Sync Contacts with iCloud

» Assign a photo to a contact

» Add social media information

» Customize contacts profiles

» Search for a contact

» View a contact's location
  in Maps

Chapter **7**

Organizing Contacts

ontacts is the iPhone equivalent of the dog-eared address book that used to sit by your phone. The Contacts app is simple to set up and use, and it has some powerful features beyond simply storing names, addresses, and phone numbers.

For example, you can pinpoint a contact's address in iPhone's Maps app. You can use your contacts to address email and Facebook messages and Twitter tweets quickly. If you store a contact record that includes a website, you can use a link in Contacts to view that website instantly. In addition, of course, you can easily search for a contact by a variety of criteria, including how people are related to you, such as family or mutual friends, or by groups you create.

In this chapter, you discover the various features of Contacts, including how to save yourself time spent entering contact information by syncing contacts with such services as iCloud.

Add a Contact

1. To access Contacts, tap Phone at the bottom of the Home screen, and then tap the Contacts icon at the bottom of the screen, or simply find and tap the Contacts app icon on a Home screen (it's on the second one by default). An alphabetical list of contacts appears, like the one shown in **Figure 7-1.**

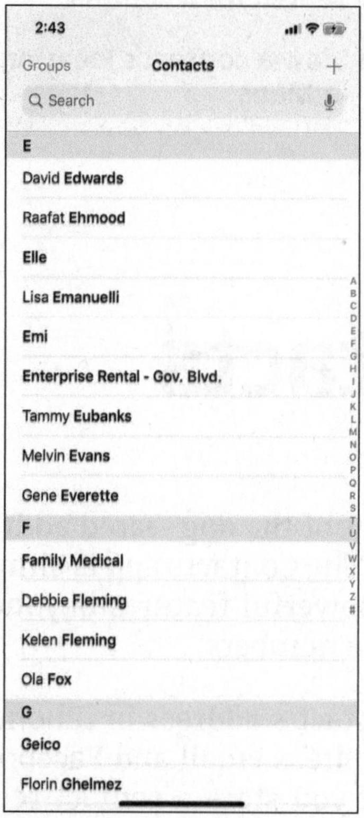

FIGURE 7-1

2. Tap the Add button, the button with the small plus sign (+) on it in the upper-right corner. A blank New Contact page opens (see **Figure 7-2**). Tap in any field and the onscreen keyboard displays.

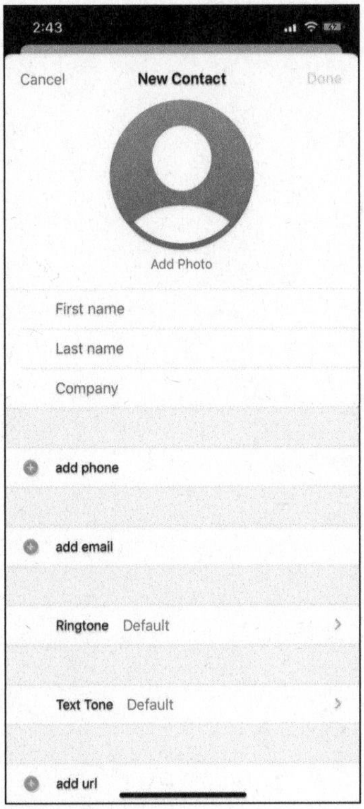

FIGURE 7-2

3. Enter any contact information you want.

   TECHNICAL STUFF

   Only one of the First name, Last name, or Company fields is required, but do feel free to add as much information as you like.

4. To scroll down the contact's page and see more fields, flick up on the screen with your finger.

5. If you want to add information (such as a mailing or street address), you can tap the relevant Add field, which opens additional entry fields.

6. To add an information field, such as Nickname or Job Title, tap the blue add field button toward the bottom of the page. In the Add Field dialog that appears (see **Figure 7-3**), choose a field to add.

   TIP

   You have to flick up or down the screen with your finger to view all the fields.

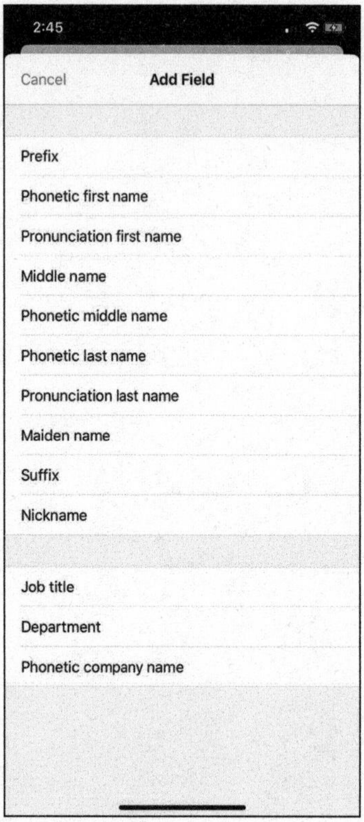

FIGURE 7-3

TIP

If your contact has a name that's difficult for you to pronounce, con-sider adding the Phonetic First Name or Phonetic Last Name field, or both, to that person's record (refer to **Figure 7-3**).

7. Tap the Done button in the upper-right corner when you finish mak-ing entries. The new contact appears in your address book. Tap it to see details (see **Figure 7-4**).

TIP

You can choose a distinct ringtone or text tone for a new contact. Just tap the Ringtone or Text Tone field in the New Contact form or when editing a contact to see a list of options. When that per-son calls either on the phone or via FaceTime, or texts you via SMS, MMS, or iMessage, you will recognize them from the tone that plays.

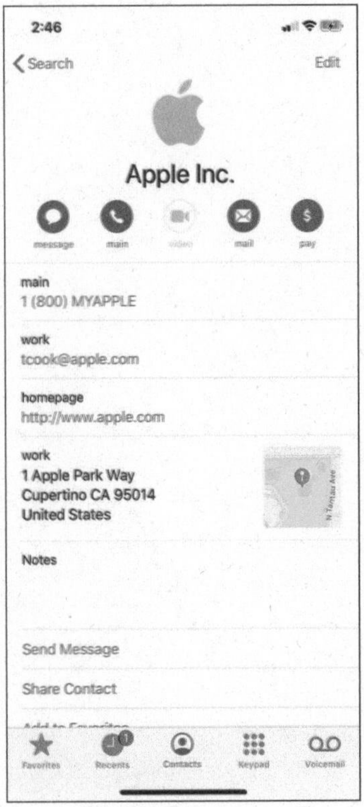

FIGURE 7-4

Sync Contacts with iCloud

You can use your iCloud account to sync contacts from your iPhone to iCloud to back them up. These also become available to your email account, if you set one up.

TIP

Mac users can also use iTunes or Finder (if your Mac is running macOS Catalina) to sync contacts among all your Apple devices; Windows PC users also use iTunes. See Chapter 4 for more about making iTunes settings.

1. On the Home screen, tap Settings, tap the name of your Apple ID account (at the top of the screen), and then tap iCloud.

2. In the iCloud settings shown in **Figure 7-5,** make sure that the On/Off switch for Contacts is set to On (green) in order to sync contacts.

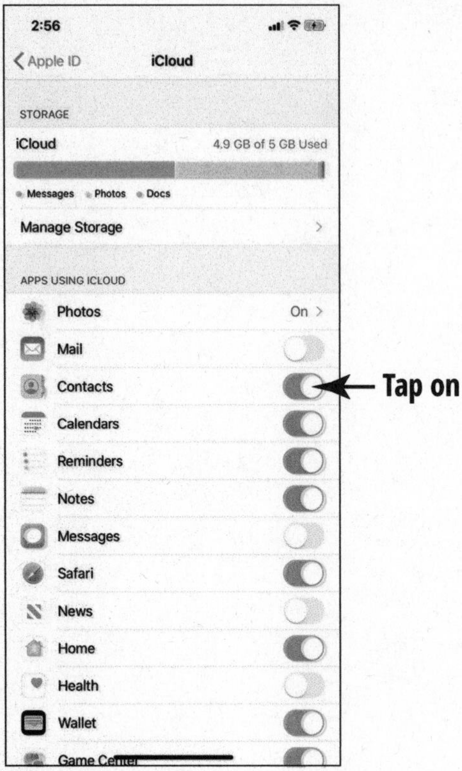

FIGURE 7-5

3. In the top-left corner of the screen, tap the Apple ID button and then tap the Settings button to return to Settings.

4. To choose which email account to sync with, first tap Passwords & Accounts. In the Accounts section, tap the email account you want to use.

5. In the following screen (see **Figure 7-6**), toggle the Contacts switch to On to merge contacts from that account via iCloud.

TIP You can use the iTunes Wi-Fi Sync feature in iPhone Settings under General to sync with iTunes wirelessly from a computer connected to the same Wi-Fi network.

Tap on

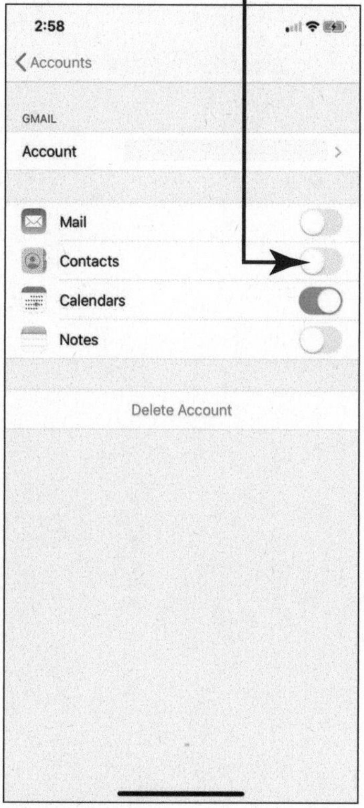

FIGURE 7-6

Assign a Photo to a Contact

1. With Contacts open, tap a contact to whose record you want to add a photo.

2. Tap the Edit button.

3. On the Info page that appears (see **Figure 7-7**), tap Add Photo.

4. In the menu that appears, tap a suggested photo or All Photos to choose an existing photo.

You could also tap the Camera icon to take that contact's photo on the spot.

TIP

5. In the Photos dialog that appears, choose a source for your photo (such as Favorites, Camera Roll, or other album).

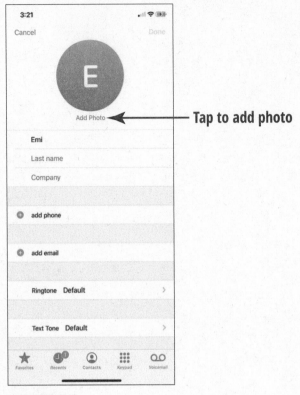

FIGURE 7-7

6. In the photo album that appears, tap a photo to select it. The Move and Scale dialog, shown in **Figure 7-8,** appears.

Center the photo the way you want it by dragging it with your finger.

7. Tap the Choose button to use the photo for this contact. If prompted, you may also select a filter to use with the photo.

8. Tap Done to save changes to the contact. The photo appears on the contact's Info page (see **Figure 7-9**).

While in the Photos dialog, in Step 6, you can modify the photo before saving it to the contact information. You can pinch or unpinch your fingers on the iPhone screen to contract or expand the photo, tap-and-drag the photo around the space to focus on a particular section, and then tap the Choose button to use the modified version.

FIGURE 7-8

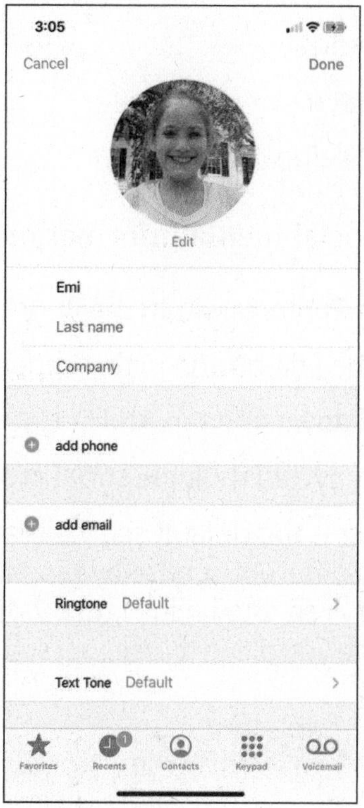

FIGURE 7-9

Add Social Media Information

iPhone users can add social media information to their Contacts so that they can quickly tweet (send a short message to) others using Twitter, comment to a contact on Facebook, and more.

You can use any of these social media platforms with Contacts:

» Twitter

» Facebook

» Flickr

» LinkedIn

» Myspace

» Sina Weibo

To add social media information to contacts, follow these steps:

1. Open Contacts within the Phone app and tap a contact.

2. Tap the Edit button in the upper-right corner of the screen.

3. Scroll down and tap Add Social Profile.

   You may add multiple social profiles if you like.

TIP

4. Twitter is the default service that pops up, but you can easily change it to a different service by tapping "Twitter" and selecting from the list of services, shown in **Figure 7-10.** Tap Done after you've selected the service you'd like to use.

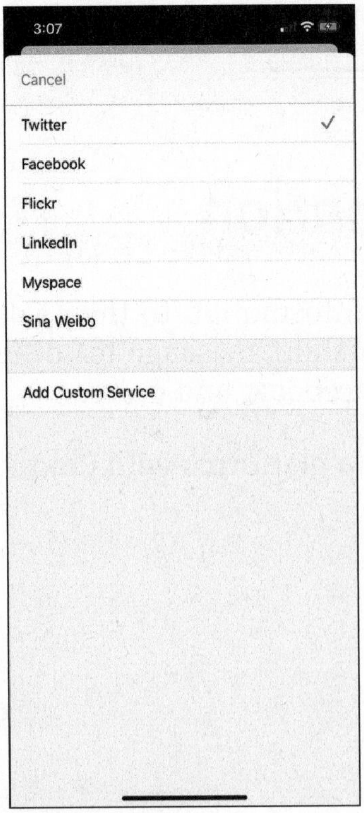

FIGURE 7-10

5. Enter the information for the social profile as needed.

6. Tap Done and the information is saved. The social profile account is now displayed when you select the contact, and you can send tweets, Facebook messages, or what-have-you by simply tapping the username, tapping the service you want to use to contact the person, and then tapping the appropriate command (such as Facebook posting).

Designate Related People

You can quickly designate relationships in a contact record if those people are saved to Contacts. One great use for this feature is using Siri to simply say, "Call Son" to call someone who is designated in your contact information as your son.

TIP

There's a setting for Linked Contacts in the Contacts app when you're editing a contact's record. Using this setting isn't like adding a relation; rather, if you have records for the same person that have been imported into Contacts from different sources, such as Google or Twitter, you can link them to show only a single contact.

1. Tap a contact and then tap Edit.

2. Scroll down the record and tap Add Related Name.

3. The field labeled Mother (see **Figure 7-11**) now appears. If the contact you're looking for is indeed your mother, leave it as is; otherwise, tap Mother and select the correct relationship from the list provided.

4. Tap the blue Info icon to the left of the Related Name field, and your Contacts list appears. Tap the related person's name, and it appears in the field (see **Figure 7-12**).

5. If you would like to add additional names, tap Add Related Name again and continue to add additional names as needed.

6. Tap Done to complete the edits.

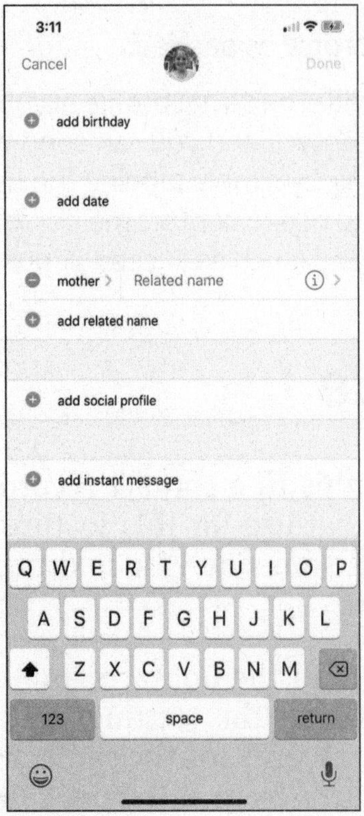

FIGURE 7-11 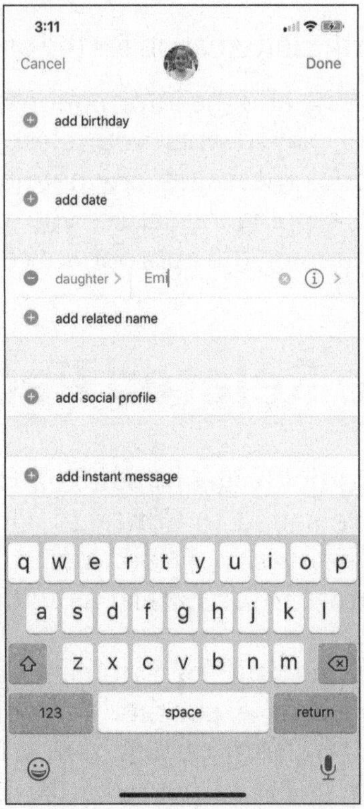　　　　**FIGURE 7-12**

TIP

After you add relations to a contact record, when you select the person in the Contacts main screen, all the related people for that contact are listed there.

Set Individual Ringtones and Text Tones

If you want to hear a unique tone when you receive a phone or Face-Time call from a particular contact, you can set up this feature in Contacts. For example, if you want to be sure that you know instantly whether your spouse, friend, or boss is calling, you can set a unique tone for that person.

TIP

If you set a custom tone for someone, that tone will be used when that person calls or contacts you by FaceTime.

To set up custom tones, follow these steps:

1. Tap to add a new contact or select a contact in the list of contacts and tap Edit.

2. Tap the Ringtone field in a new contact, or for an existing contact, tap Edit and then tap the Ringtone field, and a list of tones appears (see **Figure 7-13**).

TIP

You can set a custom text tone to be used when the person sends you a text message. Tap Text Tone instead of Ringtone, and then follow the remaining steps.

3. Scroll up and down to see the full list. Tap a tone, and it previews. When you hear one you like, tap Done.

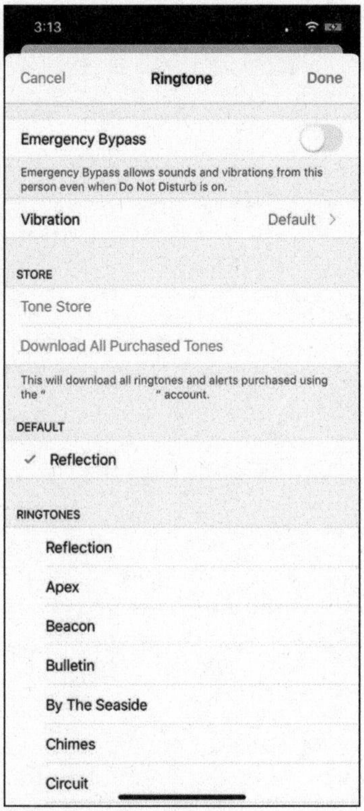

FIGURE 7-13

TIP

If your Apple devices are synced via iCloud, setting a unique ring-tone for an iPhone contact also sets it for use with FaceTime and Messages on your iPad and Mac. See Chapter 4 for more about iCloud.

Search for a Contact

1. With Contacts open, tap in the Search field at the very top of your Contacts list (see **Figure 7-14**). The onscreen keyboard opens.

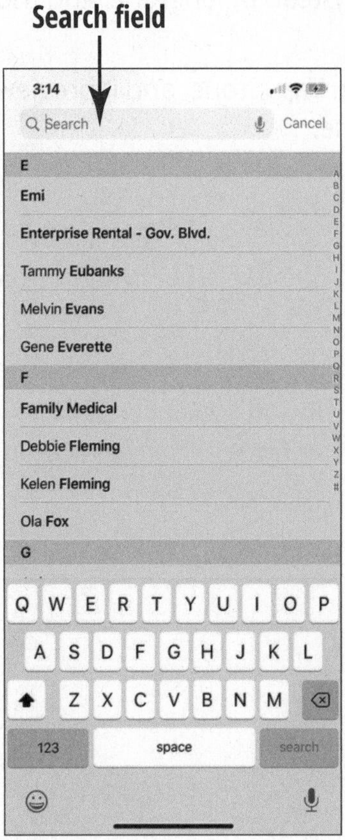

Search field

FIGURE 7-14

2. Type the first letters of either the first or last name or company. All matching results appear, as shown in **Figure 7-15.** For example, typing "App" might display Johnny Appleseed and Apple, Inc. in the results, both of which have "App" as the first three letters of the first or last part of the name or address.

TIP

You can use the alphabetical listing along the right side of All Contacts and tap a letter to locate a contact. Also, you can tap and drag to scroll down the list of contacts on the All Contacts page.

3. Tap a contact in the results to display that person's Information page.

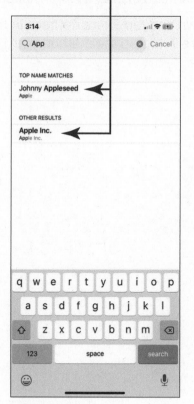

FIGURE 7-15

You can search by phone number simply by entering the phone number in the Search field until the list narrows to the person you're looking for. This might be a good way to search for all contacts in your town or company, for example.

Share a Contact

After you've entered contact information, you can share it with others via an email, text message, and other methods.

1. With Contacts open, tap a contact name to display its information.

2. On the Information page, scroll down and tap Share Contact. In the dialog that appears, shown in **Figure 7-16,** tap the method you'd like to use to share the contact.

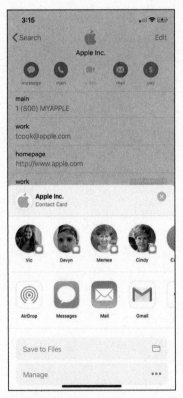

FIGURE 7-16

To share with an AirDrop-enabled device that is nearby, use the AirDrop button in the screen shown in **Figure 7-16.** Just select a nearby device, and your contact is transmitted to that person's device (such as a smartphone, a Mac with macOS with the AirDrop folder open in Finder, or a tablet).

3. Use the onscreen keyboard to enter a recipient's information if emailing or sharing via text message.

If the person is saved in Contacts, you can just type his or her name here.

4. Tap the Send button if sharing with email or text message. The message goes to your recipient with the contact information attached as a .vcf file. (This vCard format is commonly used to transmit contact information.)

When somebody receives a vCard containing contact information, he or she needs only to click the attached file to open it. At this point, depending on the email or contact management program, the recipient can perform various actions to save the content. Other iPhone, iPod touch, iPad, or iPhone users can easily import .vcf records as new contacts in their own Contacts apps.

Delete a Contact

When it's time to remove a name or two from your Contacts, it's easy to do.

1. With Contacts open, tap the contact you want to delete.

2. On the Information page (refer to **Figure 7-4**), tap the Edit button.

3. On the Info page that displays, drag your finger upward to scroll down and then tap the Delete Contact button at the bottom (see **Figure 7-17**).

4. When the confirmation dialog appears, tap the Delete Contact button to confirm the deletion.

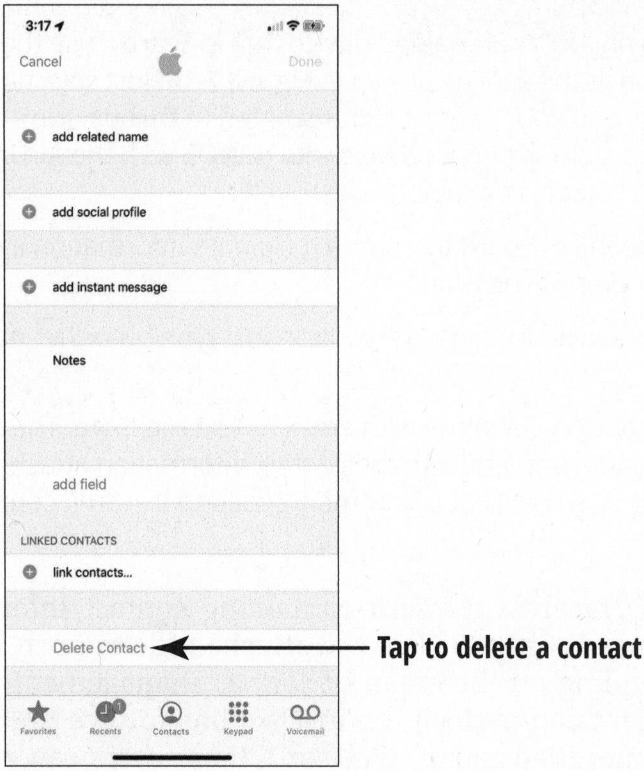
3:17
Cancel
Done
add related name
add social profile
add instant message
Notes
add field
LINKED CONTACTS
link contacts...
Delete Contact
Tap to delete a contact
Favorites
Recents
Contacts
Keypad
Voicemail

FIGURE 7-17

WARNING

During Step 4 of this process, if you change your mind simply tap the Cancel button. Be careful: Once you tap Delete Contact in the confirmation dialog, there's no going back! Your contact is deleted from your iPhone and also any other device that syncs to your iPhone via iCloud, Google, or other means.

Chapter **8**

Communicating with FaceTime and Messages

FaceTime is an excellent video-calling app that lets you call people who have FaceTime on their devices using either a phone number or an email address. You and your friend, colleague, or family member can see each other as you talk, which makes for a much more personal calling experience.

iMessage is a feature available through the preinstalled Messages app for instant messaging (IM). IM involves sending a text message to somebody's iPhone, iPod touch, Mac running macOS 10.8 or later, or iPad (using the person's phone number or email address to carry on an instant conversation). You can even send audio and video via Messages.

In this chapter, I introduce you to FaceTime and the Messages app and review their simple controls. In no time, you'll be socializing with all and sundry.

Understand Who Can Use FaceTime

Here's a quick rundown of the device and information you need for using FaceTime's various features:

» You can use FaceTime to call people over a Wi-Fi connection who have an iPhone 4 or later, an iPad 2 or a third-generation iPad or later, a fourth-generation iPod touch or later, or a Mac (running macOS 10.6.6 or later). If you want to connect over a cellular connection, you're limited to iPhone 4s or later and iPad third generation or later.

» You can use a phone number to connect with anybody with either an iOS device or a Mac and an iCloud account.

» The person you're contacting must have allowed FaceTime to be used in Settings.

Get an Overview of FaceTime

FaceTime works with the iPhone's built-in cameras so that you can call other folks who have a device that supports FaceTime. You can use FaceTime to chat while sharing video images with another person. This preinstalled app is useful for seniors who want to keep up with distant family members and friends and see (as well as hear) the latest-and-greatest news.

You can make and receive calls with FaceTime using a phone number or an email account and make calls to those with an iCloud account. When connected, you can show the person on the other end what's going on around you. Just remember that you can't adjust audio volume from within the app or record a video call. Nevertheless, on the positive side, even though its features are limited, this app is straightforward to use.

You can use your Apple ID and iCloud account to access FaceTime, so it works pretty much right away. See Chapter 4 for more about getting an Apple ID.

TIP

If you're having trouble using FaceTime, make sure that the FaceTime feature is turned on. That's quick to do: Tap Settings on the Home screen, tap FaceTime, and then tap the FaceTime On/Off switch to turn it On (green), if it isn't already. On this Settings screen, you can also select the phone number and/or email addresses that others can use to make FaceTime calls to you, as well as which one of those is displayed as your caller ID.

To view information for recent calls, open the FaceTime app and then tap the Information button on a recent call, and iPhone displays that person's information. You can tap the contact to call the person back.

TECHNICAL
STUFF

FaceTime is very secure, meaning that your conversations remain private. Apple encrypts (protects) all of your FaceTime calls, whether one-on-one or group calls, with industry-leading technology to make sure snoops are kept at bay.

Make a FaceTime Call with Wi-Fi or Cellular

If you know that the person you're calling has FaceTime available on his device, adding that person to your iPhone's Contacts is a good idea so you can initiate FaceTime calls from within Contacts if you like or from the Contacts list you can access through the FaceTime app.

TIP

When you call somebody using an email address, the person must be signed in to his Apple iCloud account and have verified that the address can be used for FaceTime calls. You can access this setting by tapping Settings and then FaceTime⇨Use Your Apple ID for FaceTime; FaceTime for Mac users make this setting by selecting FaceTime⇨Preferences.

1. Tap the FaceTime icon to launch the app. If you've made or received FaceTime calls already, you will see a list of recent calls on the screen. You can simply tap one of those to initiate a new call, or continue to learn how to start a new call from scratch.

2. Tap the + in the upper-right corner to open the New FaceTime screen. Tap the To field to enter or find a contact in your Contacts list (as shown in **Figure 8-1**).

FIGURE 8-1

3. Tap one of the green buttons to choose a Video or Audio call at the top of the screen. Video includes your voice and image; Audio includes only your voice.

TIP

You'll see a Video button if that contact's device supports FaceTime video and an Audio button if the contact's device supports FaceTime audio. (If you haven't saved this person in your contacts and you know the phone number to call or email, you can just enter that information in the Enter Name, Email, or Number field.)

4. When the person accepts the call, you see a large screen that displays the recipient's image and a small screen referred to as a Picture in Picture (PiP) containing your image superimposed (see **Figure 8-2**).

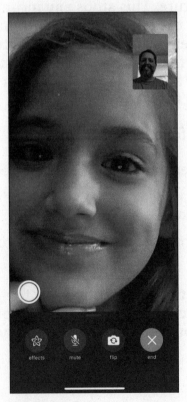

FIGURE 8-2

iOS 6 and later allow you to use FaceTime over both a Wi-Fi network and your iPhone cellular connection. However, if you use FaceTime over a cellular connection, you may incur costly data usage fees. To avoid the extra cost, in Settings under Cellular, toggle the FaceTime switch to Off (white).

Accept and End a FaceTime Call

If you're on the receiving end of a FaceTime call, accepting the call is about as easy as it gets.

If you'd rather not be available for calls, you can go to Settings and turn on the Do Not Disturb feature. This stops any incoming calls or notifications other than for the people you've designated as exceptions to Do Not Disturb. After you turn on Do Not Disturb, you can use the feature's settings to schedule when it's active, allow calls from certain people, or allow a second call from the same person in a 3-minute interval to go through.

To accept and end a FaceTime call, follow these steps:

1. When the call comes in, tap the Accept button to take the call (see **Figure 8-3**).

To reject the call, tap the Decline button.

2. Chat away with your friend, swapping video images. To end the call, tap the End button (see **Figure 8-4**).

To mute sound during a call, tap the Mute button (in the call dialog sheet), which looks like a microphone with a line through it (refer to **Figure 8-4**). Tap the button again to unmute your iPhone.

Flip button

End call button

Drag up for call options

FIGURE 8-3   **FIGURE 8-4**

FaceTime in iOS 13 allows group calls for up to 32 people! You can have a family reunion without leaving your front porch. To add more folks to a current call:

1. Swipe up on the call dialog sheet (drag the light gray line up) to see call options, shown in **Figure 8-5.**

2. Tap the Add Person button.

3. Tap the To field, enter or find a contact, tap a contact to add them to the To field, and finally, tap the green Add Person to FaceTime button to place them in the call.

Tap to add callers

FIGURE 8-5

Switch Views

When you're on a FaceTime call, you might want to use iPhone's built-in, rear-facing camera to show the person you're talking to what's going on around you.

1. Tap the Flip button (refer to **Figure 8-4**) to switch from the front-facing camera that's displaying your image to the back-facing camera that captures whatever you're looking at.

2. Tap the Switch Camera button again to switch back to the front camera displaying your image.

Set Up an iMessage Account

iMessage is a feature available through the preinstalled Messages app that allows you to send and receive instant messages (IMs) to others using an Apple iOS or iPadOS device, or suitably configured Macs. iMessage is a way of sending instant messages through a Wi-Fi network, but you can send messages through your cellular connection without having iMessage activated.

TECHNICAL STUFF

Instant messaging differs from email or tweeting in an important way. Whereas you might email somebody and wait for days or weeks before that person responds, or you might post a tweet that could sit there awhile before anybody views it, with instant messaging, communication happens almost immediately. You send an IM, and it appears on somebody's Apple device right away.

Assuming that the person wants to participate in a live conversation, the chat begins immediately, allowing a back-and-forth dialogue in real time.

1. To set up Messages, tap Settings on the Home screen.

2. Tap Messages. The settings shown in **Figure 8-6** appear.

3. If iMessage isn't set to On (refer to **Figure 8-6**), tap the On/Off switch to toggle it On (green).

TIP

Be sure that the phone number and/or email account associated with your iPhone under the Send & Receive setting is correct. (This should be set up automatically based on your iCloud settings.) If it isn't, tap the Send & Receive field, add an email or phone, and then tap Messages in the upper-left to return to the previous screen.

4. To allow a notice to be sent to the sender when you've read a message, tap the On/Off switch for Send Read Receipts. You can also choose to show a subject field in your messages.

5. Press the Home button (or swipe up from the bottom of the screen for iPhone X and newer models) to leave Settings.

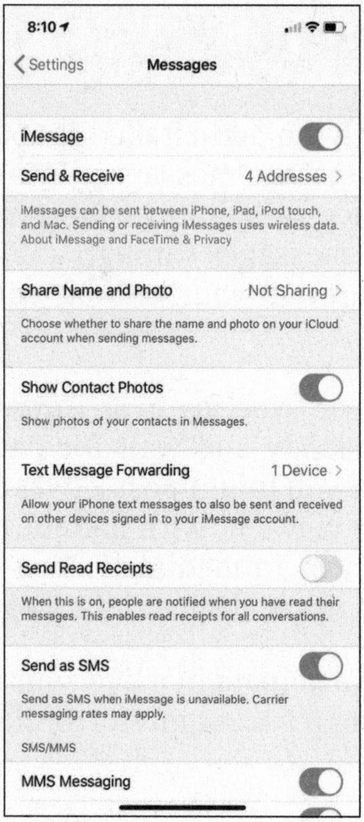

FIGURE 8-6

> To enable or disable email accounts used by Messages, tap Send & Receive and then tap an email address to either enable (check mark appears to the left) or disable it (no check mark appears to the left).

TIP

Use Messages to Address, Create, and Send Messages

Now you're ready to use Messages.

1. From the Home screen, tap the Messages button.

2. Tap the New Message button in the top-right corner to begin a conversation.

3. In the form that appears (see **Figure 8-7**), you can address a message in a few ways:

   - Begin to type a name in the To field, and a list of matching contacts appears.

   - Tap the Dictation key on the onscreen keyboard and speak the address.

   - Tap the plus (+) button on the right side of the address field, and the Contacts list is displayed.

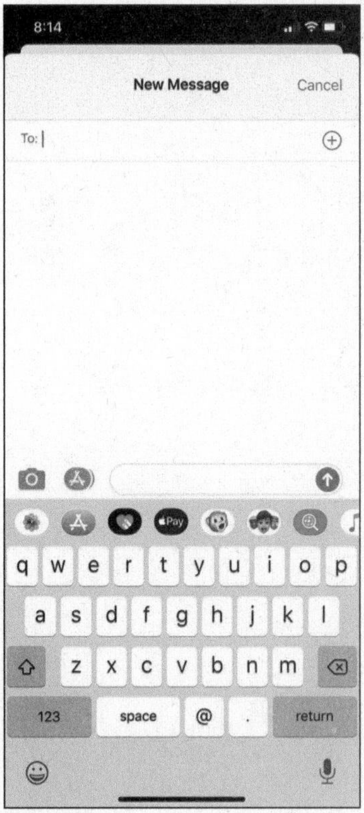

FIGURE 8-7

4. Tap a contact on the list you chose from in Step 3. If the contact has both an email address and a phone number stored, the Info dialog appears, allowing you to tap one or the other, which addresses the message.

5. To create a message, simply tap in the message field near the bottom of the screen (see **Figure 8-8**) and type your message.

6. To send the message, tap the Send button (refer to **Figure 8-8**). When your recipient (or recipients) responds, you'll see the conversation displayed on the screen. Tap in the message field again to respond to the last comment.

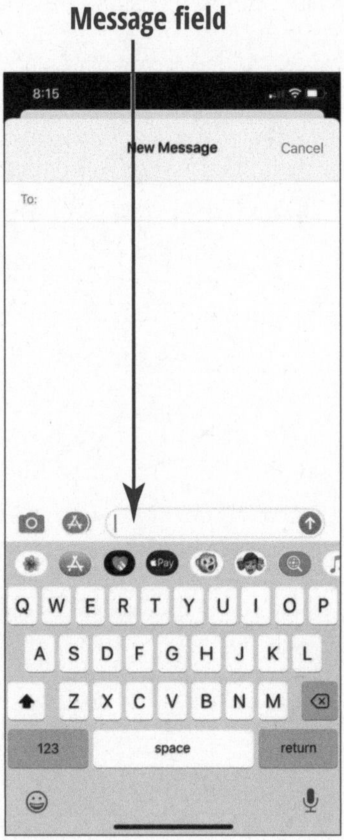

Message field

FIGURE 8-8

You can address a message to more than one person by simply choosing more recipients in Step 3 of the preceding list.

TIP

Read Messages

When you receive a message, it's as easy to read as email — easier, to be honest!

1. Tap Messages on the Home screen.

2. When the app opens, you see a list of text conversations you've engaged in.

3. Tap a conversation to see the message string, including all attachments, as shown in **Figure 8-9.**

4. To view all attachments of a message, tap Details (the encircled "i" in the upper-right corner) and scroll down.

FIGURE 8-9

Clear a Conversation

When you're done chatting, you might want to delete a conversation to remove the clutter before you start a new chat.

1. With Messages open and your conversations displayed, swipe to the left on the message you want to delete.

2. Tap the Delete button next to the conversation you want to get rid of (see **Figure 8-10**).

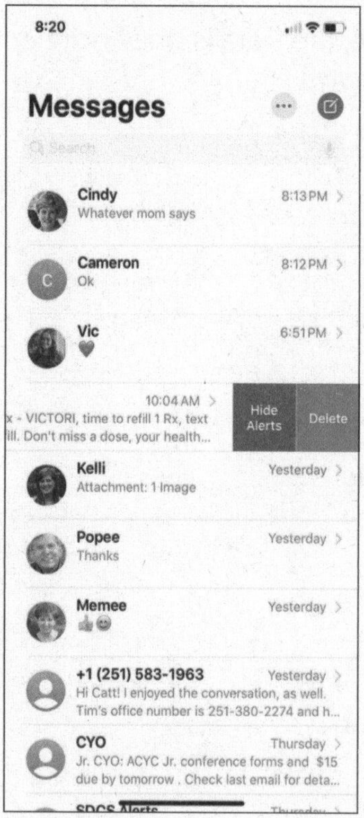

FIGURE 8-10

Tap the Hide Alerts button to keep from being alerted to new messages in the conversation. To reactivate alerts for the conversation, swipe again, and then tap the Show Alerts button.

TIP

Send Emojis in Place of Text

Emojis are small pictures that can help convey a feeling or idea. For example, smiley faces and sad faces to show emotions, thumbs up to convey approval, and the like.

1. From within a conversation, tap the Emoji key on the onscreen keyboard. If you can't see the keyboard, tap in the Message field to display it.

2. When the emojis appear (seen in **Figure 8-11**), swipe left and right to find the right emoji for the moment and tap to select it. You can add as many as you like to the conversation.

FIGURE 8-11

Use the App Drawer

The App Drawer allows you to add items that spice up your messages with information from other apps that are installed on your iPhone, as well as drawings and other images from the web.

Tap the App Drawer icon (looks like an A) to the left of the iMessage field in your conversation; the App Drawer will display at the bottom of the screen. Tap an item in the App Drawer to see what it offers your messaging.

The App Drawer is populated by

» **The App Store:** Tap the App Store all the way to the left of the App Drawer to find tons of stickers, games, and apps for your messages.

» **Digital Touch:** Allows you to send special effects in Messages. These can include sending your heartbeat, sketching a quick picture, or sending a kiss.

» **Other apps you have installed:** These may appear if they have the ability to add functions and information to your messages. For example, send the latest scores using ESPN (as I'm doing in **Figure 8-12**), or let your friend know what the weather's like nearby using icons from the AccuWeather app. Another example could be using Fandango's app to send movie information.

Digital Touch is one of the most personal ways to send special effects to others. Here's a close look at it:

1. To send a Digital Touch in a message, open a conversation and tap the Digital Touch button, shown in **Figure 8-13.**

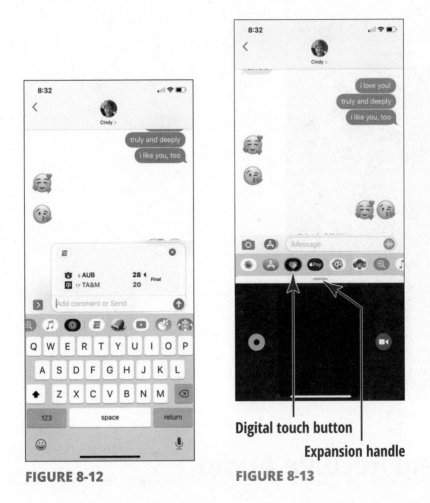

Digital touch button

Expansion handle

FIGURE 8-12   FIGURE 8-13

2. In the Digital Touch window, tap the gray expansion handle (seen in **Figure 8-13**) to open the full window. Tap the Information button in the lower-right (a gray circle with a white letter "i") and you'll see a list of the gestures and what they do.

3. Perform a gesture in the Digital Touch window and it will go to your recipient, as I've done in **Figure 8-14.**

FIGURE 8-14

Send and Receive Audio

When you're creating a message, you can also create an audio message.

1. With Messages open, tap the New Message button in the top-right corner.

2. Enter an addressee's name in the To field.

3. Tap and hold the Audio button (the microphone symbol to the right of the screen).

4. Speak your message or record a sound or music near you as you continue to hold down the Audio button.

5. Release the Audio button when you're finished recording.

6. Tap the Send button (an upward-pointing arrow at the top of the recording circle). The message appears as an audio track in the recipient's Messages inbox (see **Figure 8-15**). To play the track, she just holds the phone up to her ear or taps the Play button.

FIGURE 8-15

Send a Photo or Video

When you're creating a message, you can also send a picture or create a short video message.

1. With Messages open, tap the New Message button in the top-right corner.

2. Tap the Camera button to open the Camera app, and then take a picture.

3. Once the picture is taken, you'll be able to work with it before sending it along to your recipient. In the tools that appear (shown in **Figure 8-16**), you can

- Tap Retake to take a different picture.

- Tap Edit to edit the picture.

- Tap Markup to add notes or other text to your picture.

- Tap Done to place the picture in your message but not send it yet.

- Tap the Send button (the blue circle containing the white arrow in the lower-right) to send the picture immediately.

FIGURE 8-16

Send a Map of Your Location

When responding to a message, you can also send a map showing your current location.

1. Tap a message, tap the picture of the recipient in the upper-center of the screen, and then tap the Info button underneath (see **Figure 8-17**).

2. Tap Send My Current Location (see **Figure 8-18**) and a map will be inserted as a message attachment.

FIGURE 8-17

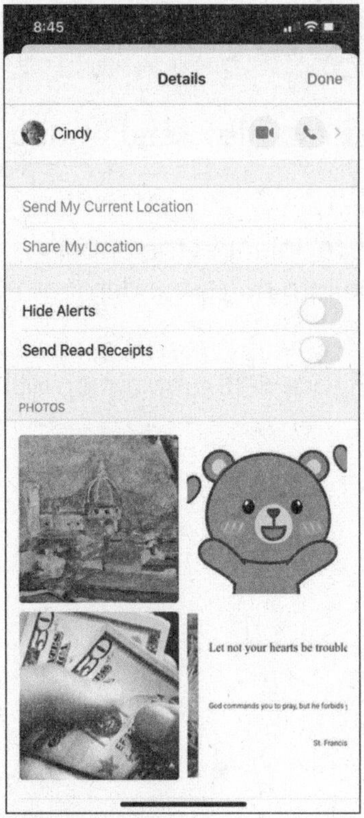

FIGURE 8-18

TIP You can also share your location in the middle of a conversation rather than send a map attachment with your message. In the screen shown in **Figure 8-18,** tap Share My Location and then tap Share for One Hour, Share Until End of Day, or Share Indefinitely. A map showing your location appears above your conversation until you stop sharing.

Understand Group Messaging

If you want to start a conversation with a group of people, you can use group messaging. Group messaging is great for keeping several people in the conversational loop.

Group messaging functionality includes the following features:

» When you participate in a group message, you see all participants in the Info for the message (see **Figure 8-19**). You can drop people whom you don't want to include any longer and leave the conversation yourself when you want to by simply tapping Info and then tapping Leave This Conversation.

» When you turn on Hide Alerts in the Details in a message (see **Figure 8-19**), you won't get notifications of messages from this group, but you can still read the group's messages at a later time (this also works for individuals).

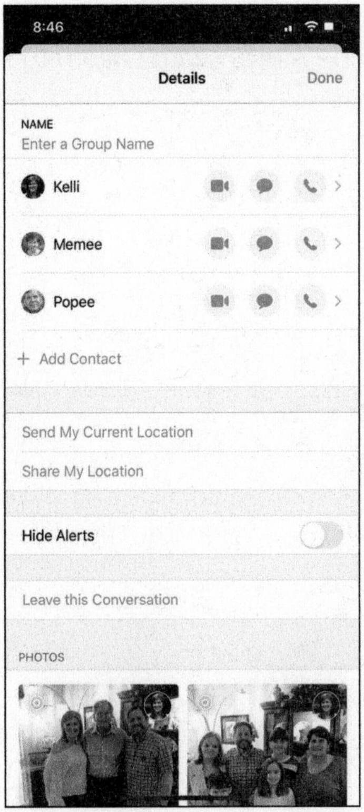

FIGURE 8-19

Taking you further into the workings of group messages is beyond the scope of this book, but if you're intrigued, go to `https://support.apple.com/en-us/HT202724` for more information.

Activate the Hide Alerts Feature

If you don't want to get notifications of new messages from an individual or group for a while, you can use the Hide Alerts feature.

1. With a message open, tap Details.

2. Tap the Hide Alerts switch to turn the feature on (refer to **Figure 8-19**).

3. Later, return to Details and tap the Hide Alerts switch again to turn the feature off.

Chapter **9**

Using Handy Utilities

U tilities are simple apps that can be very useful indeed to help with common tasks, such as calculating your meal tip or find-ing your way on a hike in the woods.

In this chapter, I help you out with using the Calculator app to keep your numbers in line. I also help you explore two other apps: Com-pass to help you find your way, and Voice Memos so that you can record your best ideas for posterity.

Use the Calculator

This one won't be rocket science. The Calculator app works like just about every calculator app (or actual calculator, for that matter) you've ever used. Follow these steps:

1. Tap the Calculator app icon (shown in **Figure 9-1**) to open it. You'll find it in the Utilities folder.

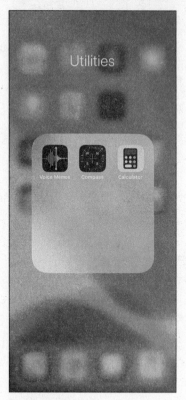

FIGURE 9-1

2. Tap a few numbers (see **Figure 9-2**), and then use any of these functions and additional numbers to perform calculations:

- **+, –, ×, and ÷:** These familiar buttons add, subtract, multiply, and divide the number you've entered.

- **+/–:** If the calculator is displaying a negative result, tap this to change it to a positive result, and vice versa.

- **AC/C:** This is the Clear button; its name will change depending on whether you've entered anything. (AC clears all; C clears just the last entry after you've made several entries.)

- **=:** This button produces the result of whatever calculation you've entered.

FIGURE 9-2

TIP

If you have a true mathematical bent, you'll be delighted to see that if you turn your phone to a landscape orientation, you get additional features that turn the basic calculator into a scientific calculator (also shown in **Figure 9-2**). Now you can play with calculations involving such functions as cosines and tangents. You can also use memory functions to work with stored calculations.

Find Your Way with Compass

Compass is a handy tool for figuring out where you are, assuming that you get cellular reception wherever you are. To find directions with Compass, follow these steps:

1. Tap the Compass icon to get started.

TECHNICAL
STUFF

The first time you do this, if you haven't enabled location access, a message appears, asking whether your iPhone can use your current location to provide information. Tap OK.

2. If you're using Compass for the first time, you may be asked to tilt the screen to roll a little red ball around a circle; this helps your iPhone calibrate the Compass app.

When you've completed this exercise, the Compass app appears (see **Figure 9-3**). Move around with your iPhone, and the compass indicates your current orientation in the world.

FIGURE 9-3

3. Tap the bold white line indicating your current location, as shown in **Figure 9-4**. The display changes to True North and indicates with a red wedge how far off True North you are when you move the compass; tap it again to display Magnetic North.

FIGURE 9-4

TECHNICAL
STUFF

True North refers to the direction you follow from where you are to get to the North Pole; *Magnetic North* is correlated relative to the Earth's magnetic field. True North is the more accurate measurement because of the tilt of the Earth.

Record Voice Memos

Voice Memos is perhaps the most robust of the apps covered in this chapter. The app allows you to record memos, edit memos by trimming them down, share them by email or instant message with Messages, synchronize recordings and edits across Apple devices (iPhone, iPad, and Mac), and label recordings so that you find them easily.

To record voice memos, follow these steps:

1. Tap the Voice Memos icon to open the app.

2. In the Voice Memos app (see **Figure 9-5**), tap the red Record button at the bottom of the screen to record a memo.

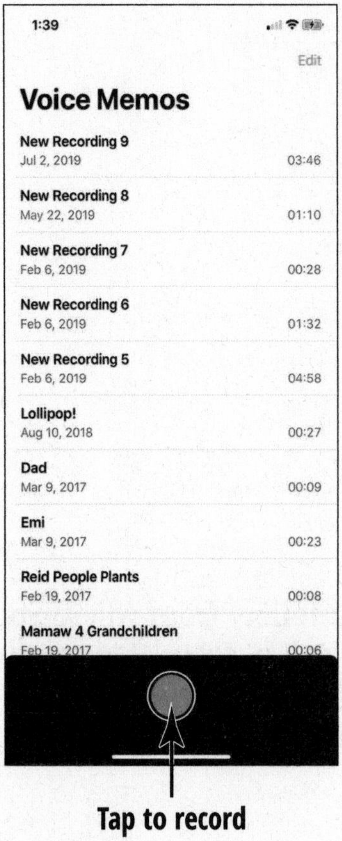

Tap to record

FIGURE 9-5

This button changes to a red Stop button (looks like a small red square in a circle) when you're recording. A red line moving from right to left indicates that you're in recording mode (see **Figure 9-6**).

Swipe up on the recording window to reveal the advanced controls, shown in **Figure 9-7**. Now the line is moving left to right, indicating the recording is continuing.

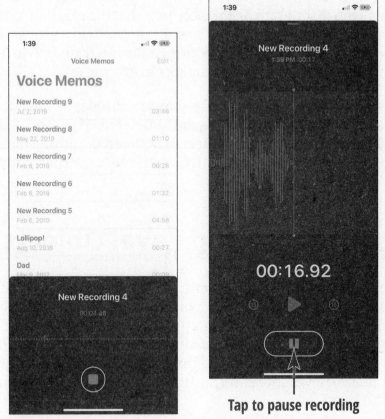

FIGURE 9-6

FIGURE 9-7

Tap to pause recording

3. While recording, you can

- Tap the name of the recording (called New Recording by default) to give it a new more descriptive name.

- Tap the red Pause button to pause the recording, and then tap Resume to continue recording.

- While paused, drag the waveform to a place in the recording you'd like to record over, and then tap the Replace button to begin recording from there.

- Tap Done to stop recording, and the new recording appears in the Voice Memos list.

4. Tap a memo in the list to open its controls. Tap the play button to play it back; tap the Forward or Reverse buttons to move forward or backward 15 seconds in the recording; or tap the Trash icon to delete it. You can also tap the name of the memo to rename it.

Deleted voice memos are kept for 30 days in a folder at the bottom of the Voice Memos list called Recently Deleted. You can retrieve a deleted memo by tapping the Recently Deleted button, tapping the name of the memo you want to retrieve, and then tapping Recover.

Measure Distances and Level Objects

iOS 13 uses the latest advancements in AR (augmented reality) and your iPhone to offer you a cool way to ditch your measuring tape and level: the Measure app! This app allows you to use your iPhone to measure distances and objects simply by pointing your iPhone at them. It also helps you check that things (such as pictures and what-not) are placed level. Measure is fun to play with and surprisingly accurate to boot.

Make sure you have plenty of light when using the Measure app, which increases the accuracy of your measurements.

1. Open the Measure app by tapping its icon and tap the Measure button on the lower left to use the measurement feature.

2. Your iPhone will prompt you to calibrate the Measure app by panning your iPhone around so that the camera gets a good look at your surroundings, as illustrated in **Figure 9-8.**

Move iPhone to start

Measure   Level

FIGURE 9-8

3. Once calibrated, you'll need to add the first reference point for your measurement. Do so by aiming the white targeting dot in the center of the screen to the location of your first reference point, as shown in **Figure 9-9.** Tap the Add a Point button (white button containing the +) to mark the point.

4. Next, mark the second reference point by placing the targeting dot on the location (shown in **Figure 9-10**) and tapping the Add a Point button again.

TIP

Should you make a mistake or simply want to start afresh, tap the Clear button in the upper-right corner to clear your reference points and begin again.

FIGURE 9-9   **FIGURE 9-10**

5. The length of your measurement is displayed as a white line, and the distance is shown in the middle of it (see **Figure 9-10**).

6. You can continue to make measurements by aiming the targeting dot at a previous reference point, tapping the Add a Point button, and moving your iPhone to the next reference point, where you again tap the Add a Point button to make a new measurement, as shown in **Figure 9-11.**

7. When you're finished measuring, tap the white Capture button (just to the right of the Add a Point button when holding your iPhone in Portrait mode; just above it in Landscape) to save an image of your measurements to the Camera Roll in the Photos app.

FIGURE 9-11

Here's how you determine if an object or surface is level. Let's say you're trying to figure out if a picture frame is perfectly straight on your wall:

1. Tap the level button in the lower right to view information about how many degrees off of zero a surface is (see **Figure 9-12**).

2. Align your iPhone along the upper border of the frame. If the surface beneath your phone is level, the screen turns green, and you'll see 0 degrees in the middle of the screen. If the frame is a little crooked, you might see 1 or 2 degrees on the iPhone screen.

TIP

The level feature of the Measure app can come in handy when working on construction projects and you need to check whether what you're working on is level or not. I've used it several times when a conventional level wasn't close by.

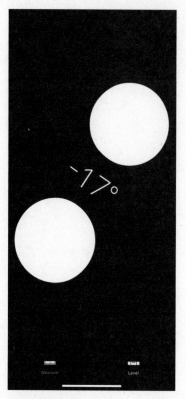

FIGURE 9-12

Get an Overview of the Home App

Since the smart home movement began a few years ago, controlling your home remotely meant juggling several apps: one for your lights, one for your garage doors, one for your thermostat, one for your oven, and on and on. While some developers have tried to create apps that worked with multiple smart home platforms by multiple manufacturers, none had the clout or the engineering manpower to pull things together — until Apple jumped in.

The Home app on your iPhone is designed to work with multiple smart home platforms and devices, and you can control everything in your home from one easy-to-use app.

Here's a list of the types of devices you can control remotely (meaning from anywhere you take your iPhone, as long as you at least have a cellular data connection): lighting, locks, windows and window shades, heating and cooling systems, speakers, humidifiers and air purifiers, security systems, garage doors, plugs and switches, sensors, video cameras, smoke and carbon monoxide detectors, and even more!

TIP

If you want to use the Home app with your smart home devices, make sure you see the Works with Apple HomeKit symbol on packaging or on the website (if you purchase the device online). Apple has an ever-growing list of HomeKit-enabled devices at www.apple.com/ios/home/accessories. You can also buy HomeKit-enabled devices on Apple's website: www.apple.com/shop/accessories/all-accessories/homekit.

Because there are so many ways to configure and use the Home app and so many different accessories you can control with it, it's really beyond the scope of this book cover the app in detail. Apple offers a great overview at www.apple.com/ios/home.

Chapter **10**

Making Your iPhone More Accessible

iPhone users are a very diverse group, and some face visual, motor, or hearing challenges. If you're one of these folks, you'll be glad to hear that Apple offers some handy accessibility features for your iPhone.

You can make your screen easier to read and set up the VoiceOver feature to read onscreen elements out loud. Voice Control, Numbers, and Grids are welcome additions to accessibility features in iOS 13. Then there are a slew of features you can turn on or off, including Zoom, Invert Colors, Speak Selection, Large Type, and more.

If hearing is your challenge, you can do the obvious and adjust the system volume. If you wear hearing aids, you can choose the correct settings for using Bluetooth or another hearing aid mode.

The iPhone also has features that help you deal with physical and motor challenges. And the Guided Access feature helps if you have difficulty focusing on one task. All of these accessibility features and more are covered in this chapter.

Set Brightness

Especially when using iPhone as an e-reader, you may find that a slightly less-bright screen reduces strain on your eyes. To manually adjust screen brightness, follow these steps:

1. Tap the Settings icon on the Home screen.

   If glare from the screen is a problem for you, consider getting a screen protector. This thin film both protects your screen from damage and reduces glare. You can easily find them on Amazon, and just about any cellphone dealer carries them.

2. In Settings, go to Accessibility ⇨ Display & Text Size.

3. Tap the Auto-Brightness On/Off switch at the bottom of the screen (see **Figure 10-1**) to turn off this feature (the button turns white when off).

4. Tap Accessibility in the upper-left corner and then tap Settings in the same location.

5. Tap Display & Brightness and then tap and drag the Brightness slider (refer to **Figure 10-2**) to the right to make the screen brighter or to the left to make it dimmer.

6. Press the Home button (or swipe up from the bottom of the screen for iPhone X models and newer) to close Settings.

In the Apple Books e-reader app, you can set a sepia tone for the page, which might be easier on your eyes. See Chapter 17 for more about using Apple Books.

Tap here

Brightness slider

FIGURE 10-1　　　　**FIGURE 10-2**

Change the Wallpaper

The default iPhone background image on your iPhone may be pretty, but it may not be the one that works best for you. Choosing different wallpaper may help you to more easily see all the icons on your Home screen. Follow these steps:

1. Tap the Settings icon on the Home screen.

2. In Settings, tap Wallpaper.

3. In the Wallpaper settings, tap Choose a New Wallpaper.

4. Tap a wallpaper category, as shown in **Figure 10-3,** to view choices. Tap a sample to select it.

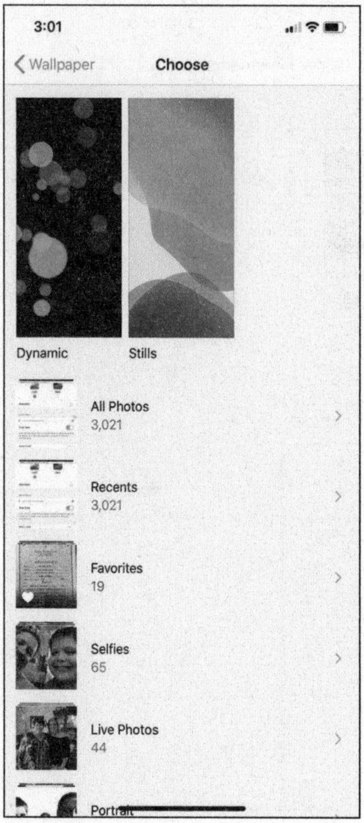

FIGURE 10-3

TIP

If you prefer to use a picture that's on your iPhone, tap an album in the lower part of the Wallpaper screen to locate a picture; tap to use it as your wallpaper.

5. In the preview that appears (see **Figure 10-4**), tap Set in the lower-right corner.

TECHNICAL STUFF

Some wallpapers may allow you to select either

- Still (the picture is static)

- Perspective (the picture will seem to move when you move your iPhone)

FIGURE 10-4

6. In the following menu, tap your choice of

- Set Lock Screen (the screen that appears when you lock the iPhone by tapping the power button)
- Set Home Screen
- Set Both

7. Press the Home button or swipe up from the bottom of the screen (iPhone X models and newer only).

You return to your Home screen with the new wallpaper set as the background.

Set Up VoiceOver

VoiceOver reads the names of screen elements and settings to you, but it also changes the way you provide input to the iPhone. In Notes, for example, you can have VoiceOver read the name of the Notes buttons to you, and when you enter notes, it reads words or characters that you've entered. It can also tell you whether such features as Auto-Correction are on.

To turn on VoiceOver, follow these steps:

1. Tap the Settings icon on the Home screen.

2. In Settings, tap Accessibility.

3. In the Accessibility pane, shown in **Figure 10-5,** tap VoiceOver.

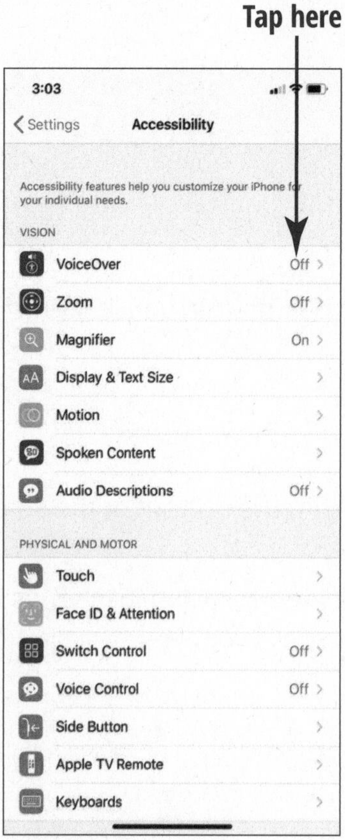

FIGURE 10-5

4. In the VoiceOver pane, shown in **Figure 10-6,** tap the VoiceOver On/Off switch to turn on this feature (the button turns green). With VoiceOver on, you must first single-tap to select an item such as a button, which causes VoiceOver to read the name of the button to you. Then you double-tap the button to activate its function.

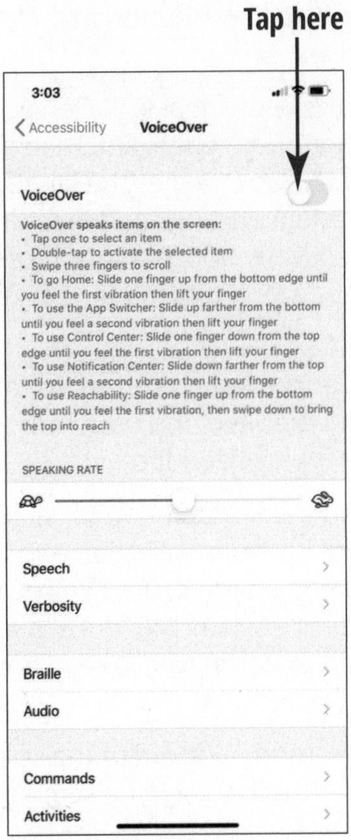

Tap here

FIGURE 10-6

5. Tap the VoiceOver Practice button to select it and then double-tap the button to open VoiceOver Practice. Practice using gestures (such as pinching or flicking left), and VoiceOver tells you what action each gesture initiates.

6. Tap the Done button and then double-tap the same button to return to the VoiceOver dialog.

7. Tap the Verbosity button once and then double-tap to open its options:

- Tap the Speak Hints On/Off switch and then double-tap the switch to turn the feature on (or off).

  VoiceOver speaks the name of each tapped item.

- Tap once and then double-tap the VoiceOver button in the upper-left corner to go back to the VoiceOver screen.

TIP

You can change the language that VoiceOver speaks. In General settings, tap Language & Region, tap iPhone Language, and then select another language. However, this action also changes the language used for labels on Home icons and various settings and fields in iPhone. Be careful with this setting, lest you choose a language you don't understand by accident and have a very difficult time figuring out how to change it back.

8. If you want VoiceOver to read words or characters to you (for example, in the Notes app), scroll down and then tap and double-tap Typing, and then tap and double-tap Typing Feedback.

9. In the Typing Feedback dialog, tap and then double-tap to select the option you prefer in both the Software Keyboards section and the Hardware Keyboards section. The Words option causes VoiceOver to read words to you, but not characters, such as the "dollar sign" ($). The Characters and Words option causes VoiceOver to read both, and so on.

10. Press the Home button or swipe up from the bottom of the screen (for iPhone X models and newer) to return to the Home screen.

The following section shows how to navigate your iPhone after you've turned on VoiceOver.

TIP

You can use the Accessibility Shortcut setting to help you more quickly turn the VoiceOver, Zoom, Switch Control, AssistiveTouch, Grayscale, or Invert Colors features on and off:

1. In the Accessibility screen, tap Accessibility Shortcut (at the very bottom of the screen).

2. In the screen that appears, choose what you want three presses of the Home button (or Side button for iPhone X models and newer) to activate. Now three presses with a single finger on the Home button or Side button provides you with the option you selected wherever you go in iPhone.

Use VoiceOver

After VoiceOver is turned on, you need to figure out how to use it. I won't kid you — using it is awkward at first, but you'll get the hang of it!

Here are the main onscreen gestures you should know how to use:

» **Tap an item to select it.** VoiceOver then speaks its name.

» **Double-tap the selected item.** This action activates the item.

» **Flick three fingers.** It takes three fingers to scroll around a page with VoiceOver turned on.

TIP

If tapping with two or three fingers seems difficult for you, try tapping with one finger from one hand and one or two from the other. When double- or triple-tapping, you have to perform these gestures as quickly as you can for them to work.

Table 10-1 provides additional gestures to help you use VoiceOver. If you want to use this feature often, I recommend the VoiceOver section of the online iPhone User Guide, which goes into great detail about using VoiceOver. You'll find the User Guide at `https://support.apple.com/manuals/iphone`. When there, just click on the model of iPhone or the version of iOS you have to read its manual. You can also get an Apple Books version of the manual through that app in the Book Store. (See Chapter 17 for more information.)

TABLE 10-1 VoiceOver Gestures

Gesture	Effect
Flick right or left.	Select the next or preceding item.
Tap with two fingers.	Stop speaking the current item.
Flick two fingers up.	Read everything from the top of the screen.
Flick two fingers down.	Read everything from the current position.
Flick three fingers up or down.	Scroll one page at a time.
Flick three fingers right or left.	Go to the next or preceding page.
Tap three fingers.	Speak the scroll status (for example, line 20 of 100).
Flick four fingers up or down.	Go to the first or last element on a page.
Flick four fingers right or left.	Go to the next or preceding section (as on a web page).

TIP

Check out some of the settings for VoiceOver, including a choice for Braille, Language Rotor for making language choices, the ability to navigate images, and a setting to have iPhone speak notifications.

Several Vision features are simple on/off settings that you can turn on or off after you tap Settings ➪ Accessibility:

» **Zoom:** The Zoom feature enlarges the contents displayed on the iPhone screen when you double-tap the screen with three fingers. The Zoom feature works almost everywhere in iPhone: in Photos, on web pages, on your Home screens, in your Mail, in Music, and in Videos — give it a try!

» **Magnifier:** Enable Magnifier to use your iPhone's built-in camera as a magnifying glass. Just triple-click the Home button (Side button for iPhone X models and newer) to activate it (after you've turned the feature on, of course).

» **Display Accommodations (under Accessibility ⇨ Display & Text Size):** Includes such features as

- Color Filters (aids in case of color blindness)

- Reduce White Point (helps reduce the intensity of bright colors)

- Invert Colors (which reverses colors on your screen so that white backgrounds are black and black text is white). Classic Invert will invert all colors, while Smart Invert will not invert colors for items like images, multimedia, and some apps that may use darker color styles.

» **Spoken Content:** Options here include the ability to have your iPhone speak items you've selected or hear the content of an entire screen, highlight content as its spoken, and more.

» **Larger Text (under Accessibility ⇨ Display & Text Size):** If having larger text in such apps as Contacts, Mail, and Notes would be helpful to you, you can turn on the Larger Text feature and choose the text size that works best for you.

» **Bold Text (under Accessibility ⇨ Display & Text Size):** Turning on this setting restarts your iPhone (after asking you for permission to do so) and then causes text in various apps and in Settings to be bold.

» **Button Shapes (under Accessibility ⇨ Display & Text Size):** This setting applies shapes to buttons so they're more easily distinguishable. For an example, check out the General button in the upper-left corner of the screen after you enable Button Shapes by toggling its switch to On. Turn it back off and notice the difference (shown in **Figure 10-7**).

» **Reduce Transparency (under Accessibility ⇨ Display & Text Size):** This setting helps increase legibility of text by reducing the blurs and transparency effects that make up a good deal of the iPhone user interface.

» **Increase Contrast (under Accessibility ⇨ Display & Text Size):** Use this setting to set up backgrounds in some areas of iPhone and apps with greater contrast, which should improve visibility.

» **Reduce Motion (under Accessibility ⇨ Motion):** Tap this accessibility feature and then tap the On/Off setting to turn off the parallax effect, which causes the background of your Home screens to appear to float as you move the phone around.

» **On/Off Labels (under Accessibility ⇨ Display & Text Size):** If you have trouble making out colors and therefore find it hard to tell when an On/Off setting is On (green) or Off (white), use this setting to add a circle to the right of a setting when it's off and a white vertical line to a setting when it's on.

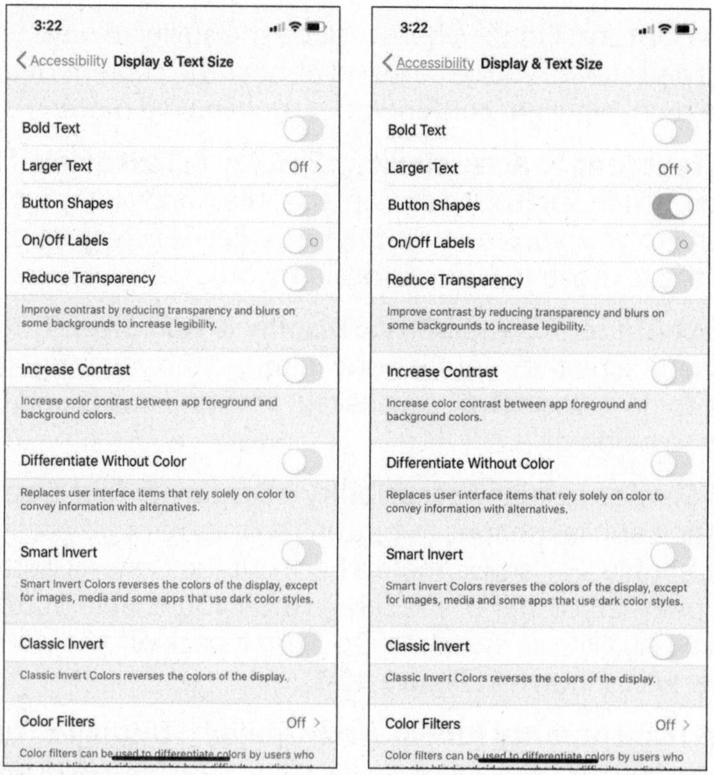

FIGURE 10-7

Use iPhone with Hearing Aids

If you have Bluetooth enabled or use another style of hearing aid, your iPhone may be able to detect it and work with its settings to improve sound on your phone calls. Follow these steps to connect your hearing aid to your iPhone.

1. Tap Settings on the Home screen.

2. Tap Accessibility and then scroll down to the Hearing section and tap Hearing Devices. On the following screen, shown in **Figure 10-8,** your iPhone searches for hearing aid devices.

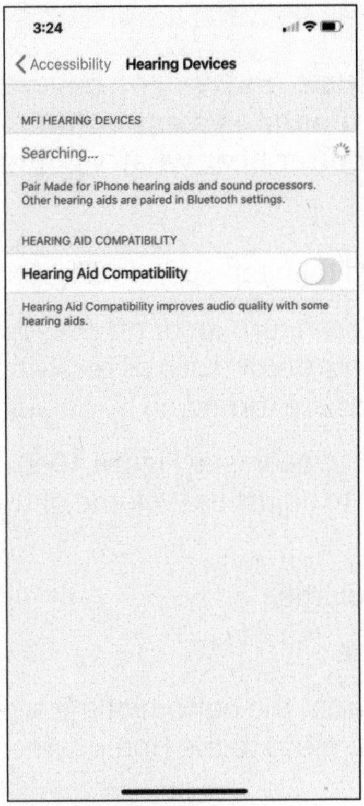

FIGURE 10-8

TIP

If you have a non-MFi (Made For iPhone) hearing aid, add your hearing aid in Bluetooth settings. To do so, go to Settings ⇨ Bluetooth, make sure the Bluetooth toggle switch is On (green), and select your hearing aid in the list of devices.

3. When your device appears, tap it.

4. Tap the Back button in the upper-left corner of the screen, scroll back down to the Hearing section (if you're not automatically returned there), and tap Hearing Aid Compatibility to turn on a feature that could improve audio quality when you're using your hearing aid.

Adjust the Volume

Though individual apps (such as Music and Video) have their own volume settings, you can set your iPhone system volume for your ringer and alerts as well to help you better hear what's going on. Follow these steps:

1. Tap Settings on the Home screen and then tap Sounds & Haptics.

TIP

In the Sounds & Haptics settings, you can turn on or off the sounds that iPhone makes when certain events occur (such as receiving new Mail or Calendar alerts). These sounds are turned on by default.

2. In the Sounds & Haptics settings that appear (see **Figure 10-9**), tap and drag the Ringer and Alerts slider to adjust the volume of these audible attention grabbers:

- Drag to the right to increase the volume.

- Drag to the left to lower the volume.

3. Press the Home button or swipe up from the bottom of the screen (iPhone X models and newer only) to return to the Home screen.

TIP

Even those with perfect hearing sometimes have trouble hearing a phone ring, especially in busy public places. Consider using the Vibrate settings in the Sounds settings to have your phone vibrate when a call is coming in.

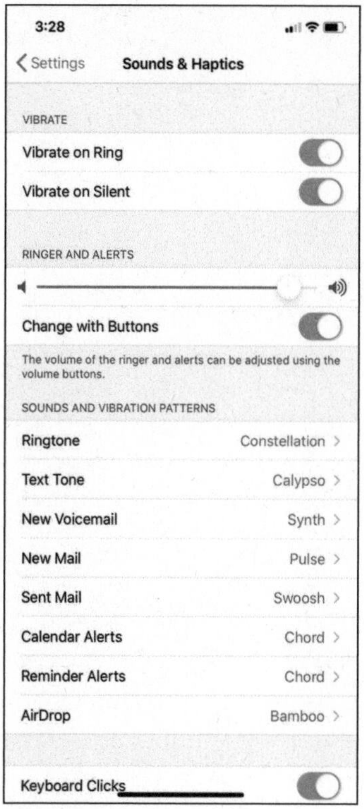

FIGURE 10-9

Set Up Subtitles and Captioning

Closed captioning and subtitles help folks with hearing challenges enjoy entertainment and educational content. Follow these steps:

1. Tap Settings on the Home screen, and then tap Accessibility.

2. Scroll down to the Hearing section and tap Subtitles & Captioning.

3. On the following screen, tap the On/Off switch to turn on Closed Captions + SDH (Subtitles for the Deaf and Hard of Hearing).

   You can also tap Style and choose a text style for the captions, as shown in **Figure 10-10.** A neat video helps show you what your style will look like when the feature is in use.

4. Press the Home button or swipe up from the bottom of the screen (for iPhone X models and newer) to return to the Home screen.

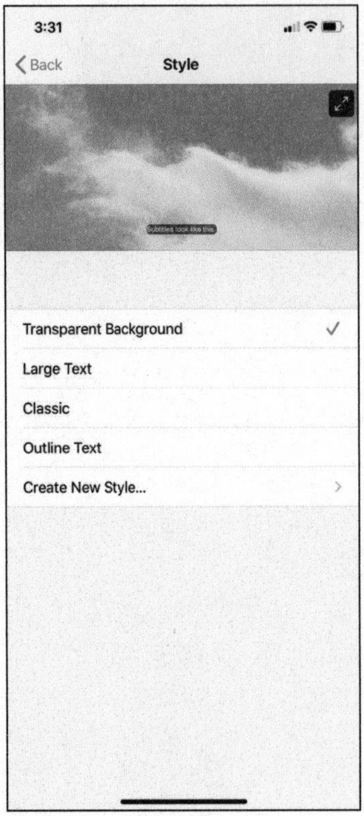

FIGURE 10-10

Manage Other Hearing Settings

Several hearing accessibility settings are simple On/Off settings, including

>> **Mono Audio (under Accessibility ⇨ Audio/Visual):** Using the stereo effect in headphones or a headset breaks up sounds so that you hear a portion in one ear and a portion in the other ear. The purpose is to simulate the way your ears process sounds. If there is only one channel of sound, that sound is sent to both ears. However, if you're hard of hearing or deaf in one ear, you're hearing only a portion of the sound in your hearing ear, which can be frustrating. If you have such hearing challenges and want to use iPhone with a headset connected, you should turn on

Mono Audio. When it's turned on, all sound is combined and distributed to both ears. You can use the slider below Mono Audio to direct more sound to the ear you hear best with.

» **RTT/TTY:** RTT stands for Real-Time Text, which provides better text support during calls. TTY is a symbol indicating teletype machine capabilities. The iPhone is compatible with teletype machines via the iPhone TTY Adapter, which can be purchased from Apple. The TTY option allows you to enable either Software TTY, Hardware TTY, or both. RTT and TTY are only available for your iPhone if your cell carrier supports one or both of them.

» **LED Flash for Alerts (under Accessibility ⇨ Audio/Visual):** If you need a visual clue when an alert is spoken, turn this setting on.

» **Phone Noise Cancellation (under Accessibility ⇨ Audio/Visual):** If you're annoyed at ambient noise when you make a call in public (or noisy private) settings, with an iPhone 5 or later, turn on the Phone Noise Cancellation feature. When you hold the phone to your ear during a call, this feature reduces background noise to some extent.

Turn On and Work with AssistiveTouch

If you have difficulty using buttons, the AssistiveTouch Control panel aids input using the touchscreen.

1. To turn on AssistiveTouch, tap Settings on the Home screen and then tap Accessibility.

2. In the Accessibility pane, tap Touch and then tap AssistiveTouch. In the pane that appears, tap the On/Off switch for AssistiveTouch to turn it on (see **Figure 10-11**). A dark circle (called the AssistiveTouch Control panel) then appears on the right side of the screen. This circle now appears in the same location in whatever apps you display on your iPhone, though you can move it around with your finger.

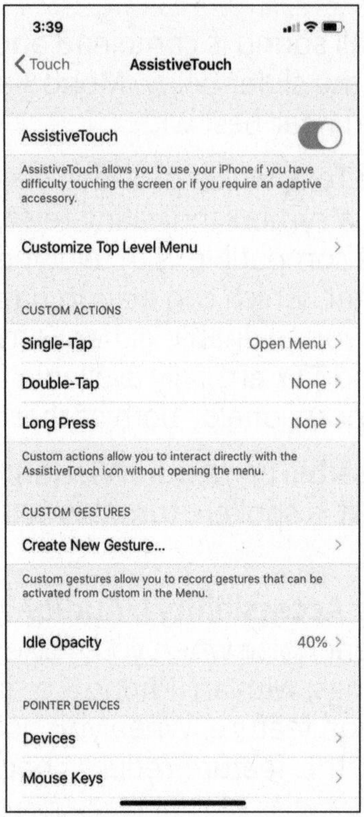

FIGURE 10-11

3. Tap the AssistiveTouch Control panel to display options, as shown in **Figure 10-12.** The panel includes Notifications and Control Center options.

4. You can tap Custom or Device on the panel to see additional choices, tap Siri to activate the personal assistant feature, tap Notifications or Control Center to display those panels, or press Home to go directly to the Home screen. After you've chosen an option, pressing the Home button or swiping up from the bottom of the screen (for iPhone X models and newer) takes you back to the Home screen.

Table 10-2 shows the major options available in the AssistiveTouch Control panel and their purpose.

FIGURE 10-12

TABLE 10-2 ## AssistiveTouch Controls

Control	Purpose
Siri	Activates the Siri feature, which allows you to speak questions and make requests of your iPhone.
Custom	Displays a set of gestures with only the Pinch gesture preset; you can tap any of the other blank squares to add your own favorite gestures.
Device	You can rotate the screen, lock the screen, turn the volume up or down, mute or unmute sound, or shake iPhone to undo an action using the presets in this option.
Home	Sends you to the Home screen.
Control Center	Open Control Center common commands.
Notifications	Open Notifications with reminders, Calendar appointments, and so on.

Turn On Additional Physical and Motor Settings

Use these On/Off settings in the Accessibility settings to help you deal with how fast you tap and how you answer phone calls:

» **Home Button (non-iPhone X models and newer only):** Sometimes if you have dexterity challenges, it's hard to double-press or triple-press the Home button fast enough to make an effect. Choose the Slow or Slowest option when you tap this setting to allow you a bit more time to make that second or third tap. Also, the Rest Finger to Open feature at the bottom of the screen is helpful by allowing you to simply rest your finger on the Home button to open your iPhone using Touch ID (if enabled), as opposed to needing to press the Home button.

» **Call Audio Routing (under Accessibility ➪ Touch):** If you prefer to use your speaker phone to receive incoming calls, or you typically use a headset with your phone that allows you to tap a button to receive a call, tap this option and then choose Headset or Speaker. Speakers and headsets can both provide a better hearing experience for many.

TIP

If you have certain adaptive accessories that allow you to control devices with head gestures, you can use them to control your iPhone, highlighting features in sequence and then selecting one. Use the Switch Control feature in the Accessibility settings to turn this mode on and make settings.

Focus Learning with Guided Access

Guided Access is a feature that you can use to limit a user's access to iPhone to a single app, and even limit access in that app to certain features. This feature is useful in several settings, ranging from a classroom, for use by someone with attention deficit disorder, and even to a public setting (such as a kiosk where you don't want users to be able to open other apps).

1. Tap Settings and then tap Accessibility.

2. Scroll down and tap Guided Access; then, on the screen that follows (see **Figure 10-13**), tap Guided Access to turn the feature on.

FIGURE 10-13

3. Tap Passcode Settings and then tap Set Guided Access Passcode to activate a passcode so that those using an app can't return to the Home screen to access other apps. You may also activate Touch ID or Face ID (iPhone X models and newer only) to perform the same function.

4. In the Set Passcode dialog that appears (see **Figure 10-14**), enter a 4-digit passcode using the numeric pad. Enter the number again when prompted.

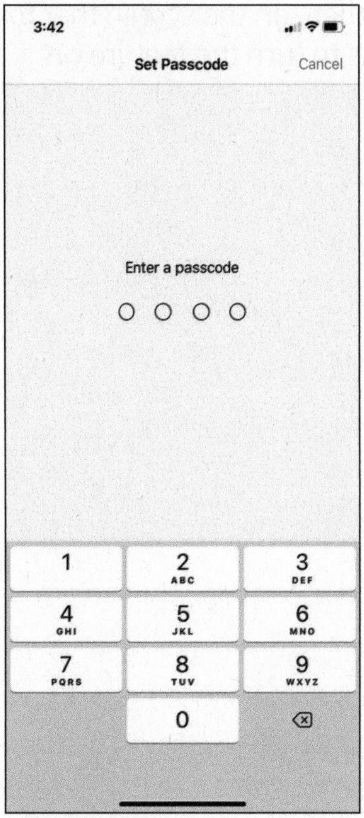

FIGURE 10-14

5. Press the Home button or swipe up from the bottom of the screen (iPhone X models and newer only) and tap an app to open it.

6. Rapidly press the Home button (Side button for iPhone X models and newer) three times. You're presented with some options at the bottom of the screen; tap the Guided Access button and then tap Options at the bottom to display these options:

- **Sleep/Wake Button or Side button:** You can put your iPhone to sleep or wake it up with three presses of the Home button or Side button, depending on your iPhone model.

- **Volume Buttons:** You can tap Always On or Always Off. If you don't want users to be able to adjust volume using the volume toggle on the side of the iPhone, for example, use this setting.

- **Motion:** Turn this setting off if you don't want users to move the iPhone around — for example, to play a race car driving game.

- **Keyboards:** Use this setting to prohibit people using this app from entering text using the keyboard.

- **Touch:** If you don't want users to be able to use the touchscreen, turn this off.

- **Time Limit:** Tap this and use settings that are displayed to set a time limit for the use of the app.

7. Tap Done to hide the options.

> **TIP** At this point, you can also use your finger to circle areas of the screen that you want to disable, such as a Store button in the Music app.

8. Press the Start button (upper-right corner) and then press the Home button (Side button for iPhone X models and newer) three times. Enter your passcode, if you set one, and tap End.

9. Tap the Home button or swipe up from the bottom of the screen (iPhone X models and newer only) again to return to the Home screen.

One-Handed Keyboard

The one-handed keyboard is a much-needed feature to make typing on the onscreen keyboard that much easier. For those with dexterity issues, or simply for those of us with smaller hands using the larger iPhones, this option allows the onscreen keyboard to "slide over" to one side or the other to better facilitate typing.

1. Open any app that uses the onscreen keyboard. I'm using Notes for this example.

2. With the onscreen keyboard displayed, tap-and-hold the emoji (smiley face) or International (globe) icon to display the Keyboard Settings menu, seen in **Figure 10-15.**

Tap-and-hold here

FIGURE 10-15

3. At the bottom of the Keyboard Settings menu, tap either the left-sided keyboard icon or the right-sided keyboard icon to shift the keyboards keys in the desired direction.

4. Your keyboard will now appear either shifted to the left or right, as shown in **Figure 10-16.**

5. To quickly return to the standard keyboard, tap the white arrow to the left or right side of your shifted keyboard (its position depends on which side you shifted your keyboard).

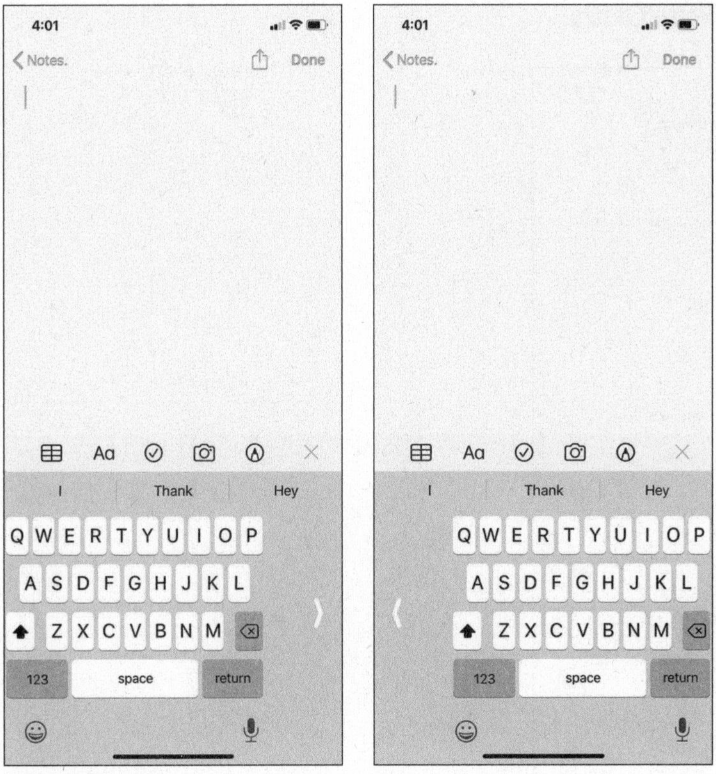

FIGURE 10-16

Control Your iPhone with Voice Control

iOS 13 introduces an exciting accessibility innovation: the ability to control your iPhone using your voice! As part of Voice Control, you can also use numbers and grid overlays to command your iPhone to perform tasks. This feature is a real game-changer for a lot of folks.

1. Tap Settings and then tap Accessibility.

2. Scroll down and tap Voice Control; then, on the screen that follows (see **Figure 10-17**), tap Set Up Voice Control to begin.

> **TIP**
> You can easily tell when Voice Control is on, as there will be a blue circle containing a microphone in the upper-left corner of your iPhone's screen.

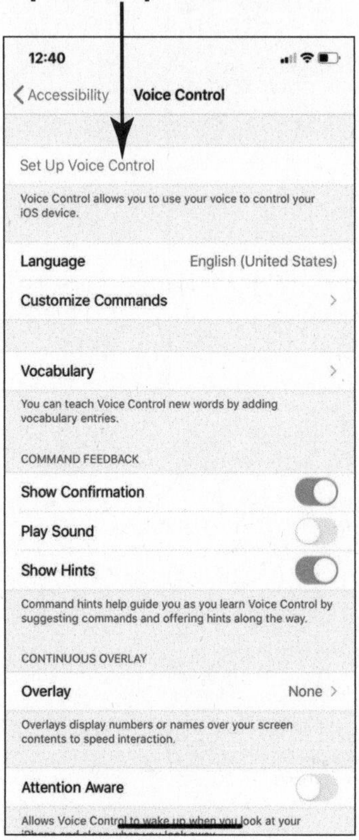

Tap to set up Voice Control

FIGURE 10-17

3. Read through the information screens, tapping Continue to advance through them. Afterwards, you'll see the Voice Control toggle switch is set to On (green).

   Pay particular attention to the What can I say? screen. It tells you in simple terms commands you can use to get started with Voice Control, such as "Go home" and "Show grid."

   TIP

4. Tap Customize Commands to see what commands are built-in to Voice Control (shown in **Figure 10-18**), enable or disable commands, and even create your own custom commands. I suggest taking your time in this section of the Voice Control options; you'll be surprised at just what all you can do out-of-the-gate with this amazing tool. Tap Back in the upper-left to return to the main Voice Control options.

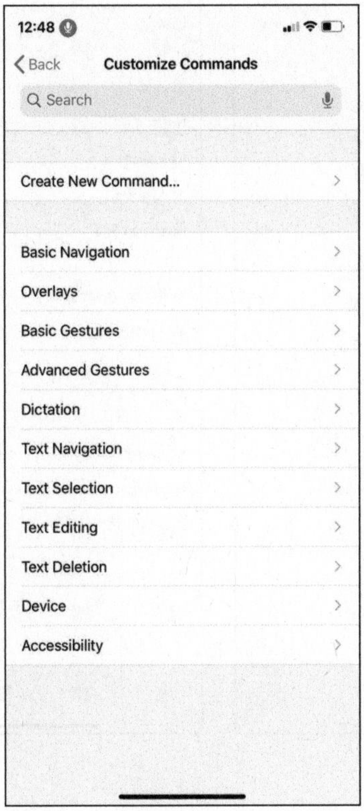

FIGURE 10-18

5. You may need or want to use words that Voice Control doesn't know or understand, so Apple's given you the ability to add words. This is particularly useful with dictation. In the Voice Control options, tap Vocabulary and then tap the + in the upper-right to add your own words. Type the word or phrase you'd like to add in the Add New Entry window and then tap the Save button. Tap Voice Control in the upper-left to return to the main Voice Control screen.

6. Overlays are a fantastic accessibility addition to iOS 13. If you use them, clickable items on the screen are labeled with numbers, names, or a numbered grid. Whenever you want to click an item, simply execute a command such as "tap three" to "tap" the item with your voice. Each of the three overlays is displayed in **Figure 10-19.**

FIGURE 10-19

TIP

The number and name labels will fade to a light gray so that you can more clearly see the screen when not actively using the feature, but it will darken again when you do use it.

- » **Get suggestions and call contacts**
- » **Create reminders and alerts**
- » **Add tasks to your calendar**
- » **Play music and get directions**
- » **Ask for facts and search the web**
- » **Send messages, dictate, and translate**

Chapter **11**

Conversing with Siri

One of the most talked about (pun intended) features on your iPhone is Siri, a personal assistant that responds to the commands you speak to your iPhone (models 4s or later). With Siri, you can ask for nearby restaurants, and a list appears. You can dictate your email messages rather than type them. You can open apps with a voice command. Calling your mother is as simple as saying, "Call Mom." Want to know the capital of Rhode Island? Just ask. Siri checks several online sources to answer questions ranging from the result of a mathematical equation to the next scheduled flight to Rome (Italy or Georgia). You can have Siri search photos and videos and locate what you need by date, location, or album name. Ask Siri to remind you about an app you're working in, such as Safari, Mail, or Notes at a later time so you can pick up where you left off.

You can also have Siri perform tasks, such as returning calls and controlling Music. Siri can play music at your request and identify tagged songs (songs that contain embedded information that identifies them by categories such as artist or genre of music) for you. You can also hail a ride with Uber or Lyft, watch live TV just by saying "Watch ESPN" (or say another app you might use, such as CBS), find tagged photos, make payments with some third-party apps, and more.

With iOS 13, Siri can offer you curated suggestions for Safari, Maps, and Podcasts. Siri also utilizes new voice technology that allows it to sound more natural and smooth, particularly when speaking long phrases.

Activate Siri

When you first go through the process of registering your phone, you'll see a screen similar to **Figure 11-1**; tap Get Started to begin making settings for your location, using iCloud, and so on, and at one point you will see the option to activate Siri. As you begin to use your phone, iPhone reminds you about using Siri by displaying a message.

Siri is available only on iPhone 4s and later with Internet access, and cellular data charges could apply when Siri checks online sources. In addition, Apple warns that available features may vary by area.

If you didn't activate Siri during the registration process, you can use Settings to turn Siri on by following these steps:

1. Tap the Settings icon on the Home screen.

2. Tap Siri & Search (see **Figure 11-2**).

Tap here

Settings

3:07

Do Not Disturb
Screen Time

General
Control Center
Display & Brightness
Accessibility
Wallpaper
Siri & Search
Face ID & Passcode
Emergency SOS
Battery
Privacy

iTunes & App Store
Wallet & Apple Pay

Passwords & Accounts
Mail

Welcome to
iPhone

Get Started

FIGURE 11-1   **FIGURE 11-2**

3. In the dialog in **Figure 11-3,** toggle the On/Off switch to On (green) to activate any or all of the following features:

- If you want to be able to activate Siri for hands-free use, toggle the Listen for "Hey Siri" switch to turn on the feature. When you first enable "Hey Siri," you'll be prompted to set up the feature. Just walk through the steps to enable it and continue.

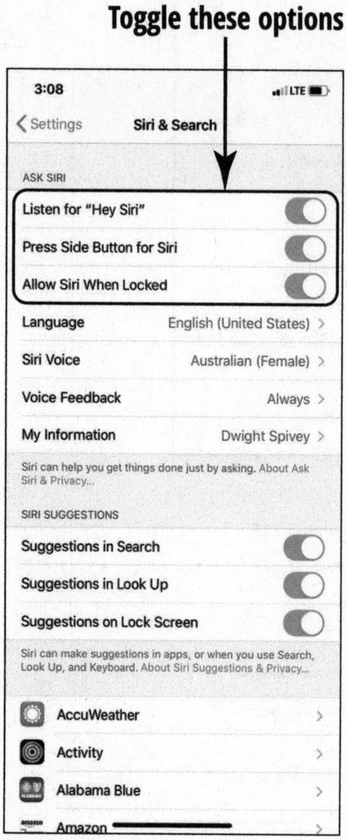

Toggle these options

> 3:08   .ıll LTE 🔋
>
> ‹ Settings   **Siri & Search**
>
> ASK SIRI
>
> Listen for "Hey Siri"   🔘
>
> Press Side Button for Siri   🔘
>
> Allow Siri When Locked   🔘
>
> Language   English (United States) ›
>
> Siri Voice   Australian (Female) ›
>
> Voice Feedback   Always ›
>
> My Information   Dwight Spivey ›
>
> Siri can help you get things done just by asking. About Ask Siri & Privacy...
>
> SIRI SUGGESTIONS
>
> Suggestions in Search   🔘
>
> Suggestions in Look Up   🔘
>
> Suggestions on Lock Screen   🔘
>
> Siri can make suggestions in apps, or when you use Search, Look Up, and Keyboard. About Siri Suggestions & Privacy...
>
> ◻ AccuWeather   ›
>
> ◻ Activity   ›
>
> ◻ Alabama Blue   ›
>
> ◻ Amazon   ›

FIGURE 11-3

With this feature enabled, just say "Hey, Siri" and Siri opens up, ready for a command. In addition, with streaming voice recognition, Siri displays in text what it's hearing as you speak, so you can verify that it has understood you correctly. This streaming feature makes the process of interacting with Siri faster.

REMEMBER

iPhone models older than the 6s and 6s Plus must be plugged into an outlet, car, or computer to use the "Hey Siri" feature.

- Press Home for Siri requires you to press the Home button to activate Siri. Alternatively, iPhone X and newer model users will see Press Side Button for Siri, requiring the press of the Side button to activate Siri.

- Allow Siri When Locked allows you to use Siri even when the iPhone is locked.

4. If you want to change the language Siri uses, tap Language and choose a different language in the list that appears.

5. To change the nationality or gender of Siri's voice from American to British or Australian (for examples), or from female to male, tap Siri Voice and make your selections.

6. Let Siri know about your contact information by tapping My Information and selecting yourself from your Contacts.

TIP

If you want Siri to verbally respond to your requests only when the iPhone isn't in your hands, tap Voice Feedback and choose Hands-Free Only. Here's how this setting works and why you might want to use it: In general, if you're holding your iPhone, you can read responses on the screen, so you might choose not to have your phone talk to you out loud. But if you're cooking dinner while helping your spouse make travel plans and want to speak requests for destinations and hear the answers rather than have to read them, Hands-Free is a useful setting.

Understand All That Siri Can Do

Siri allows you to interact by voice with many apps on your iPhone.

REMEMBER

No matter what kind of action you want to perform, first press and hold the Home button (or Side button for iPhone X models) until Siri opens.

You can pose questions or ask to do something like make a call or add an appointment to your calendar, for example. Siri can also search the Internet or use an informational service called Wolfram|Alpha to provide information on just about any topic.

Siri also checks with Wikipedia, Bing, and Twitter to get you the information you ask for. In addition, you can use Siri to tell iPhone to return a call, play your voice mail, open and search the App Store, control Music playback, dictate text messages, and much more.

With iOS 13, Siri learns your daily habits and will offer suggestions throughout the day when appropriate. For example, say you usually stop by the local coffee shop around the same time each morning and use the shop's app to order a drink from your iPhone. Siri will pick up on this activity and eventually begin asking if you'd like to order a drink when you're within proximity of the coffee shop.

Siri knows what app you're using, though you don't have to have that app open to make a request involving it. However, if you are in the Messages app, you can make a statement like "Tell Susan I'll be late," and Siri knows that you want to send a message. You can also ask Siri to remind you about what you're working on and Siri notes what you're working on, in which app, and reminds you about it at a later time you specify.

TIP If you want to dictate text in an app like Notes, use the Dictation key on the onscreen keyboard to do so. See the task "Use Dictation," later in this chapter, for more about this feature.

Siri requires no preset structure for your questions; you can phrase things in several ways. For example, you might say, "Where am I?" to see a map of your current location, or you could say, "What is my current location?" or "What address is this?" and get the same results.

If you ask a question about, say, the weather, Siri responds to you both verbally and with text information (see **Figure 11-4**) or by opening a form, as with email, or by providing a graphic display for some items, such as maps. When a result appears, you can tap it to make a choice or open a related app.

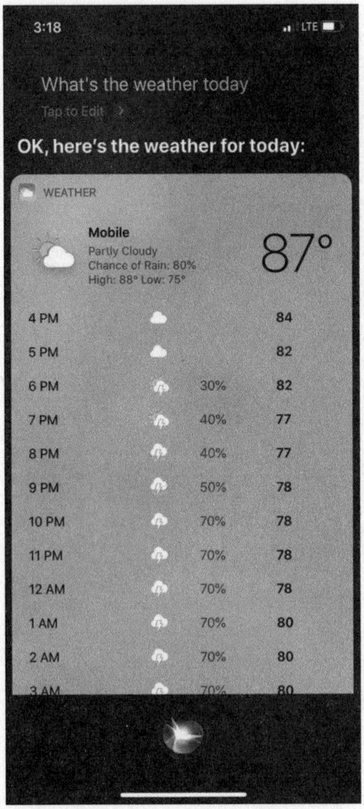

FIGURE 11-4

Siri works with Phone, the App Store, Music, Messages, Reminders, Calendar, Maps, Mail, Weather, Stocks, Clock, Contacts, Notes, social media apps (such as Twitter), and Safari (see **Figure 11-5**). In the following tasks, I provide a quick guide to some of the most useful ways you can use Siri.

TIP

Siri now supports many different languages, so you can finally show off those language lessons you took in high school. Some languages supported include Chinese, Dutch, English, French, German, Italian, Spanish, Arabic, Danish, Finnish, Hebrew, Japanese, Korean, and more!

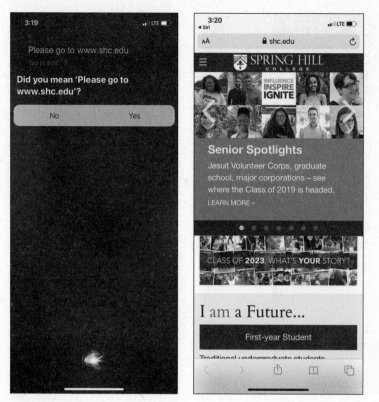

FIGURE 11-5

Get Suggestions

Siri anticipates your needs by making suggestions when you swipe from left to right on the initial Home screen and tap within the Search field at the top of the screen. Siri will list contacts you've communicated with recently, apps you've used, and nearby businesses, such as restaurants, gas stations, or coffee spots. If you tap on an app in the suggestions, it will open displaying the last viewed or listened to item.

Additionally, Siri lists news stories that may be of interest to you based on items you've viewed before.

Call Contacts

First, make sure that the person you want to call is entered in your Contacts app and include that person's phone number in his or her record. If you want to call somebody by stating your relationship to her, such as "Call sister," be sure to enter that relationship in the Add Related Name field in her contact record. Also make sure that the settings for Siri (refer to **Figure 11-3**) include your own contact name in the My Information field. (See Chapter 7 for more about creating contact records.) Follow these steps:

1. Press and hold the Home button or Side button (or say "Hey Siri," if you're using that feature) until Siri appears.

2. Speak a command, such as "Call Harold Smith," "Return Joe's call," or "Call Mom." If you want to make a FaceTime call, you can say "FaceTime Mom."

3. If you have two contacts who might match a spoken name, Siri responds with a list of possible matches (see **Figure 11-6**). Tap one in the list or state the correct contact's name to proceed.

4. The call is placed. To end the call before it completes, press the Home button (Side button for iPhone X models), and then tap End.

TIP

To cancel any spoken request, you have three options: Say "Cancel," tap the Siri button on the Siri screen (looks like swirling bands of light), or press the Home or Side (iPhone X and newer models) button. If you're using a headset or Bluetooth device, tap the End button on the device.

You can also access your voice mail using Siri. Just press and hold the Home button (Side button for iPhone X and newer models) until Siri activates, and then say something like "Check voice mail." Siri responds by telling you whether you have a new voice mail message and displays a list of any new messages. Tap one and then tap the Play button (looks like a blue arrow) to play it back. If you want to get rid of it, tap Delete (the red circle containing a white trash can). It's that simple.

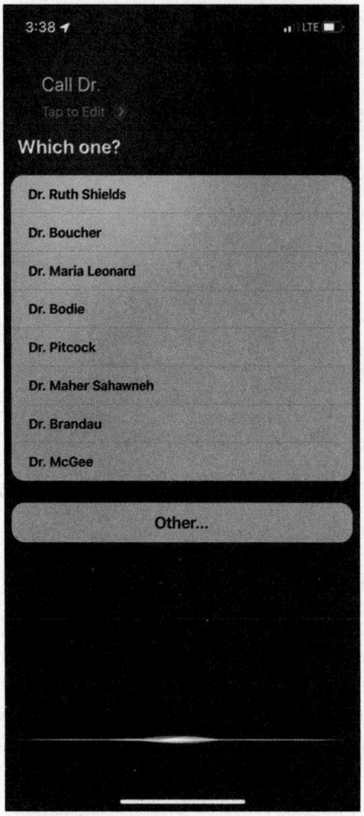

FIGURE 11-6

Create Reminders and Alerts

You can also use Siri with the Reminders app.

1. To create a reminder or alert, press and hold the Home button or Side button (iPhone X and newer models) and then speak a command, such as "Remind me to call Dad on Thursday at 10 a.m." or "Wake me up tomorrow at 6:15 a.m."

2. A preview of the reminder or alert is displayed (see **Figure 11-7**). Tell Siri to Cancel or Remove if you change your mind.

3. If you want a reminder ahead of the event that you created, activate Siri and speak a command, such as "Remind me tonight about the play on Thursday at 8 p.m." A second reminder is created, which you can confirm or cancel if you change your mind.

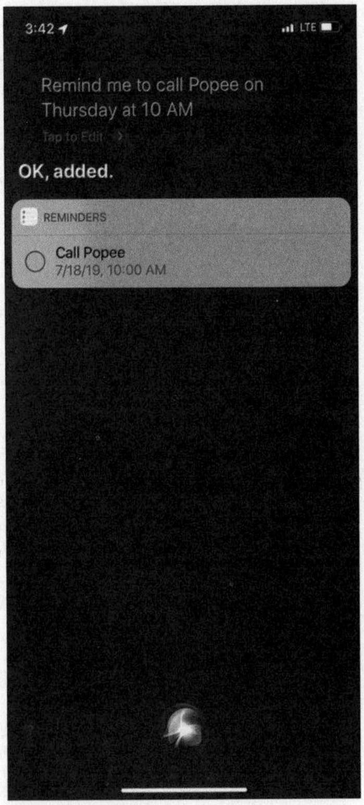

FIGURE 11-7

Add Tasks to Your Calendar

You can also set up events on your Calendar using Siri.

1. Press and hold the Home button or Side button (iPhone X and newer models) and then speak a phrase, such as "Set up a meeting for 3 p.m. tomorrow."

2. Siri sets up the appointment (see **Figure 11-8**) and informs you that you can let it know if you'd like to make any changes.

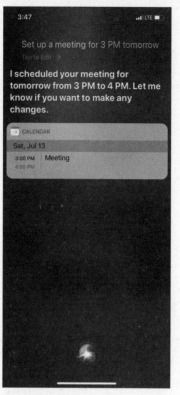

FIGURE 11-8

Play Music

You can use Siri to play music from the Music app.

1. Press and hold the Home button or Side button (iPhone X and newer models) until Siri appears.

2. To play music, speak a command, such as "Play music" or "Play Jazz radio station" to play a specific song, album, or radio station, as seen in **Figure 11-9.**

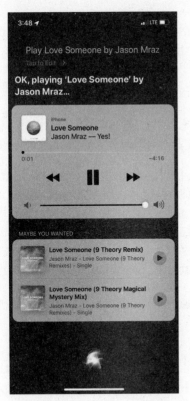

FIGURE 11-9

You can use the integration of Siri with Shazam, a music identifier app, to identify tagged music.

1. First, when you're near an audio source playing music, press and hold the Home button or Side button (iPhone X and newer models) to activate Siri.

2. Ask Siri a question, such as "What music is playing?" or "What's this song?"

3. Siri listens for a bit and if Siri recognizes the song, it shows you the song name, artist, any other available information, and the ability to purchase the music in the iTunes Store.

TIP

If you're listening to music or a podcast with earphones plugged in, and stop midstream, the next time you plug in earphones, Siri recognizes that you might want to continue with the same item.

Get Directions

You can use the Maps app and Siri to find your current location, get directions, find nearby businesses (such as restaurants or a bank), or get a map of another location. Be sure to turn on Location Services to allow Siri to know your current location (go to Settings and tap Privacy⇨Location Services; make sure Location Services is on and that Siri & Dictation is turned on further down in these settings).

Here are some of the commands that you can try to get directions or a list of nearby businesses:

» **"Where am I?":** Displays a map of your current location.

» **"Where is Cammie's Old Dutch Ice Cream?":** Displays a map of that business's location, as shown in **Figure 11-10.**

» **"Find pizza restaurants.":** Displays a list of restaurants near your current location; tap one to display a map of its location.

» **"Find Bank of America.":** Displays a map with the location of the indicated business (or in some cases, several nearby locations, such as a bank branch and all ATMs).

» **"Get directions to the Empire State Building.":** Loads a map with a route drawn and provides a narration of directions to the site from your current location.

TIP

After a location is displayed on a map, tap the Information button on the location's label to view its address, phone number, and website address, if available.

FIGURE 11-10

Ask for Facts

Wolfram|Alpha is a self-professed online computational knowledge engine. That means that it's more than a search engine because it provides specific information about a search term rather than multiple search results. If you want facts without having to spend time browsing websites to find those facts, Wolfram|Alpha is a very good resource.

Siri uses Wolfram|Alpha and such sources as Wikipedia and Bing to look up facts in response to questions, such as: "What is the capital of Kansas?" "What is the square root of 2,300?" "How large is Mars?" Just press and hold the Home button or Side button (for iPhone X and newer models) and ask your question; Siri consults its resources and returns a set of relevant facts.

You can also get information about other things, such as the weather, stocks, or the time. Just say a phrase like one of these to get what you need:

» **"What is the weather?":** This shows the weather report for your current location. If you want weather in another location, just specify the location in your question.

» **"What is the price of Apple stock?":** Siri tells you the current price of the stock or the price of the stock when the stock market last closed.

» **"How hot is the sun?":** Siri tells you the temperature of the sun, and even breaks it down into various unit conversions.

Search the Web

Although Siri can use its resources to respond to specific requests such as "Who is the Queen of England?" more general requests for information will cause Siri to search further on the web. Siri can also search Twitter for comments related to your search.

For example, if you speak a phrase, such as "Find a website about birds" or "Find information about the World Series," Siri can respond in a couple of ways. The app can simply display a list of search results by using the default search engine specified in your settings for Safari or by suggesting, "If you like, I can search the web for such and such." In the first instance, just tap a result to go to that website. In the second instance, you can confirm that you want to search the web or cancel.

Send Email, Messages, or Tweets

You can create an email or an instant message using Siri and existing contacts. For example, if you say, "Email Porter," a form opens that is already addressed to that stored contact. Siri asks for a subject and then a message. Speak your message contents and then say, "Send" to speed your message on its way.

Siri also works with messaging apps, such as Messages. If you have the Messages app open and you say, "Tell Devyn I'll call soon," Siri creates a message for you to approve and send.

Use Dictation

Text entry isn't Siri's strong point. Instead, you can use the Dictation key that appears with a microphone symbol on the onscreen keyboard to speak text rather than type it. This feature is called Dictation.

1. Go to any app where you enter text, such as Notes or Mail, and tap in the document or form. The onscreen keyboard appears.

2. Tap the Dictation key on the keyboard and speak your text.

3. To end the dictation, tap Done.

TIP

When you finish speaking text, you can use the keyboard to make edits to the text Siri entered, although as voice recognition programs go, Dictation is pretty darn accurate. If a word sports a blue underline, which means there may be an error, you can tap to select and make edits to it.

Exploring the Internet

3

IN THIS CHAPTER

» **Connect to the Internet**

» **Navigate web pages and tabs**

» **View history and search the web**

» **Use bookmarks**

» **Download files**

Chapter **12**

Browsing with Safari

Getting on the Internet with your iPhone is easy, by using its Wi-Fi or cellular capabilities. After you're online, the built-in browser (software that helps you navigate the Internet's contents), Safari, is your ticket to a wide world of information, entertainment, education, and more. Safari will look familiar to you if you've used a web browser on a PC or Mac computer, though the way you move around by using the iPhone touchscreen may be new to you. If you've never used Safari, this chapter takes you by the hand and shows you all the basics of making Safari work for you.

In this chapter, you see how to go online with your iPhone, navigate among web pages, and use iCloud tabs to share your browsing experience between devices. Along the way, you see how to place a bookmark for a favorite site or place a web clip on your Home screen. You can also view your browsing history, save online images to your Photo Library, post photos to sites from within Safari, or email or tweet a link to a friend. You also explore Safari's Reader and Reading List features and learn how to keep yourself safer while online by using private browsing. Finally, you review the simple steps involved in printing what you find online.

Connect to the Internet

How you connect to the Internet depends on which types of connections are available:

>> You can connect to the Internet via a Wi-Fi network. You can set up this type of network in your own home using your computer and some equipment from your Internet provider. You can also connect over public Wi-Fi networks, referred to as *hotspots*.

You'll probably be surprised to discover how many hotspots your town or city has. Look for Internet cafés, coffee shops, hotels, libraries, and transportation centers (such as airports or bus stations). Many of these businesses display signs alerting you to their free Wi-Fi.

>> You can use the paid data network provided by AT&T, Sprint, T-Mobile, Verizon, or most any other cellular provider, to connect from just about anywhere you can get cellphone coverage through a cellular network.

To enable cellular data, tap Settings and then Cellular. Toggle the switch (just tap it) to turn on the Cellular Data setting.

WARNING

Browsing the Internet using a cellular connection can eat up your data plan allotment quickly if your plan doesn't include unlimited data access. If you think you'll often use the Internet with your iPhone away from a Wi-Fi connection, double-check your data allotment with your cellular provider or consider getting an unlimited data plan.

To connect to a Wi-Fi network, you have to complete a few steps:

1. Tap Settings on the Home screen and then tap Wi-Fi.

2. Be sure that Wi-Fi is set to On (green) and then choose a network to connect to by tapping it.

Network names should appear automatically when you're in range of them. When you're in range of a public hotspot or if access to several nearby networks is available, you may see a message asking you to tap a network name to select it. After you select a network you may see a message asking for your password. Ask the owner of the hotspot (for example, a hotel desk clerk or business owner) for this password, or enter your own network password if you're connecting to your home network.

Free public Wi-Fi networks usually don't require passwords, or the password is posted prominently for all to see. (If you can't find the password, don't be shy to ask someone.)

3. Tap the Join button when prompted. Once done, you're connected! Your iPhone will now recognize the network and connect without repeatedly entering the password.

After you connect to public Wi-Fi, someone else could possibly track your online activities because these are unsecured networks. Avoid accessing financial accounts, making online purchases, or sending emails with sensitive information in them, when connected to a public hotspot.

Explore Safari

1. After you're connected to a network, tap Safari on the Dock at the bottom of the Home screen. Safari opens, possibly displaying the Apple iPhone Home page the first time you go online (see **Figure 12-1**).

Address/Search field

Next   **Bookmarks**

Previous   **Share**   **Show/Hide Tabs**

FIGURE 12-1

2. Put two fingers together on the screen and spread them apart to expand the view (also known as zooming in). Place your fingers on the screen about an inch or so apart and quickly bring them together to zoom back out. You can also double-tap the screen with a single finger to restore the default view size (if you tap a link, though, your gesture will just open that link).

Using your fingers on the screen to enlarge or reduce the size of a web page allows you to view what's displayed at various sizes, giving you more flexibility than the double-tap method.

3. Put your finger on the screen and flick upward to scroll down on the page.

4. To return to the top of the web page, put your finger on the screen and drag downward or tap the Status bar at the very top of the screen twice.

Navigate among Web Pages

1. Tap in the Address field just under the Status bar. The onscreen keyboard appears (see **Figure 12-2**).

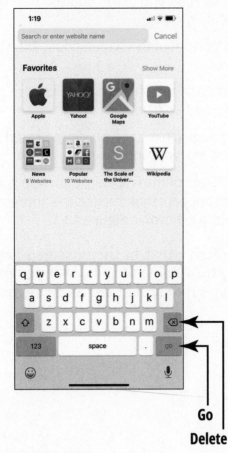

Go
Delete

FIGURE 12-2

2. Enter a web address; for example, you can go to www.dummies.com.

By default, AutoFill is turned on in iPhone, causing entries you make in fields, such as the Address field and password fields, to automatically display possible matching entries. You can turn off AutoFill by using iPhone Settings for Safari.

3. Tap the Go key on the keyboard (refer to **Figure 12-2**). The website appears.

   • If a page doesn't display properly, tap the Reload button at the right end of the Address field.

   • If Safari is loading a web page and you change your mind about viewing the page, you can stop loading the page. Tap Cancel (looks like an X), which appears at the right end of the Address field during this process, to stop loading the page.

4. Tap the Previous button at the bottom of the screen (looks like <) to go to the last page you displayed.

5. Tap the Next button at the bottom of the screen (looks like >) to go forward to the page you just backed up from.

6. To follow a link to another web page (links are typically indicated by colored text or graphics), tap the link with your finger.

To view the destination web address of the link before you tap it, just touch and hold the link; a menu appears that displays the address at the top and a preview of the site, as shown in **Figure 12-3**.

Apple QuickType supports predictive text in the onscreen keyboard. This feature adds the capability for iPhone to spot what you probably intend to type from text you've already entered and suggests it to save you time typing.

FIGURE 12-3

Use Tabbed Browsing

Tabbed browsing is a feature that allows you to have several websites open at one time so that you can move easily among those sites.

1. With Safari open and a web page already displaying, tap the Show/Hide Tabs button in the bottom-right corner (refer to **Figure 12-1**). The new Tab view appears.

2. To add a new page (meaning that you're opening a new website), tap the New Page button (shaped like a plus [+] symbol) in the lower middle of the screen (see **Figure 12-4**). A page with your favorite sites and an address bar appears.

You can get to the same new page by simply tapping in the address bar from any site.

TIP

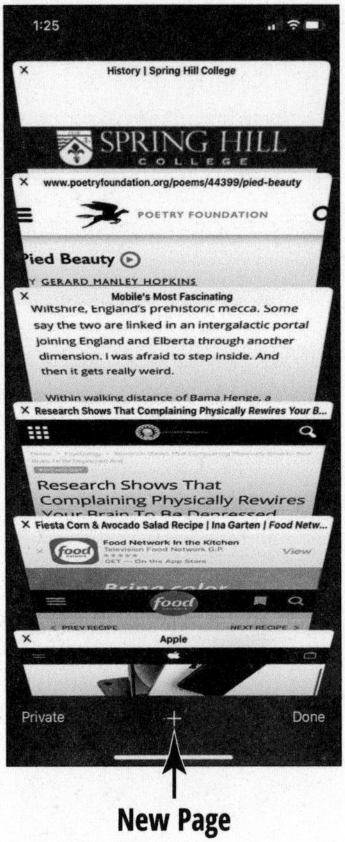

New Page

FIGURE 12-4

3. Tap in the Address field and use the onscreen keyboard to enter the web address for the website you want to open. Tap the Go key. The website opens on the page.

Repeat Steps 1 to 3 to open as many new web pages as you'd like.

TIP

4. You can now switch among open sites by tapping outside the keyboard to close it and tapping the Show/Hide Tabs button and scrolling among recent sites. Find the one you want and then tap it.

You can easily rearrange sites in the tabs window. Just touch-and-hold the tab you want to move and then drag it up or down the list until it's in the spot you'd like it to be (the other sites in the window politely move to make room). To drop it in the new location, simply remove your finger from the screen.

TIP

5. To delete a tab, tap the Show/Hide Tabs button, scroll to locate the tab, and then tap the Close button in the upper-left corner of the tab (looks like an X; it may be difficult to see on some sites, but trust me, it's there).

View Browsing History

As you move around the web, your browser keeps a record of your browsing history. This record can be handy when you want to visit a site that you viewed previously but whose address you've now forgotten.

1. With Safari open, tap the Bookmarks button.

After you master the use of the Bookmarks button options, you might prefer a shortcut to view your History list. Tap and hold the Previous button at the bottom left on any screen, and your browsing history for the current session appears. You can also tap and hold the Next button to look at sites you backtracked from.

2. On the menu shown in **Figure 12-5,** tap the History tab (looks like a clock).

3. In the History list that appears (see **Figure 12-6**), tap a site to navigate to it. Tap Done to leave History and return to browsing.

To clear the history, tap the Clear button (refer to **Figure 12-6**) and on the screen that appears, tap an option: The Last Hour, Today, Today and yesterday, or All time. This button is useful when you don't want your spouse or grandchildren to see where you've been browsing for anniversary, birthday, or holiday presents!

FIGURE 12-5

FIGURE 12-6

Search the Web

If you don't know the address of the site that you want to visit (or you want to research a topic or find other information online), get acquainted with Safari's Search feature on iPhone. By default, Safari uses the Google search engine.

1. With Safari open, tap in the Address field (refer to **Figure 12-1**). The onscreen keyboard appears.

TIP

To change your default search engine from Google to Yahoo!, Bing, or DuckDuckGo, from the Home screen, tap Settings, tap Safari, and then tap Search Engine. Tap Yahoo!, Bing, or DuckDuckGo, and your default search engine changes.

2. Enter a search term. With recent versions of Safari, the search term can be a topic or a web address because of what's called the Unified smart search field. You can tap one of the suggested sites or complete your entry and tap the Go key (see **Figure 12-7**) on your keyboard.

3. In the search results that are displayed, tap a link to visit that site.

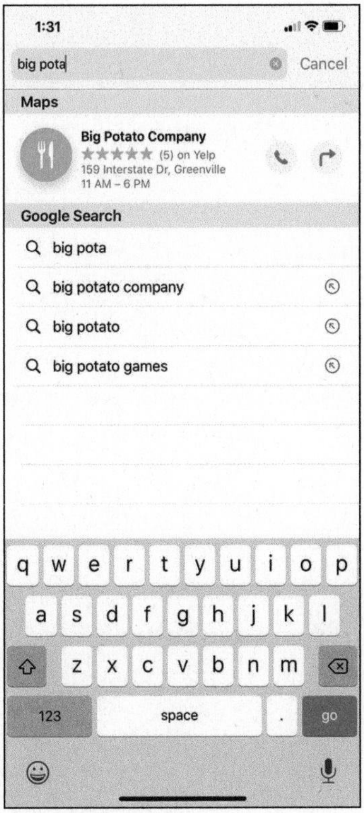

FIGURE 12-7

Add and Use Bookmarks

Bookmarks are a way to save favorite sites so that you can easily visit them again.

1. With a site open that you want to bookmark, tap the Share button at the bottom of the screen (looks like a box with an upward-pointing arrow).

TIP

If you want to sync your bookmarks on your iPhone browser, go to Settings on iPhone and make sure that iCloud is set to sync with Safari.

2. On the menu that appears (see **Figure 12-8**), tap Add Bookmark. (You may need to swipe up the page to see it.)

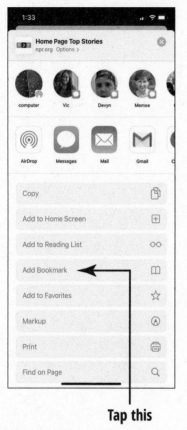

Tap this

FIGURE 12-8

3. In the Add Bookmark dialog, shown in **Figure 12-9**, edit the name of the bookmark if you want. Tap the name of the site and use the onscreen keyboard to edit its name.

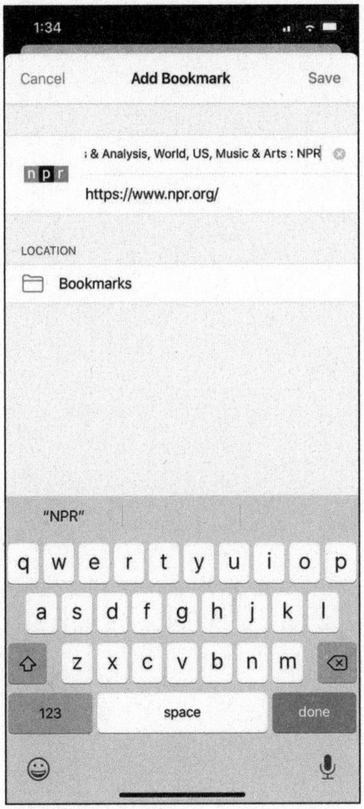

FIGURE 12-9

4. Tap the Save button in the upper-right corner. The item is saved to your Favorites by default; to save to another location, click Favorites (or whatever is listed in the Location section of the Add Bookmark dialog) and choose the desired location from the list.

5. To go to the bookmark, tap the Bookmarks button.

6. On the Bookmarks menu that appears (see **Figure 12-10**), if you saved a site to a folder, tap to open the folder, and then tap the book-marked site that you want to visit.

When you tap the Bookmarks button, you can tap Edit in the lower-right corner and then use the New Folder option (in the lower-left corner) to create folders to organize your bookmarks or folders. When you next add a bookmark, you can then choose, from the dialog that appears, any folder to which you want to add the new bookmark.

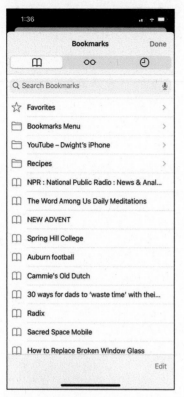

FIGURE 12-10

TIP

You can reorder your bookmarks quite easily. Tap the Bookmarks button, tap the Edit button (lower-right), find the bookmark you'd like to rearrange, tap-and-hold the three parallel lines to the right of the bookmark, and then drag it up and down the list, releasing it once you get to the place you'd like it to reside. You can also delete bookmarks from the same screen by tapping the red circle to the left of a bookmark and then tapping the red Delete button that appears to the right.

Download Files

iOS 13 introduces a new Download Manager for Safari to help you efficiently download files from websites and store them to a location of your choosing. You can choose to store downloaded files on your iPhone or in iCloud.

TIP

Set the default download location for files you download in Safari. Go to Settings ➪ Safari ➪ Downloads and tap the location you want to use.

1. Open a site in Safari that contains a file you'd like to download.

2. Tap-and-hold the link for the file until the menu in **Figure 12-11** appears.

3. Tap the Download Linked File button to download the file to your iPhone, iCloud, or another destination.

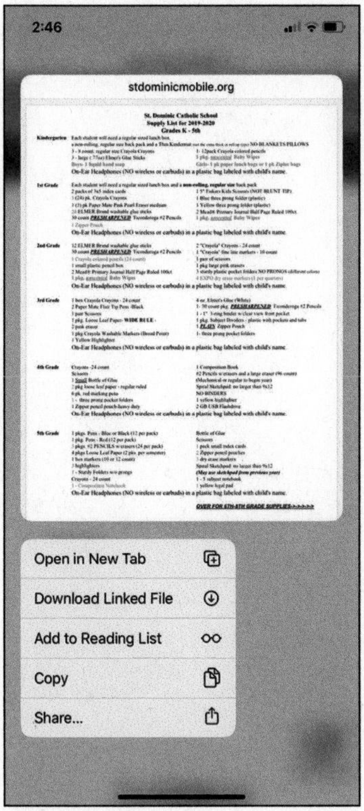

FIGURE 12-11

4. The Downloads button (a circle containing a downward-pointing arrow) appears to the right of the address field at the top of the screen (see **Figure 12-12**); tap it to see the progress of the download. If the download is finished, tap it in the Download Manager menu to open it, or tap the magnifying glass to see where the file is stored.

Downloads button

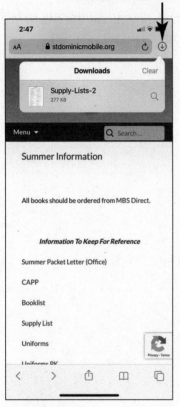

FIGURE 12-12

IN THIS CHAPTER

» **Add an email account**

» **Read, reply to, or forward email**

» **Create, format, and send emails**

» **Search email**

» **Mark or flag email**

» **Create events with email contents**

» **Delete and organize email**

» **Create a VIP list**

Chapter **13**

Working with Email in Mail

S taying in touch with others by email is a great way to use your iPhone. You can access an existing account using the handy Mail app supplied with your iPhone or sign in to your email account using the Safari browser. In this chapter, you take a look at using Mail, which involves adding an existing email account. Then you can use Mail to write, format, retrieve, and forward messages from that account.

Mail offers the capability to mark the messages you've read, delete messages, and organize your messages in a small set of folders, as well as use a handy search feature. You can create a VIP list so that you're notified when that special person sends you an email.

In this chapter, you read all about the Mail app and its various features.

Add an Email Account

You can add one or more email accounts, including the email account associated with your iCloud account, using your iPhone's Settings app. If you have an iCloud, Microsoft Exchange (often used for business accounts), Gmail, Yahoo!, AOL, or Outlook.com (this includes Microsoft accounts from Live, Hotmail, and so on) account, iPhone pretty much automates the setup.

TIP

If this is the first time you're adding an account, and if you only need to add one, save yourself a few taps; just open Mail and begin from Step 4 below.

1. To set up iPhone to retrieve messages from your email account at one of these popular providers, first tap the Settings icon on the Home screen.

2. In Settings, tap Passwords & Accounts. The screen shown in **Figure 13-1** appears.

3. Tap Add Account, found under the Accounts section. The options shown in **Figure 13-2** appear.

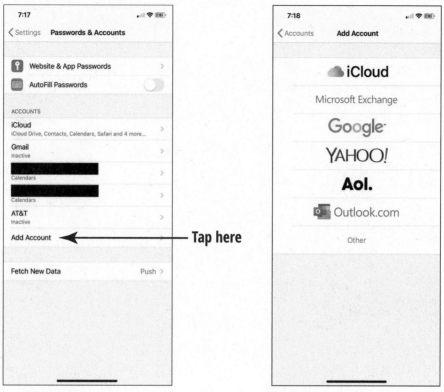

FIGURE 13-1

FIGURE 13-2

4. Tap iCloud, Microsoft Exchange, Google, Yahoo!, AOL, or Outlook. com. Enter your account information in the form that appears and follow any instructions to complete the process. (Each service is slightly different, but none are complicated.) If you have a different email service than these, skip to the next section called "Manually Set Up an Email Account."

5. After iPhone takes a moment to verify your account information, on the next screen (shown in **Figure 13-3**), you can tap any On/Off switch to have services from that account synced with iPhone.

6. When you're done, tap Save in the upper-right corner of the screen. The account is saved, and you can now open it using Mail.

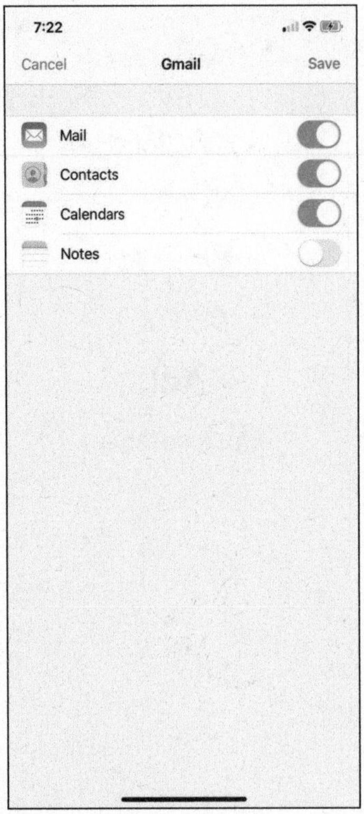

FIGURE 13-3

Manually Set Up an Email Account

You can also set up most popular email accounts, such as those available through Earthlink or a cable provider's service, by obtaining the host name from the provider. To set up an existing account with a provider other than iCloud (Apple), Microsoft Exchange, Gmail (Google), Yahoo!, AOL, or Outlook.com, you enter the account settings yourself.

TIP

If this is the first time you're adding an account, and if you only need to add one, just open Mail and begin from Step 3 below.

1. First, tap the Settings icon on the Home screen.

2. In Settings, tap Mail, tap Accounts, and then tap the Add Account button (refer to **Figure 13-1**).

3. On the screen that appears (refer to **Figure 13-2**), tap Other.

4. On the screen shown in **Figure 13-4**, tap Add Mail Account.

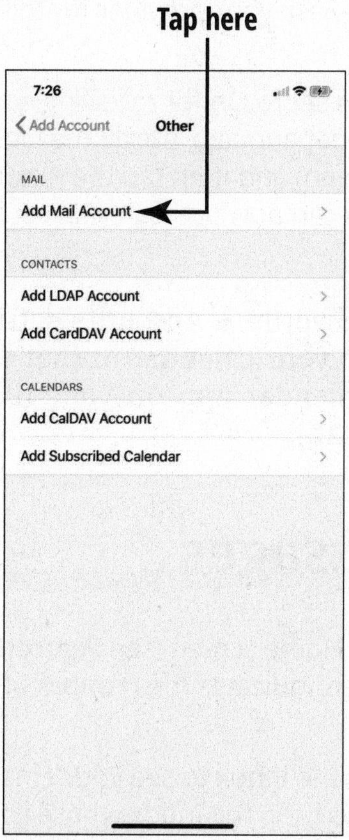

Tap here

FIGURE 13-4

5. In the form that appears, enter your name and an account email address, password, and description, then tap Next. iPhone takes a moment to verify your account, then returns you to the Passwords & Accounts page, with your new account displayed.

TIP

iPhone will probably add the outgoing mail server (SMTP) information for you. If it doesn't, you may have to enter it yourself. If you have a less mainstream email service, you may have to enter the mail server protocol (POP3 or IMAP — ask your provider for this information) and your password.

6. To make sure that the Account field is set to On for receiving email, tap the account name. In the dialog that appears, toggle the On/Off switch for the Mail field to On (green) and then tap the Accounts button to return to Mail settings. You can now access the account through iPhone's Mail app.

TIP

If you turn on Calendars in the Passwords & Accounts settings, any information that you've put into your calendar in that email account is brought over into the Calendar app on your iPhone (discussed in more detail in Chapter 22).

Open Mail and Read Messages

1. Tap the Mail app icon located on the Home screen (see **Figure 13-5**). A red circle on the icon, called a badge, indicates the number of unread emails in your Inbox.

2. In the Mail app (see **Figure 13-6**), tap the Inbox to see your emails. If you have more than one account listed, tap the Inbox whose contents you want to display.

Tap the Mail icon

FIGURE 13-5   **FIGURE 13-6**

3. Tap a message to read it. It opens, as you can see **Figure 13-7**.

TIP

The 3D Touch feature allows you to preview an email before you open it. Simply press lightly on an email in the Inbox to open a preview of the message. From within the preview, you can elect to perform several functions, such as Reply, Forward, or send it to the Trash.

4. If you need to scroll to see the entire message, just place your finger on the screen and flick upward to scroll down. You can swipe right while reading a message to open the Inbox's list of messages, then swipe right again to return to your list of mailboxes.

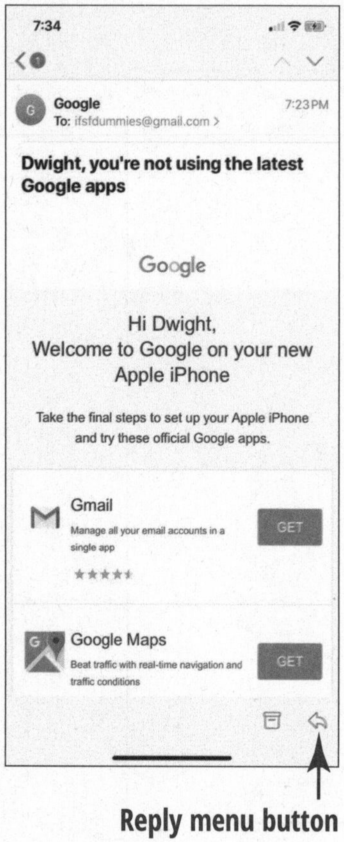

Reply menu button

FIGURE 13-7

You can tap the Next or Previous buttons (top-right corner of the message) to move to the next or previous message in the Inbox or tap All Inboxes in the top-left corner to return to your Inbox.

Email messages that you haven't read are marked with a blue circle in your Inbox. After you read a message, the blue circle disappears. You can mark a read message as unread to help remind you to read it again later. With the Inbox displayed, swipe to the right (starting your swipe just a little in from the left edge of the screen) on a message, and then tap Unread. If you swipe quickly and all the way to the right you don't need to tap; it will just mark as unread automatically.

If you have a Plus iPhone model (iPhone 8 Plus, for example) or an iPhone X model or newer and you hold it horizontally, you will view both the Inbox and currently selected message. The larger screen of these models can accommodate more content, and such apps as Mail and Weather take advantage of this.

Reply To or Forward Email

1. With an email message open, tap the Reply menu button, which looks like a left-facing arrow (refer to **Figure 13-7**). Then tap Reply, Reply All (available if there are multiple recipients), or Forward in the menu that appears (see **Figure 13-8**).

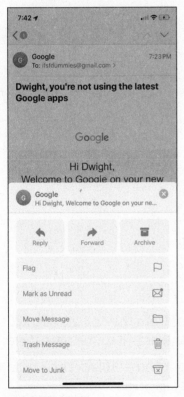

FIGURE 13-8

2. In the new email message that appears (see **Figure 13-9**), tap in the To field and enter another addressee if you like (you have to do this if you're forwarding). Next, tap in the message body and enter a message (see **Figure 13-10**).

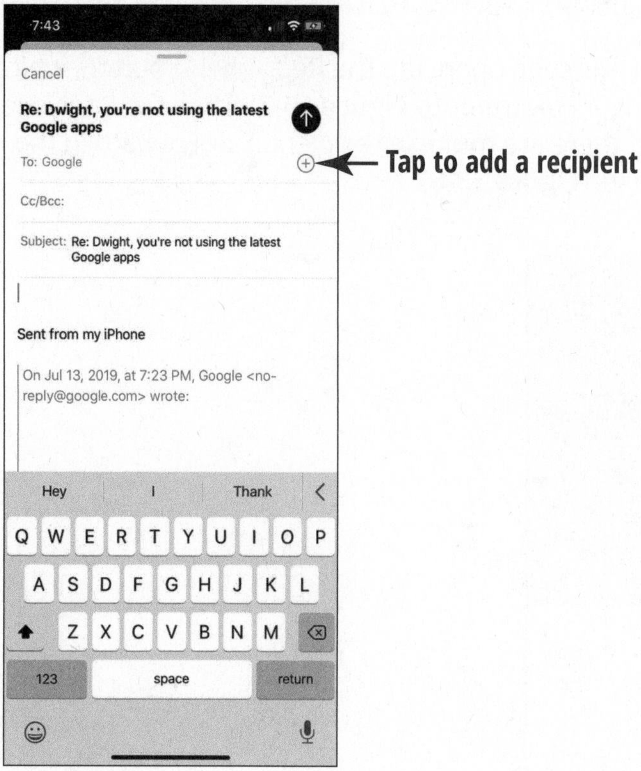

FIGURE 13-9

TIP
If you want to move an email address from the To field to the Cc or Bcc field, tap and hold the address and drag it to the other field.

3. Tap the Send button in the upper-right corner (black circle with an upward-pointing arrow). The email goes on its way.

TIP
If you tap Forward to send the message to somebody else and the original message had an attachment, you're offered the option of including or omitting the attachment.

Tap in the message
body to add content

FIGURE 13-10

Create and Send a New Message

1. With Mail open, tap the New Message button in the bottom-right corner (this looks like a page with a pencil on it). A blank email appears (see **Figure 13-11**).

2. Enter a recipient's address in the To field by tapping the field and typing the address. If you have addresses in Contacts, tap the plus sign (+) in the To field to choose an addressee from the Contacts list that appears.

3. If you want to send a copy of the message to other people, tap the Cc/Bcc field. When the Cc and Bcc fields open, enter addresses in either or both. Use the Bcc field to specify recipients of blind carbon copies, which means that no other recipients are aware that that person received this reply.

4. Enter the subject of the message in the Subject field.

5. Tap in the message body and type your message.

6. If you want to check a fact or copy and paste some part of another message into your draft message, swipe down near the top of the email to display your Inbox and other folders. Locate the message, and when you're ready to return to your draft, tap the Subject of the email, which is displayed near the bottom of the screen.

7. When you've finished creating your message, tap Send.

FIGURE 13-11

Format Email

You can apply some basic formatting to email text. You can use bold, underline, and italic formats, and indent text using the Quote Level feature.

1. Press and hold the text in a message you're creating and choose Select or Select All to select a single word or all the words in the email (see **Figure 13-12**).

TIP

When you make a selection, blue handles appear that you can drag to add adjacent words to your selection. If the menu disappears after you select the text, just tap one of the selection handles and it will reappear.

FIGURE 13-12

2. To see more tools, tap the arrow on the toolbar that appears. To apply bold, italic, or underline formatting, tap the BIU button.

3. In the toolbar that appears (see **Figure 13-13**), tap Bold, Italic, or Underline to apply formatting.

FIGURE 13-13

4. To change the indent level, tap and hold at the beginning of a line and then tap Quote Level.

5. Tap Increase to indent the text or Decrease to move indented text farther toward the left margin.

To use the Quote Level feature, make sure that it's on. From the Home screen, tap Settings, tap Mail, tap Increase Quote Level, then toggle (tap) the Increase Quote Level On/Off switch to turn it On (green).

Mail in iOS 13 allows you to go beyond the basics, though. It introduces much-improved text formatting and font support, freeing you up to create some really great looking emails. However, it doesn't stop there: The new format bar (which appears above the keyboard, shown in **Figure 13-14**) allows you to easily jazz up your email with a variety of options.

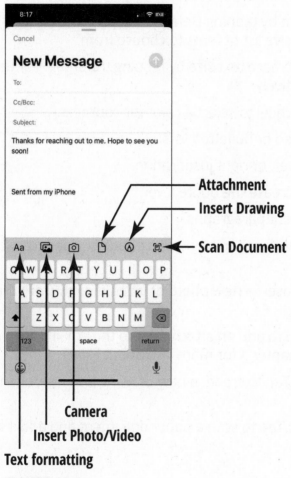

Attachment

Insert Drawing

Scan Document

Camera

Insert Photo/Video

Text formatting

FIGURE 13-14

If you see words above the keyboard and not the format bar, tap the arrow to the right of the words to bring the format bar back into view.

TIP

Here's a quick look at the options in the new format bar:

» **Desktop-class text formatting:** Tap the Aa button to see a bevy of formatting options (seen in **Figure 13-15**) hitherto not available in Mail, such as

- Choose Bold, Italic, Underline, and Strikethrough. (Okay, these options aren't new, but the rest are.)

- Change the font by tapping Default Font and browsing a surprisingly extensive list of fonts to choose from.

- Decrease or increase text size by tapping the small A or the large A, respectively.

- Tap the color wheel to select a color for your text.

- Insert numbered or bulleted lists.

- Select left, center, or right justification.

- Increase or decrease the quote level.

- Indent or outdent paragraphs.

» **Insert Photo or Video:** Tap to insert a photo or video from the Photos app.

» **Camera:** Tap to insert a new photo or video directly from the Camera app.

» **Attachment:** Tap to add an attachment to the email from the Files app. (See Chapter 4 for more info about Files.)

» **Insert Drawing:** Tap to create a new drawing and insert it into your email.

» **Scan Document:** Tap to scan a paper document and add it to your email.

FIGURE 13-15

Search Email

What do you do if you want to find all messages from a certain person or containing a certain word? You can use Mail's handy Search feature to find these emails.

1. With Mail open, tap an account to display its Inbox.

2. In the Inbox, tap and drag down near the top email to display the Search field. Tap in the Search field, and the onscreen keyboard appears.

You can also use the Search feature covered in Chapter 2 to search for terms in the To, From, or Subject lines of mail messages.

TIP

3. Tap the All Mailboxes tab to view messages that contain the search term in any mailbox, or tap the Current Mailbox tab to see only matches within the current mailbox. (These options may vary slightly depending on which email service you use.)

4. Enter a search term or name, as shown in **Figure 13-16.** If multiple types of information are found, such as People or Subjects, tap the one you're looking for. Matching emails are listed in the results.

Enter search terms here

Search results appear here

FIGURE 13-16

To start a new search or go back to the full Inbox, either tap the Delete icon (the gray circled X) on the far-right end of the Search field to delete the term and start over or tap the Cancel button to end your search.

TIP

Mark Email as Unread or Flag for Follow-Up

You can use a simple swipe to access tools that either mark an email as unread after you've read it (placing a blue dot before the message) or flag an email (which places an orange flag to the right of it). If the email is both marked as unread and is flagged, both a blue dot and an orange flag will appear on the message. These methods help you to remember to reread an email that you've already read or to follow up on a message at a later time.

1. With Mail open and an Inbox displayed, swipe to the left on an email to display three options: More, Flag, and Trash (or Archive).

TECHNICAL STUFF

You may see Archive in place of Trash. This depends on the type of email account you're using and how it has been set up by the email provider.

2. Tap More. On the menu shown in **Figure 13-17,** you're given several options, including Mark. Tapping Mark accesses both the Mark As Read/Unread and Flag commands. Tapping either command applies it and returns you to your Inbox.

TIP

You can also get to the Mark As Read/Unread command by swiping to the right on a message displayed in your Inbox.

3. There's another way to get to the Flag command. Swipe to the left on another email, then tap Flag. An orange flag appears to the right of the email. Perform the same action to Unflag it, if you like.

TIP

There's an alternative way to flag emails that allows you to select custom colors for flags. Open the email, tap the Reply menu button in the lower-right corner (looks like a left-pointing arrow), and tap Flag. Select a color from the options and click the gray circled X in the upper-right of the Reply menu to return to the email.

TIP

On the menu shown in **Figure 13-17,** you can also select Notify Me or Mute. Notify Me causes Mail to notify you whenever somebody replies to this email thread. Mute allows you to mute a thread of emails that just won't stop bugging you.

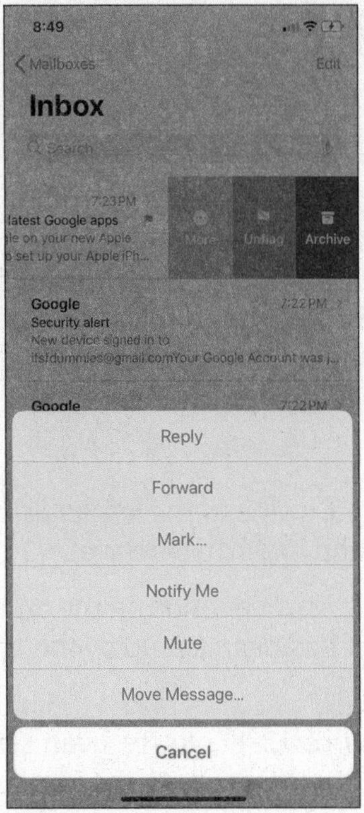

FIGURE 13-17

Create an Event from Email Contents

A neat feature in Mail is the ability to create a Calendar event from within an email.

1. To test this out, create an email to yourself mentioning a reservation on a specific airline on a specific date and time; you can also mention another type of reservation, such as for dinner, or mention a phone number.

2. Send the message to yourself and then open Mail.

3. In your Inbox, open the email. (The pertinent information is displayed in underlined text.)

4. Tap the underlined text, and in the menu shown in **Figure 13-18,** tap Create Event. A New Event form from Calendar appears. Enter additional information about the event, then tap Done.

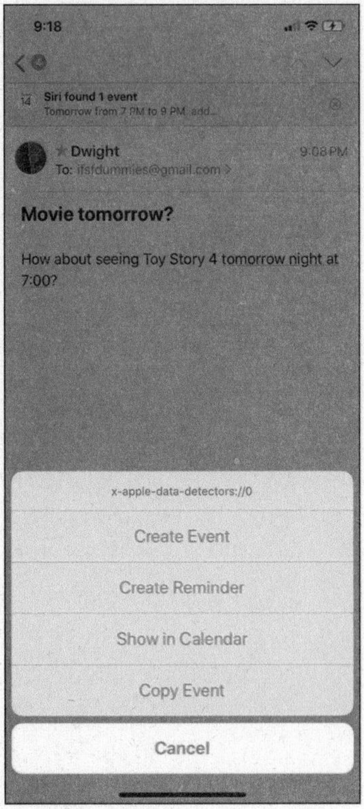

FIGURE 13-18

TIP

Siri may also detect an event in your email; if so, you'll see a notification at the top of the email that Siri did indeed find an event. Tap the tiny blue add. . . button to quickly create the event.

Delete Email

When you no longer want an email cluttering your Inbox, you can delete it.

1. With the Inbox displayed, tap the Edit button in the upper-right corner. Circular check buttons are displayed to the left of each message (see **Figure 13-19**).

Tap to select a message

Selected message

FIGURE 13-19

2. Tap the circle next to the message(s) that you want to delete. A message marked for deletion shows a check mark in the circular check button (refer to **Figure 13-19**).

TIP

You can tap multiple items if you have several emails to delete.

3. Tap the Trash or Archive button at the bottom-left of the screen. The selected messages are moved to the Trash or Archive folder.

TECHNICAL STUFF

What's the difference between Trash and Archive? Basically, email sent to a Trash folder typically is deleted forever after a certain amount of time (usually 30 days); email sent to an Archive folder is removed from the Inbox but kept indefinitely for future use.

TIP

You can also delete an open email by tapping the Trash or Archive icon on the toolbar at the bottom of the screen, or swiping left on a message displayed in an Inbox and tapping the Trash or Archive button that appears.

Organize Email

You can move messages into any of several predefined folders in Mail (these will vary depending on your email provider and the folders you've created on your provider's server).

1. After displaying the folder containing the message that you want to move (for example, Inbox), tap the Edit button. Circular check buttons are displayed to the left of each message (refer to **Figure 13-19**).

2. Tap the circle next to the message you want to move. You may select multiple messages if you like.

3. Tap the Move button at the bottom of the screen.

4. In the Mailboxes list that appears (see **Figure 13-20**), tap the folder where you want to store the message. The message is moved.

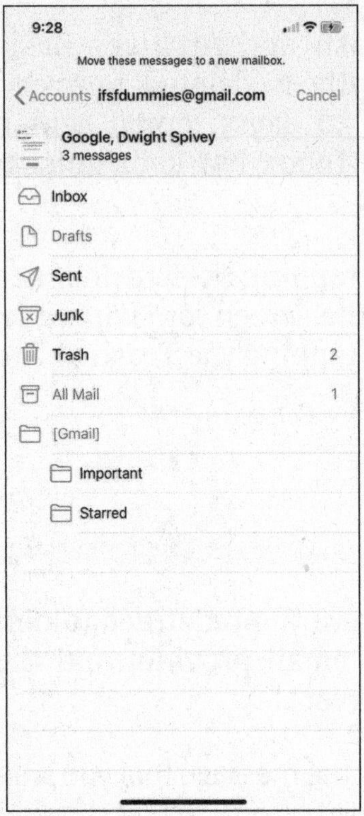

FIGURE 13-20

Create a VIP List

A VIP list is a way to create a list of senders you deem to be more important than others. When any of these senders sends you an email, you'll be notified of it through the Notifications feature of iPhone.

1. In the main list of Mailboxes, tap the Info button (circle with lower-case "i") in the VIP option (see **Figure 13-21**).

2. Tap Add VIP (see **Figure 13-22**), and your Contacts list appears.

3. Tap a contact to make that person a VIP.

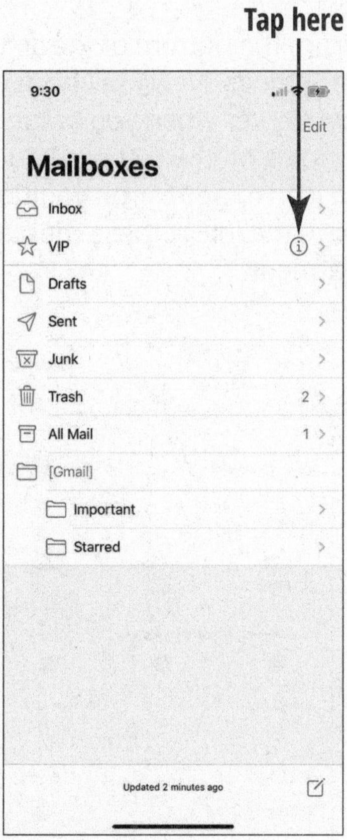

Tap here

FIGURE 13-21

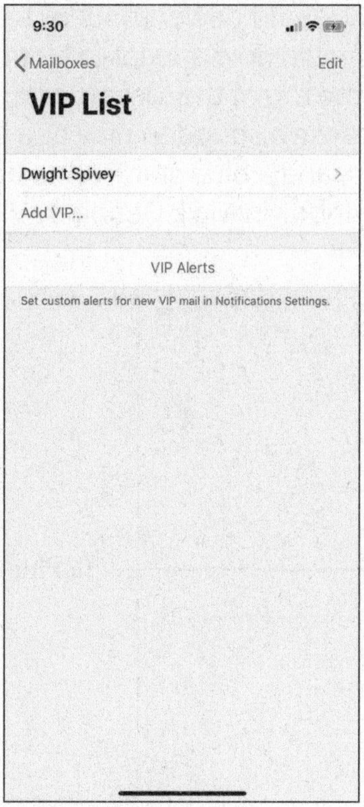

FIGURE 13-22

4. To make settings for whether VIP mail is flagged on Notification Center (the screen where notifications appear on your iPhone), press the Home button or swipe up from the bottom of the screen (iPhone X and newer models), then tap Settings.

5. Tap Notifications, then tap Mail. In the settings that appear, shown in **Figure 13-23,** tap VIP.

6. Toggle the Allow Notifications switch to On (green), and then tap one or all of the Lock Screen, Notification Center, and Banners icons to customize how you receive notifications for VIP mail.

7. Select a banner style and choose what sound should play or whether badges should appear (see **Figure 13-24**).

8. Press the Home button or swipe up from the bottom of the screen (iPhone X and newer models) to close Settings. New mail from your VIPs should now appear in Notification Center when you swipe down from the top of the screen, and, depending on the settings you chose, may cause a sound to play or a badge icon to appear on your lock screen, and a blue star icon to appear to the left of these messages in the Inbox in Mail. Definitely VIP treatment.

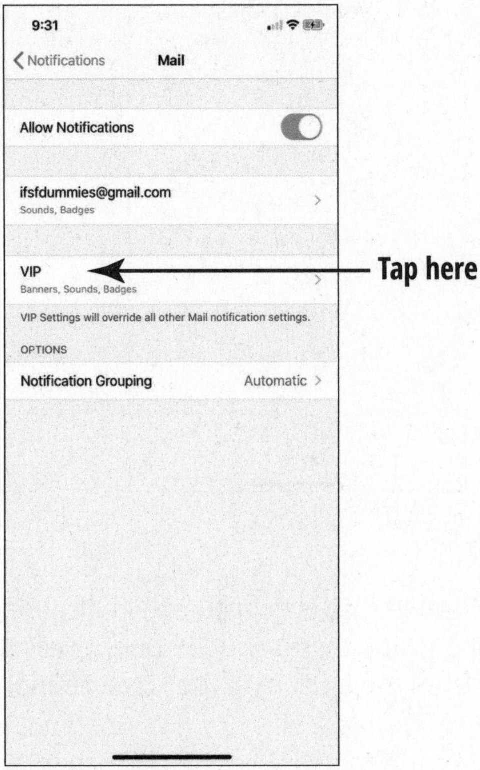

Tap here

FIGURE 13-23

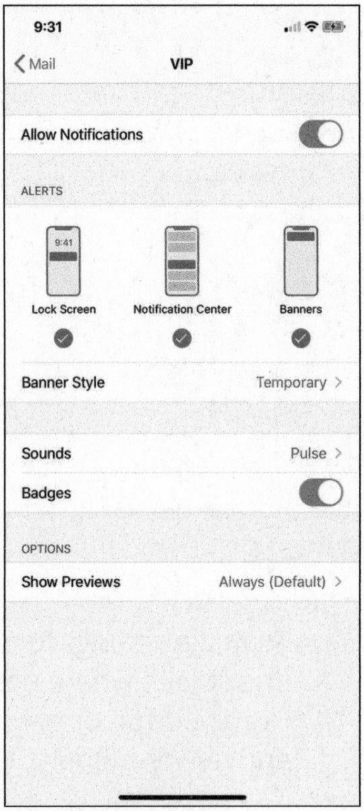

FIGURE 13-24

IN THIS CHAPTER

» Explore and get senior-recommended apps in the App Store

» Organize your apps on Home screens and in folders

» Delete apps you no longer need

» Update apps

» Purchase and download games

» Challenge friends in Game Center

Chapter **14**

Expanding Your iPhone Horizons with Apps

S ome apps (short for applications), such as News and Weather, come preinstalled on your iPhone with iOS 13. But you can choose from a world of other apps out there for your iPhone, some for free (such as Facebook) and some for a price (typically, ranging from 99 cents to about $10, though some can top out at much steeper prices).

Apps range from games to financial tools (such as loan calculators) to apps that help you when you're planning an exercise regimen or taking a trip. There are still more apps that are developed for use by private entities, such as hospitals and government agencies.

In this chapter, I suggest some apps that you might want to check out and explain how to use the App Store feature of your iPhone to find, purchase, and download apps, and detail how to organize your apps. You also find out a bit about having fun with games on your iPhone.

Explore Senior-Recommended Apps

As I write this book, new iPhone apps are in development, so even more apps that could fit your needs are available seemingly every day. Still, to get you exploring what's possible, I provide a quick list of apps that might whet your appetite.

Access the App Store by tapping the App Store icon on the Home screen. You can start by exploring either the Today tab (which features special apps and articles), by Categories, or by the Top Charts (see the buttons along the bottom of the screen). Or you can tap Search and find apps on your own. Tap an app to see more information about it.

Here are some interesting apps to explore:

» **Sudoku (free):** If you like this mental logic puzzle in print, try it out on your iPhone. It has three lessons and several levels ranging from easiest to nightmare, making it a great way to make time fly by in a doctor's or dentist's waiting room. There are also several sudoku apps to choose from, so find the one that's right for you.

» **Epicurious (free):** If you enjoy cooking and are always on the lookout for new recipes to try, Epicurious (shown in **Figure 14-1**) is THE app for you. Thousands of recipes are at your fingertips, and you won't need to thumb through a recipe book to find them.

» **Mint: Personal Finance & Money (free):** This highly rated financial app (almost a perfect 5 stars with over 400,000 reviews on the App Store!) helps you manage all your finances in one easy-to-use tool. View account balances, track spending and bills, create budgets, and more!

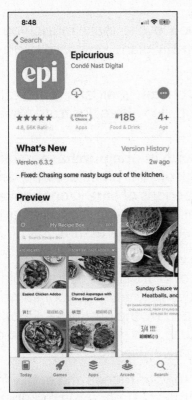

FIGURE 14-1

» **Goodreads (free):** If you're a reader, this is an app you won't want to be without. This app will keep you up-to-date on the latest releases, and you can browse reading lists and reviews from thousands of other users.

» **Procreate Pocket ($4.99):** If you're a serious artist, you will love Procreate Pocket. It's perhaps the most complete painting, sketching, and illustration app out there.

» **Pigment – Adult Coloring Book (free, with in-app purchases available):** Adult coloring books have exploded in popularity over the years, and they're a wonder at helping us unwind and unleash our creativity. This app is one of the best coloring book apps for iPhone.

» **Virtuoso Piano Free 4 (free):** If you love to make music, you'll love this app, which gives you a virtual piano keyboard to play and compose on the fly.

» **Travelzoo (free):** Get great deals on hotels, airfare, rental cars, entertainment, and more. This app also offers tips from travel experts.

» **Blood Pressure Monitor (free, with in-app purchases available):** This app helps you keep track of your blood pressure and maintain records over extended periods of time in one convenient place: your iPhone. Use the accompanying reports to give your doctor a good overview of your blood pressure.

» **GoodRx (free):** This app is a gem when it comes to finding the lowest prescription prices in town. It's saved users untold amounts of money as opposed to simply going to your same old pharmacy and hoping you're getting the best price. GoodRx will even find coupons for you to use, and you won't have to clip them out of a flyer or newspaper advertisement!

» **Skype (free):** Make Internet calls to your friends and family for free. While your iPhone comes with FaceTime, some members of your circle may not have iPhones, so in those instances Skype would be the best way to communicate.

» **Nike Training Club (free):** Use this handy utility to help design personalized workouts, see step-by-step instructions to help you learn new exercises, and watch video demonstrations. The reward system in this app may just keep you going toward your workout goals.

TIP

Note that you can work on documents using apps in the cloud. Use Keynote, Numbers, Pages, and more apps to get your work done from any device. See Chapter 4 for more about using iCloud Drive.

Search the App Store

1. Tap the App Store icon on the Home screen; by default, the first time you use App Store it will open to the Today tab, as seen in **Figure 14-2.**

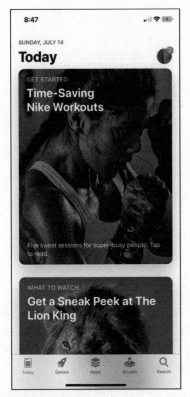

FIGURE 14-2

2. At this point, you have several options for finding apps:

   - Scroll downward to view featured apps and articles, such as The Daily List and Our Favorites.

     Tap a category to see more apps in it.

   - Tap the Apps tab at the bottom of the screen to browse by the type of app you're looking for or search by categories (tap the See All button in the Top Categories section), such as Lifestyle or Medical, as shown in **Figure 14-3.**

FIGURE 14-3

- Tap the Games tab at the bottom of the screen to see the newest releases and bestselling games. Explore by either Paid apps or free apps, by categories, and by special subjects, such as What We're Playing Today and New Games We Love.

- Tap the Search button at the bottom of the screen and then tap in the Search field, enter a search term, and tap the result you want to view.

Get Applications from the App Store

Buying or getting free apps requires that you have an iTunes account, which I covered in Chapter 4. After you have an account, you can use the saved payment information there to buy apps or download free apps with a few simple steps.

1. With the App Store open, tap the Apps tab and then tap the See All button in the Free Apps section, as shown in **Figure 14-4.**

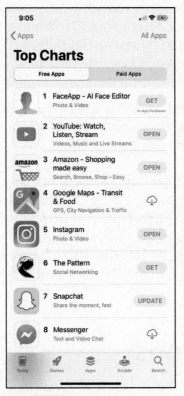

FIGURE 14-4

2. Tap the Get button for an app that appeals to you, or simply tap the app's icon if you want more information. If you already have the app and an update is available for it, the button will be labeled Update. If you've previously downloaded the app, but it's no longer on your iPhone, the icon looks like a cloud with a downward arrow; tap to download it again.

   To get a paid app, you tap the same button, which is then labeled with a price.

TIP

   If you've opened an iCloud account, you can set it up so that anything you purchase on your iPhone is automatically pushed to other Apple iOS devices and your iTunes library, and vice versa. See Chapter 4 for more about iCloud.

3. A sheet opens on the screen, listing the app and the iTunes account being used to get/purchase the app. To complete the download/purchase of the app, tap Enter Password at the bottom of the sheet, tap the Password field, and then enter the password. Alternatively, you may simply only need to use Touch ID or Face ID (iPhone X models only) to approve the download/purchase. The Get button changes to the Installing button, which looks like a circle; the thick blue line on the circle represents the progress of the installation.

4. The app downloads and can be found on one of the Home screens. If you purchase an app that isn't free, your credit card or gift card is charged at this point for the purchase price.

TIP

Out of the box, only preinstalled apps are located on the first iPhone Home screen, with a few (such as Files and Activity) located on the second Home screen. Apps that you download are placed on available Home screens, and you have to scroll to view and use them; this procedure is covered later in this chapter. See the next task for help in finding your newly downloaded apps using multiple Home screens.

Organize Your Applications on Home Screens

iPhone can display up to 11 to 15 Home screens, depending on your iPhone model. By default, the first Home screen contains preinstalled apps, and the second contains a few more preinstalled apps. Other screens are created to contain any apps you download or sync to your iPhone. At the bottom of any iPhone Home screen (just above the Dock), dots indicate the number of Home screens you've filled with apps; a solid dot specifies which Home screen you're on now, as shown in **Figure 14-5.**

1. Press the Home button or swipe up from the bottom of the screen (iPhone X models only) to open the last displayed Home screen.

2. Flick your finger from right to left to move to the next Home screen. To move back, flick from left to right.

Dots indicating the number of home screens

Screen you're on

FIGURE 14-5

3. To reorganize apps on a Home screen, press and hold any app on that page. The app icons begin to jiggle (see **Figure 14-6**), and many (not all) apps will sport a Delete button (a gray circle with a black X on it).

4. Press, hold, and drag an app icon to another location on the screen to move it.

TIP

To move an app from one page to another, while the apps are jiggling, you can press, hold, and drag an app to the left or right to move it to the next Home screen.

5. Press the Home button to stop all those icons from jiggling! iPhone X model users need to tap the Done button (upper-right corner of the screen) or simply swipe up from the bottom of the screen.

A delete button

FIGURE 14-6

TIP

You can use the multitasking feature for switching between apps easily. Press the Home button twice and you get a preview of open apps. iPhone X model users will swipe up from the bottom of the screen and keep your fingers on the screen until the App Switcher opens. Swipe right or left to scroll among the apps and tap the one you want to go to. You can also swipe an app upward from this preview list to close it.

Organize Apps in Folders

iPhone lets you organize apps in folders so that you can find them more easily. The process is simple:

1. Tap and hold an app until all apps start jiggling.

2. Drag one app on top of another app.

The two apps appear in a box with a placeholder name in a box above them (see **Figure 14-7**).

FIGURE 14-7

3. To change the name, tap in the field at the end of the placeholder name, and the keyboard appears.

4. Tap the Delete key to delete the placeholder name and type one of your own.

5. Tap Done and then tap anywhere outside the box to close it.

6. Press the Home button (or swipe up from the bottom of the screen for iPhone X models) to stop the icons from dancing around. You'll see your folder on the Home screen where you began this process.

Here's a neat trick that allows you to move multiple apps together at the same time. Follow these steps:

1. Tap and hold the first app you'd like to move. When the apps are jiggling, you're ready for the next step.

2. Move the app just a bit so that it's no longer in its original place.

3. With your free hand, tap the other app(s) you'd like to move along with the first app. As you tap additional apps, their icons "attach themselves" to the first app.

4. When you've selected all your apps, drag them to their new location. They'll all move together in a caravan!

Delete Apps You No Longer Need

When you no longer need an app you've installed, it's time to get rid of it. You can also remove most of the preinstalled apps that are native to iOS 13. If you use iCloud to push content across all Apple iOS devices, deleting an app on your iPhone won't affect that app on other devices.

1. Display the Home screen that contains the app you want to delete.

If you remove a native iOS 13 app, it's hidden, not deleted. If you need it later you can go to the App Store, find the name of the app there, and reinstall it (or technically, just unhide it).

2. Press and hold the app until all apps begin to jiggle.

3. Tap the Delete button for the app you want to delete (refer to **Figure 14-6**). A confirmation like the one shown in **Figure 14-8** appears.

4. Tap Delete to proceed with the deletion.

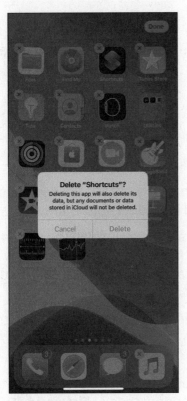

FIGURE 14-8

TIP

Don't worry about wiping out several apps at one time by deleting a folder. When you delete a folder, the apps that were contained within the folder are placed back on a Home screen where space is available, and you can still find the apps using the Search feature.

Offload Apps to Keep Data

When you delete an app from your iPhone, usually you're simultaneously deleting its data and documents. iOS 13 gives you the ability to delete an app without removing its data and documents. This feature is called Offloading. If you find later that you'd like to revisit the app, simply download it again from the App Store and its data and settings will be retained.

To offload apps, follow these steps:

TECHNICAL STUFF

1. Open Settings and go to General ⇨ iPhone Storage.

   You may need to wait a few seconds for content to load.

2. You can allow your iPhone to automatically offload unused apps as storage gets low, or you can offload individual apps manually:

   - To automatically offload unused apps, scroll down the screen to the Offload Unused Apps option (if you don't see it, tap Show All next to Recommendations) and tap the Enable button, shown in **Figure 14-9.**

     To disable the feature, go to Settings ⇨ iTunes & App Store, scroll to the bottom of the page, and then toggle the Offload Unused Apps switch to Off (white).

   - To offload an individual app, scroll down to find the app and tap it, and then tap the Offload App option, seen in **Figure 14-10;** tap Offload App again to confirm. The offloaded app's icon is grayed out on your iPhone's Home screen, indicating that the app is not loaded but its data still is.

3. You can restore an app by either tapping its grayed-out icon (when the app is ready to use the icon will no longer be grayed out) or by reinstalling it from the App Store.

TIP

Often, most of your iPhone's memory is taken by the data used in apps, not by the apps themselves. Offloading apps is a great idea if the app itself is of a significant size, but otherwise may not be very handy unless you're just super-strapped for space.

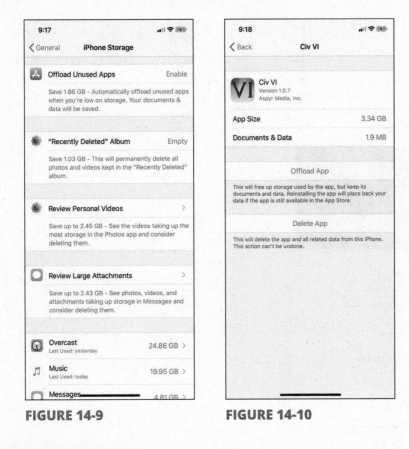

FIGURE 14-9

FIGURE 14-10

Update Apps

App developers update their apps all the time, so you might want to check for those updates. The App Store icon on the Home screen displays the number of available updates in a red circle. To update apps, follow these steps:

1. Tap the App Store icon on the Home screen.

2. Tap the Account button (an icon in the upper-right on the Apps screen, similar to the one seen in **Figure 14-11**); it will display a red badge with a number in it if updates are available.

Account button

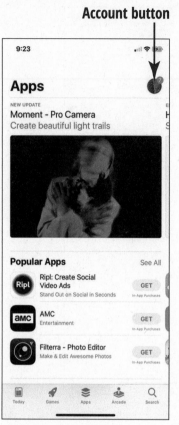

FIGURE 14-11

3. Scroll down to the Available Updates section and tap the Update button (see **Figure 14-12** for examples) for any item you want to update. Note that if you have Family Sharing turned on, there will be a folder titled Family Purchases that you can tap to display apps that are shared across your family's devices. To update all at once, tap the blue Update All button to the left.

TIP

You can download multiple apps at one time. If you choose more than one app to update instead of downloading apps sequentially, several items will download simultaneously.

4. You may be asked to confirm that you want to update, or to enter your Apple ID; after you do, tap OK to proceed. You may also be asked to confirm that you are over a certain age or agree to terms and conditions; if so, scroll down the terms dialog and, at the bottom, tap Agree. The download progress is displayed.

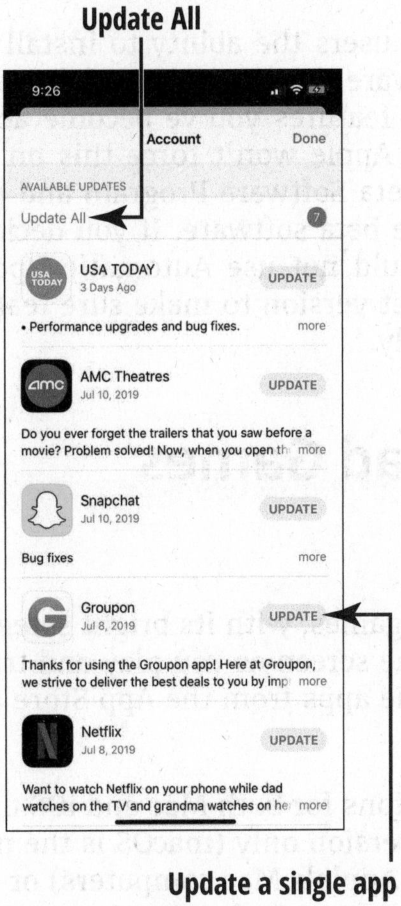

Update All

Update a single app

FIGURE 14-12

> If you have an iCloud account that you have activated on several devices and update an app on your iPhone, any other Apple iOS devices are also updated automatically and vice versa.

iOS 12 introduced a new feature that allows your iPhone to update iOS automatically as updates become available. If you'd like to enable this feature, go to Settings ⇨ General ⇨ Software Update ⇨ Automatic Updates. Toggle the Automatic Updates to On (green) or disable it by toggling it Off (white).

WARNING

Sometimes Apple offers iPhone users the ability to install beta software for iOS, which is software that's not been fully tested and could cause problems with features you've become accustomed to. Don't worry because Apple won't force this on you; you have to opt-in to Apple's Beta Software Program and jump through a series of hoops to use beta software. If you decide to use the beta software, you should not use Automatic Updates until you've researched the latest version to make sure features you rely on still function correctly.

Purchase and Download Games

Time to get your game on!

The iPhone is super for playing games, with its bright screen, portable size, and ability to rotate the screen as you play and track your motions. You can download game apps from the App Store and play them on your device.

TIP

Although a few games have versions for both Mac and iOS users, the majority are either macOS-version only (macOS is the name of the operating system used on Apple's Mac computers) or iOS-version only — something to be aware of when you buy games.

1. Open the App Store.

2. Tap the Games button at the bottom of the screen (see **Figure 14-13**).

3. Navigating the Games screen is simple:

   • Swipe from right to left to see featured apps in such categories as "What We're Playing Today" and "Editors' Choice."

   • Swipe down to find the Top Paid and Free games or to shop by categories. (Tap See All to view all of the available categories.)

FIGURE 14-13

4. Explore the list of games in the type you selected until you find something you like; tap the game to see its information screen.

5. To buy a game, tap the button labeled with either the word Get or the price (such as $2.99).

6. When the dialog opens appears at the bottom of the screen (as illustrated in **Figure 14-14**), tap Purchase (if it's a Paid game) or Install (if it's a Free game), type your password in the Password field on the next screen, and then tap Sign In to download the game. Alternatively, use Touch ID or Face ID (for iPhone X models) if it's enabled for iTunes and App Store purchases. The dialog box will display "Pay with Touch ID," or you'll be prompted to double-click the Side button to initiate Face ID authentication (iPhone X models only).

FIGURE 14-14

WARNING

I would warn against using Touch ID or Face ID for iTunes and App Store purchases. I know it's simpler than entering a password, but it can also make it easier for others to make purchases. In case you're wondering how that could be so, my children have actually tried holding my iPhone in front of my face while I was asleep in a clandestine attempt at purchasing the latest game craze with Face ID. Imagine your grandkids trying to do the same and I believe you'll see where I'm coming from.

7. **After** the game downloads, tap the Open button to go to the downloaded game or find the game's icon on your Home screen and tap to open it.

8. Have fun!

Challenge Friends in Game Center

If you and a friend or family member have both downloaded the same games, you can challenge your friend to beat your scores and even join you in a game — if the game supports Game Center interaction. You'll have to consult the developer's game information to find out if that's the case.

If it turns out that the game developer does support Game Center features in the game you'd like to play with a friend, you'll need to make sure your Apple ID information is registered for Game Center interaction. To do so, follow these steps:

1. Open the Settings app.

2. Scroll down a bit and tap Game Center.

3. Tap to toggle the Game Center switch to On (green) and then click Continue if prompted. You will be logged in using your Apple ID and password.

4. When signed in, toggle the Nearby Players switch to On (green) if it isn't already. This option enables you to find and invite nearby players who connect with you over Wi-Fi or Bluetooth, assuming the game you want to play supports this functionality.

GAMING WITH APPLE ARCADE

Apple Arcade is a new Apple service that allows unlimited gaming for a monthly fee of $4.99, after a free one-month trial. A subscription grants access to more than a hundred top-flight games (and that number is sure to grow) that you can play online or download for offline gaming. Up to six family members can use a single subscription, so Apple Arcade is a great way for families to interact and have fun. Games are able to be played on iPhone, iPad, Apple TV, and Macs. You can even continue a game across devices, jumping from one device to another! The games in Apple Arcade are state-of-the-art and are created by the top developers in the business. Enjoy, gamers!

IN THIS CHAPTER

» **Learn some social media dos and don'ts**

» **Find and install social media apps**

» **Create a Facebook account**

» **Customize Facebook settings**

» **Create a Twitter account**

» **Create an Instagram account**

Chapter **15**

Socializing with Facebook, Twitter, and Instagram

Social media apps keep us in close digital contact with friends, family, and the rest of the world, and have become as important a digital staple as email, if not more so for some folks. Facebook, Twitter, and Instagram are some of the most popular social media apps, and therefore I focus on obtaining and setting up these apps for use with your iPhone in this chapter.

Facebook is a platform for sharing posts about your life, with or without photos and video, and allows you to be as detailed as you please in your posts. Twitter, on the other hand, is meant to share information in quick bursts, allowing users only 280 characters in which to alert you to their latest comings and goings. Instagram is basically a photo sharing app, allowing you to add captions to personalize your pictures.

A Few Social Media Dos and Don'ts

Social media, like most things, has its up side and its down side. While you can connect with old friends, swap stories with others, and share vacation pics of the family, you're also in danger of being preyed upon by cyber thugs and other ne'er-do-wells prowling the Internet. This short list (it's by no means exhaustive) of dos and don'ts will help keep you safe on social media:

» Do connect with family and friends, but keep your social media circle close.

» Do use strong and unique passwords for your accounts.

» Do set up privacy controls for each social media account you use. You may want some people to see everything you post, but you may also want to keep some things (such as birthdays and other personal information) closer to the vest.

» Don't ever share your social security number or banking information!

» Don't type in ALL CAPS. It's considered the Internet equivalent of yelling.

» Don't accept a friend request from someone you are already friends with on a social media platform. If you're already friends with them on the platform, it's a good indication something fishy's going on.

» Don't believe everything you read! If something sounds too crazy to be true, it probably is. It's always best to research the topic before commenting on it in social media environs.

» Don't advertise that you're on vacation. Wait until you return to post pictures of your dream trip. If people with ill intent know that you're away, it's possible they'll take advantage of the opportunity to pay your home an unannounced visit.

Find and Install Social Media Apps

To begin using social media apps, you first need to find and install them on your iPhone. I focus on Facebook, Twitter, and Instagram in this chapter because they're currently three of the most popular social media apps, and frankly, I don't have the space here to discuss more. To find and install the apps using the App Store, follow these steps:

1. Open the App Store.

2. Tap the Search tab at the bottom of the screen.

3. Tap the Search field and enter Facebook, Twitter, Instagram, or any other social media app you might be interested in.

4. To download and install the app, tap the button labeled Get or the price (such as $2.99).

5. When the dialog appears at the bottom of the screen, tap Purchase (if it's a Paid app) or Install (if it's Free), type your password in the Password field on the next screen, and then tap Sign In to download the app. Alternatively, use Touch ID if you have it enabled for iTunes and App Store purchases; the dialog will display "Pay with Touch ID" if you do. iPhone X and newer model users will use Face ID instead of Touch ID. When you're prompted to pay (with Face ID enabled), double-click the Side button and glance at your iPhone to initiate payment.

The app will download and install on one of your Home screens.

Create a Facebook Account

You can create a Facebook account from within the app.

TIP

If you already have a Facebook account, you can simply use that account information to log in.

To create an account in the Facebook app, follow these steps:

1. Launch the newly downloaded Facebook app.

2. Tap the Create New Account option near the bottom of the screen, as seen in **Figure 15-1** (you almost need binoculars to see it).

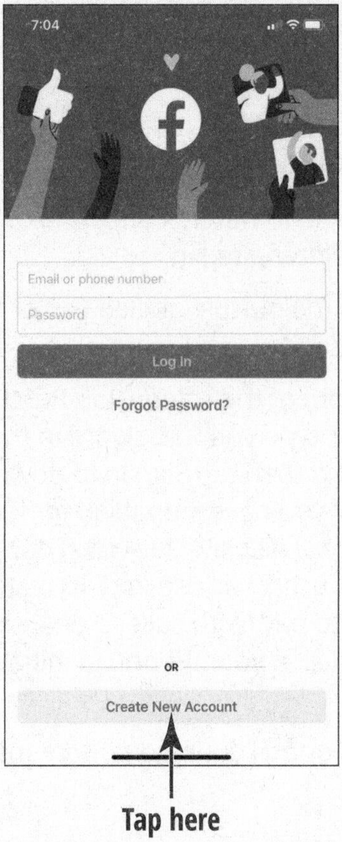

Tap here

FIGURE 15-1

3. Tap Get Started and walk through the steps to complete the registration of your account.

4. When finished, you'll be logged into your account in the Facebook app.

You may also create a Facebook account by visiting its website at www.facebook.com.

TIP

Customize Facebook Settings for Your iPhone

Facebook has a few settings that you'll want to configure when entering your account information into the Settings app.

1. Open the Settings app.

2. Tap Facebook.

3. Toggle the switches, seen in **Figure 15-2**, On (green) or Off for the following options:

- **Background App Refresh:** This option allows Facebook to refresh its content in the background, or put another way, when you aren't actually using it.

- **Cellular Data:** Turning this On allows Facebook to refresh itself and allows you to post updates when you aren't connected to a Wi-Fi network.

- **Upload HD:** If you record HD video on your iPhone, this setting allows you to upload that high-quality video to Facebook. Keep in mind that HD video files are very large files and will therefore consume vast quantities of your cellular data allotment, as well as take much longer to upload.

4. Tap the remaining items in the Allow Facebook to Access section (Bluetooth Sharing, Siri & Search, and Notifications) to customize how Facebook can interact with these iOS 13 features. For example, tap Siri & Search and allow or deny Facebook to use Ask Siri.

If you're a frequent Facebook user and you tend to upload quite a bit of photos and videos, consider toggling the Cellular Data switch to Off. If you have an account with a cellular provider that provides a limited amount of data, you could be in danger of exceeding your data allotment if you're a heavy Facebook user.

WARNING

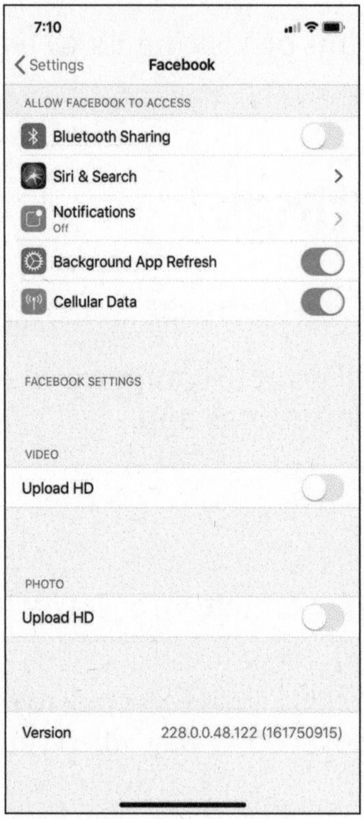

FIGURE 15-2

Create a Twitter Account

To create an account in the Twitter app, follow these steps:

1. Open the Twitter app by tapping its icon.

2. Tap the blue Create account button in the middle of the screen, as illustrated in **Figure 15-3**.

   If you already have a Twitter account, tap the tiny Log In button at the very bottom of the screen to log in.

3. The app will ask you some questions to help you create your account.

4. When you're done, the app will log you into your new account.

TIP

Tap here

FIGURE 15-3

TIP

Just like Facebook, you can create an account on the Twitter website at www.twitter.com. You can also configure options for Twitter in the Settings app, as I showed you for Facebook earlier in this chapter.

Create an Instagram Account

To create an account in the Instagram app:

1. Open the Instagram app by tapping its icon.

2. Tap the blue Create New Account button in the middle of the screen, as shown in **Figure 15-4.**

Tap here

FIGURE 15-4

TIP

If you already have an Instagram account, tap the really small Log In button to access it.

3. The app will ask you several questions to help you create your account.

4. When completed, the app will log you into your new account.

TIP

You can also create an account on the Instagram website at www.instagram.com. You may also configure options for Instagram in the Settings app as I showed you for Facebook earlier in this chapter (although the options are a bit more limited than those for Facebook).

4
Enjoying Media

IN THIS CHAPTER

» **Explore the iTunes Store**

» **Buy selections**

» **Rent movies**

» **Use Apple Pay and Wallet**

» **Set up Family Sharing**

Chapter **16**

Shopping the iTunes Store

The iTunes Store app that's built in to iOS 13 lets you easily shop for music, movies, and TV shows. As Chapter 17 explains, you can also get electronic and audio books via the Apple Books app.

In this chapter, you learn how to find content in the iTunes Store. You can download the content directly to your iPhone or to another device, and then sync it to your iPhone. With the Family Sharing feature, which I cover in this chapter, as many as six people in a family can share purchases using the same credit card. Finally, I cover a few options for buying content from other online stores and using Apple Pay to make real-world purchases using a stored payment method.

TIP

I cover opening an iTunes account and downloading iTunes software to your computer in Chapter 4. If you need to, read Chapter 4 to see how to handle these two tasks before digging into this chapter.

Explore the iTunes Store

Visiting the iTunes Store from your iPhone is easy with the iTunes Store app.

TIP

If you're in search of other kinds of content, the Podcasts app (discussed in detail in Chapter 18) and iTunes U app allow you to find and then download podcasts and online courses to your phone.

To check out the iTunes Store, follow these steps:

1. If you aren't already signed in to iTunes, tap Settings and go to iTunes & App Stores. Tap Sign In and enter your Apple ID and Password in their respective fields, as shown in **Figure 16-1,** and then tap Sign In.

FIGURE 16-1

2. Go to your Home screen and tap the iTunes Store icon.

3. Tap the Music button (if it isn't already selected) in the row of buttons at the bottom of the screen. Swipe up and down the screen and you'll find several categories of selections, such as New Music, Best of the Week, and Recent Releases (these category names change from time to time).

290   PART 4 **Enjoying Media**

4. Flick your finger up to scroll through the featured selections or tap the See All button to see more selections in any category, as shown in **Figure 16-2.**

FIGURE 16-2

TIP

The navigation techniques in these steps work essentially the same in any of the content categories (the buttons at the bottom of the screen), which include Music, Movies, and TV Shows.

5. Tap the Charts tab at the top of the screen. This displays lists of bestselling songs, albums, and music videos in the iTunes Store.

6. Tap any listed item to see more detail about it, as shown in **Figure 16-3,** and hear a brief preview when you tap the number to the left of a song.

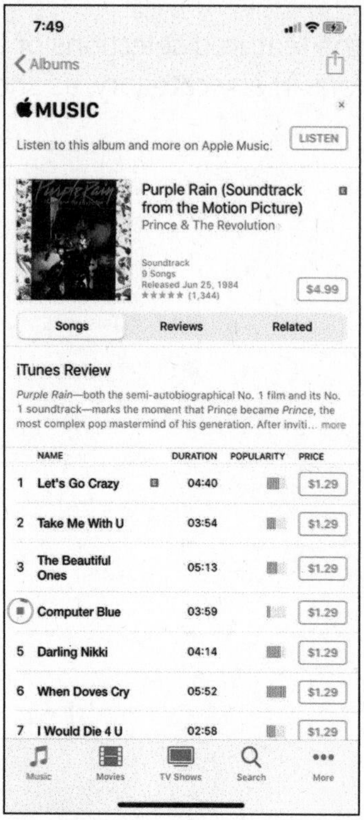

FIGURE 16-3

TIP

If you want to use the Genius playlist feature, which recommends additional purchases based on the contents of your library in the iTunes app on your iPhone, tap the More button at the bottom of the screen, and then tap Genius. If you've made enough purchases in iTunes, song and album recommendations appear based on those purchases as well as the content in your iTunes Match library (a fee-based service discussed in Chapter 18), if you have one.

Buy a Selection

1. When you find an item that you want to buy, tap the button that shows either the price (if it's a selection available for purchase; see **Figure 16-4**) or the button labeled Get (if it's a selection available for free).

Price button

The Essential Yo-Yo Ma screenshot showing:

8:18

‹ Search

The Essential Yo-Yo Ma
Yo-Yo Ma

Classical
35 Songs
Released Apr 6, 2004
★★★★★ (113) $16.99

| Songs | Reviews | Related |

iTunes Review

Yo-Yo Ma enjoyed so much well-deserved success early on that by
his mid-30s he was able to start exploring in earnest music outside
the European Classical canon. His Essential collection is hel... more

	NAME	DURATION	POPULARITY	PRICE
1	Cello Suite No... Yo-Yo Ma	02:19		$1.29
2	The Four Seas... Ton Koopman, Yo...	01:46		$1.29
3	Cantata, BWV... Yo-Yo Ma, Ton K...	02:42		$1.29
4	Cantata, BWV... Ton Koopman, Yo...	03:37		$1.29
5	Cantata, BWV... Ton Koopman, Yo...	03:48		$1.29
6	Carnival of the... Yo-Yo Ma, Philip...	03:08		$1.29
7	Havanaise, O... Yo-Yo Ma & Kath...	08:50		$1.29
8	Thaïs: Méditat... Yo-Yo Ma & Kath...	05:48		$1.29
9	Liebesfreud Yo-Yo Ma & Patri...	03:11		$1.29

Music   Movies   TV Shows   Search   More

FIGURE 16-4

TIP

If you want to buy music, you can open the description page for an
album and tap the album price, or buy individual songs rather than
the entire album. Tap the price for a song and then proceed to purchase it.

2. When the dialog appears at the bottom of the screen, tap Purchase,
type your password in the Password field on the next screen, and
then tap Sign In to buy the item. Alternatively, use Touch ID if you
have it enabled for iTunes and App Store purchases; the dialog will
display "Pay with Touch ID" if you do. Also, iPhone X and newer users
can use Face ID; when asked to pay, double-click the Side button and
look at your iPhone to authenticate.

3. The item begins downloading, and the cost, if any, is automatically charged against your account. When the download finishes, tap OK in the Purchase Complete message and you can then view the content using the Music or TV app, depending on the type of content it is.

TIP

You can allow content to be downloaded over your cellular network if you aren't near a Wi-Fi hotspot. If you aren't near a Wi-Fi hotspot, downloading over your cellular network might be your only option. Tap Settings, tap iTunes & App Store, scroll down, and set the Use Cellular Data setting switch to On (green).

WARNING

Music files are large, usually several megabytes per track. You could incur hefty data charges with your cellular provider if you run over your allotted data.

Rent Movies

In the case of movies, you can either rent or buy content. If you rent, which is less expensive but only a one-time deal, you have 30 days from the time you rent the item to begin watching it. After you have begun to watch it, you have 24 hours from that time left to watch it on the same device, as many times as you like.

TIP

Some movies are offered in high-definition versions. These HD movies look pretty good on that crisp, colorful iPhone screen. If your selection is available in SD it won't have quite as high quality (still very good, mind you), but it will take up less bandwidth to download or stream it to your phone. SD is also a bit cheaper than an HD movie to rent or purchase. Scroll all the way to the bottom of the movie you want to rent to see if a different quality version is available. If you see "Also Available in SD" or "Also Available in Higher Quality," tap to view pricing for the option you prefer.

1. With the iTunes Store open, tap the Movies button.

2. Locate the movie you want to rent and tap it, as shown in **Figure 16-5.**

FIGURE 16-5

3. In the detailed description of the movie that appears, tap the Rent button (if it's available for rental); see **Figure 16-6.**

4. When the dialog appears at the bottom of the screen, tap Rent, type your password in the Password field on the next screen, and then tap Sign In to rent the item. Alternatively, use Touch ID if you have it enabled for iTunes and App Store purchases; the dialog will display "Pay with Touch ID" if you do. iPhone X and newer users can use Face ID; when asked to pay, double-click the side button and look at your iPhone to authenticate. The movie begins to download to your iPhone immediately, and your account is charged the rental fee.

5. After the download is complete, you can use the TV app to watch it. (See Chapter 20 to read about how this app works.)

You can also download content to your computer and sync it to your iPhone. Refer to Chapter 4 for more about this process.

Rent button

FIGURE 16-6

Use Apple Pay and Wallet

Apple is the creator of a relatively new, and increasingly popular, method of paying for items by using your iPhone (or other Apple devices). It's called Apple Pay. Fancied as a mobile wallet, this service uses the Touch ID feature in your iPhone's Home button (or Face ID if you own an iPhone X or newer model) to identify you and any credit cards you've stored at the iTunes Store to make payments via a feature called Wallet.

Your credit card information isn't stored on your phone, and Apple doesn't know a thing about your purchases. In addition, Apple considers Apple Pay safer because the store cashier doesn't even have to know your name.

There are millions of merchant locations that are set up to use Apple Pay. Originally supported by Amex, Visa, MasterCard, and six of the largest banks in the United States, you'll find that even more credit cards (such as Discover) and store cards (such as Kohls or JCPenney) work with Apple Pay.

To set up Apple Pay, go to Settings and tap Wallet & Apple Pay. Add information about a credit card and then double-tap the Home button (Side button for iPhone X and newer models) when the lock screen is displayed to initiate a purchase. You can also make settings from within the Wallet app itself.

For more information on Apple Pay, check out `www.apple.com/apple-pay`.

Set Up Family Sharing

Family Sharing is a feature that allows as many as six people in your family to share whatever anybody in the group has purchased from the iTunes, Book, and App Stores even though you don't share Apple IDs. Your family must all use the same credit card to purchase items (tied to whichever Apple ID is managing the family), but you can approve purchases by children under 13 years of age (this age can vary depending on your country or region). You can also share calendars, photos, and a family calendar (see Chapter 22 for information about Family Sharing and Calendar and Chapter 19 for information on sharing photos in a family album). Start by turning on Family Sharing.

1. Tap Settings and then tap the Apple ID at the top of the screen.
2. Tap Set Up Family Sharing.
3. Tap Get Started. On the next screen, you can add a photo for your family. Tap Continue.
4. On the Share Purchases screen, tap Share Purchases from a different account to use another Apple account.

5. Tap Continue and check the payment method that you want to use. Tap Continue.

6. On the next screen, tap Add Family Member. Enter the person's name (assuming that this person is listed in your contacts) or email address. An invitation is sent to the person's email. When the invitation is accepted, the person is added to your family.

TECHNICAL STUFF

The payment method for this family is displayed under Shared Payment Method in this screen. All those involved in a family have to use a single payment method for family purchases.

There's also a link called Create a Child Account. When you click this link and enter information to create the ID, the child's account is automatically added to your Family and retains the child status until he or she turns 13. If a child accesses iTunes to buy something, he or she gets a prompt to ask permission. You get an Ask to Buy notification on your phone as well as via email. You can then accept or decline the purchase, giving you control over family spending in the iTunes Store.

Chapter **17**

Reading Books

A traditional e-reader is a device that's used primarily to read the electronic version of books, magazines, and newspapers. Apple's free app that turns your iPhone into an e-reader is Apple Books (formerly known as iBooks). This app also enables you to buy and download books (and audiobooks) from the Apple Book Store (offering millions of books and growing by the day).

In this chapter, you discover the options available for reading material and how to buy books. You also learn how to navigate a book or periodical and adjust the brightness and type.

Find Books with Apple Books

1. To shop using Apple Books, tap the Apple Books application icon to open it. (It's on your first Home screen and looks like a white book against an orange background; it's also simply labeled Books.)

2. Tap the Book Store tab at the bottom of the screen.

3. In the Book Store, shown in **Figure 17-1,** featured titles and suggestions (based on your past reading habits and searches) are shown. You can do any of the following to find a book:

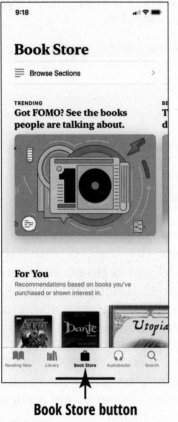

Book Store button

FIGURE 17-1

- Tap the Search button in the bottom-right of the screen, tap in the Search field that appears, and then type a search word or phrase, using the onscreen keyboard.

- Swipe left or right to see and read articles and suggestions for the latest books in various categories, such as Books We Love (suggestions from Apple, as shown in **Figure 17-2**), Trending (currently popular titles), and the like.

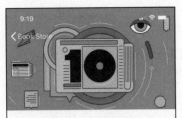

FIGURE 17-2

- Scroll down on the Book Store's main page to see links to popular categories of books, as shown in **Figure 17-3.** Tap a category to view those selections.

- Scroll down to Top Charts to view both Paid and Free books listed on top bestseller lists. Tap the See All button under Top Charts to focus on books that are the latest hits.

- Swipe further down the screen to find a list of Genres. Tap All Genres to see everything the Book Store has to offer.

- Back on the main screen of the Book Store, tap the Browse Sections button under "Book Store" (at the top of the Book Store screen, if you've scrolled down) to open the Browse Sections menu, shown in **Figure 17-4**. From here you can easily scroll up and down the screen to browse book store sections and genres.

- Tap a suggested selection or featured book to read more information about it.

FIGURE 17-3

FIGURE 17-4

Many books let you download free samples before you buy. You get to read several pages of the book to see whether it appeals to you, and it doesn't cost you a dime! Look for the Sample button when you view book details. (The button usually is below the price of the book.)

Buy Books

If you've set up an account with iTunes, you can buy books at the Apple Books Store using the Apple Books app. (See Chapter 4 for more about iTunes.)

1. Open Apple Books, tap Book Store, and begin looking for a book.

2. When you find a book in the Book Store, you can buy it by tapping it and then tapping the Buy | Price button or the Get button (if it's free), as shown in **Figure 17-5.**

FIGURE 17-5

You may also tap the Want to Read button if you'd like to keep this book in mind for a future purchase, or tap Sample to download a few pages to read before you commit your hard-earned dollars to it.

3. When the dialog appears at the bottom of the screen, tap Purchase, type your password in the Password field on the next screen, and then tap Sign In to buy the book. Alternatively, use Touch ID (or Face ID for iPhone X and newer models) if you have it enabled for iTunes and App Store purchases; the dialog will display "Pay with Touch ID" or iPhone X and newer model users will see a prompt on the right side of their screen to double-click the Side button and glance at their iPhone to authenticate with Face ID.

4. The book begins downloading, and the cost, if any, is automatically charged to your account. When the download finishes, tap OK in the Purchase Complete message, and you can find your new purchase by tapping the Library button at the bottom of the screen.

Books that you've downloaded to your computer can be accessed from any Apple device through iCloud. Content can also be synced with your iPhone by using the Lightning to USB Cable and your iTunes account, or by using the wireless iTunes Wi-Fi Sync setting on the General Settings menu. See Chapter 4 for more about syncing.

Navigate a Book

Getting around in Apple Books is half the fun!

1. Open Apple Books and, if your Library (which looks a tiny bit like a bookshelf) isn't already displayed, tap the Library button at the bottom of the screen.

2. Tap a book to open it. The book opens to its title page or the last spot you read on any compatible device.

3. Take any of these actions to navigate the book:

   • To go to the book's Table of Contents: Tap the Table of Contents button at the top of the page (refer to **Figure 17-6**) and then tap the name of a chapter to go to it (see **Figure 17-6**).

   If you don't see the Table of Contents button, simply tap the screen once to display the navigation controls.

   • To turn to the next page: Place your finger anywhere along the right edge of the page and tap or flick to the left.

   • To turn to the preceding page: Place your finger anywhere on the left edge of a page and tap or flick to the right.

   • To move to another page in the book: Tap and drag the slider at the bottom of the page (see **Figure 17-6**) to the right or left.

Table of Contents button

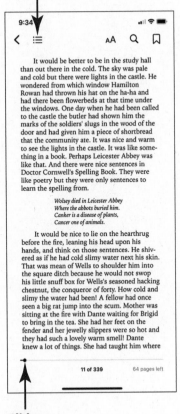

Slider

FIGURE 17-6

TIP

To return to the Library to view another book at any time, tap the Back button, which looks like a left-pointing arrow and is found in the upper-left corner of the screen. If the button isn't visible, tap anywhere on the page, and the button and other tools appear.

Adjust Brightness in Apple Books

Apple Books offers an adjustable brightness setting that you can use to make your book pages more comfortable to read.

1. With a book open, tap the Display Settings button (looks like aA), shown in **Figure 17-7**.

Display Settings button

Brightness slider

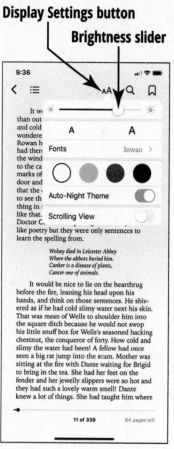

FIGURE 17-7

2. On the Brightness setting that appears at the top, tap and drag the slider to the right to make the screen brighter, or to the left to dim it.

3. Tap anywhere on the page to close the Display Settings dialog.

Bright-white screens are commonly thought to be hard on the eyes, so setting the brightness halfway relative to its default setting or less is probably a good idea (and saves on battery life).

Change the Font Size and Type

If the type on your screen is a bit small for you to make out, you can change to a larger font size or choose a different font for readability.

1. With a book open, tap the Display Settings button.

2. In the dialog box that appears (shown in **Figure 17-8**), tap the button with a smaller A, on the left, to use smaller text, or the button with the larger A, on the right, to use larger text.

Tap for larger text

Tap for smaller text

FIGURE 17-8

3. Tap the Fonts button. The list of fonts shown in **Figure 17-9** appears.

4. Tap a font name to select it. The font changes on the book page.

5. If you want a sepia tint on the pages, which can be easier on the eye, tap the Back button in the upper-left of the Fonts list to go back to the Display Settings dialog, and then tap one of the screen color options (the colored circles) to activate it.

6. Tap outside the Display Settings dialog to return to your book.

> Some fonts appear a bit larger on your screen than others because of their design. If you want the largest font, use Iowan.

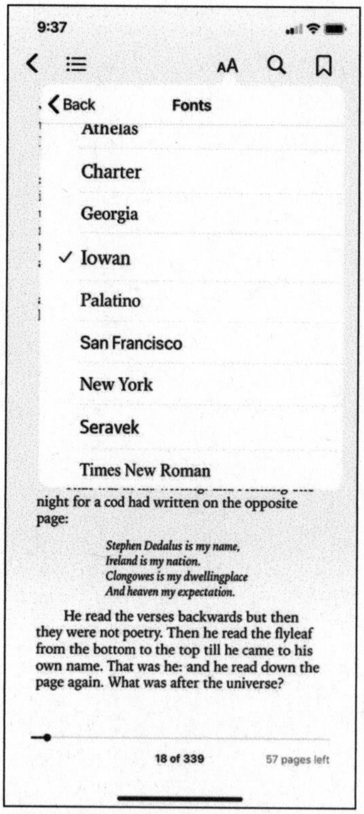

TIP

FIGURE 17-9

Chapter **18**

Enjoying Music and Podcasts

iOS 13 includes an app called Music that allows you to take advantage of your iPhone's amazing little sound system to play your favorite music or other audio files.

In this chapter, you get acquainted with the Music app and its features that allow you to sort and find music and control playback. You also get an overview of AirPlay for accessing and playing your music over a home network or over any connected device (this also works with videos and photos). Finally, I introduce you to Podcasts for your listening pleasure.

View the Library Contents

The Library in Music contains the music or other audio files that you've placed on your iPhone, either by purchasing them through the iTunes Store or copying them from your computer. Let's see how to work with those files on your iPhone.

1. Tap the Music app, located in the Dock on the Home screen. The Music library appears, as shown **Figure 18-1**.

2. Swipe down the screen to scroll through the Recently Added section of the Music app's Library.

3. Tap a category (see **Figure 18-2**) to view music by Playlists, Artists, Albums, Songs, or Downloaded Music. Tap Library in the upper-left corner to return to the main Library screen.

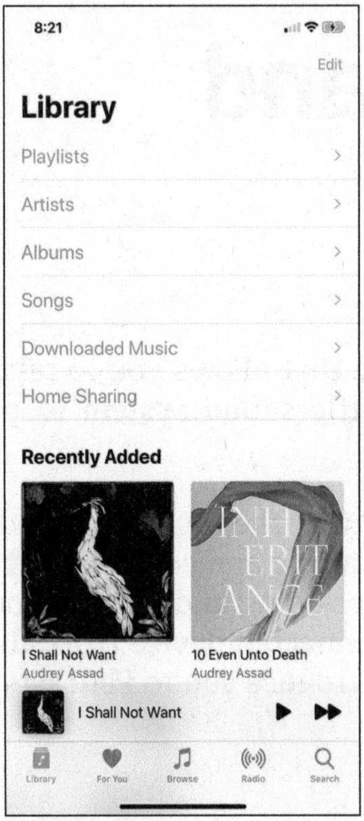

FIGURE 18-1

FIGURE 18-2

TIP

iTunes has several free items that you can download and use to play around with the features in Music. You can also sync content (such as iTunes Smart Playlists stored on your computer or other Apple devices) to your iPhone, and play it using the Music app. (See Chapter 4 for more about syncing and Chapter 16 for more about getting content from iTunes.)

4. Tap Edit in the upper-right corner to edit the list of categories, as seen in **Figure 18-3**. Tap the check box to the left of categories that you'd like to sort your Music Library by; uncheck those you don't want to use.

5. Tap Done when you're finished.

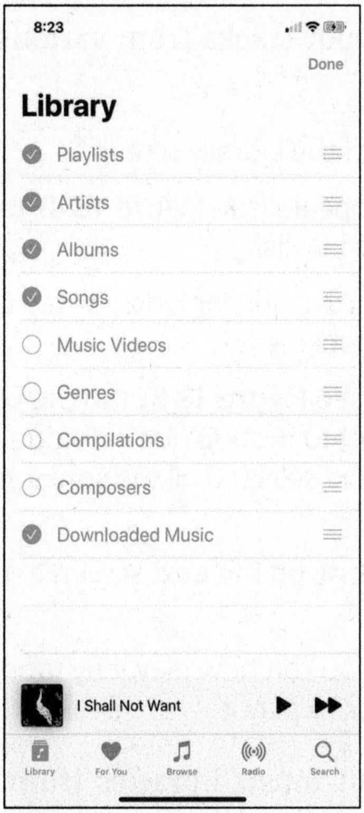

FIGURE 18-3

Apple offers a service called iTunes Match (visit `https://support.apple.com/en-us/HT204146` for more information). You pay $24.99 per year for the capability to match the music you've bought from other providers (and stored in the iTunes Library on your computer)

TIP

to what's in the iTunes Library. If there's a match (and there usually is), that content is added to your iTunes Library on iCloud. Then, using iCloud, you can sync the content among all your Apple devices. Is this service worth $24.99 a year? That's entirely up to you, my friend. However, for a few bucks more, you can have the benefits of iTunes Match plus access to millions of songs across all your Apple devices using another Apple service: Apple Music. There's more about Apple Music later in this chapter.

Create Playlists

You can create your own playlists to put tracks from various sources into collections of your choosing.

1. Tap the Playlists category at the top of the Library screen.

2. Tap New Playlist. In the dialog that appears (see **Figure 18-4**), tap Playlist Name and enter a title for the playlist.

3. Tap Add Music; search for music by artist, title, or lyrics; or tap Library and browse to find the tracks you're looking for.

4. In the list of selections that appears (see **Figure 18-5**), tap the plus sign to the right of each item you want to include (for individual songs or entire albums). Continue until you've selected all the songs you want to add to the playlist.

5. Tap the Done button and then tap Done on the next screen to return to the Playlists screen.

6. Your playlist appears in the list, and you can now play it by tapping the list name and then tapping a track to play it.

TIP

To search for and play a song in your music libraries from your Home screen (without even opening the Music app), use the Search feature. From your Home screen, you can swipe down from the screen outside the Dock and enter the name of the song in the Search field. A list of search results appears. Just tap the Play button and rock on!

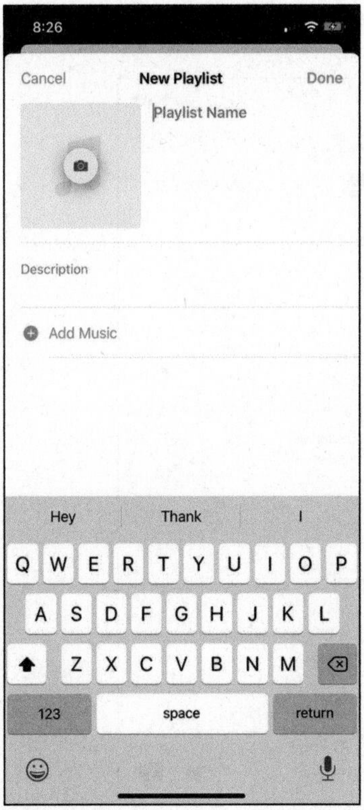

Tap to add an album to your playlist

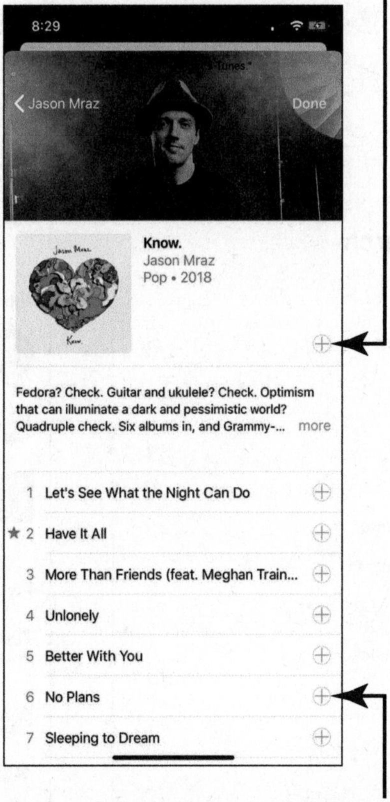

FIGURE 18-4

FIGURE 18-5

Tap to add a song to your playlist

Search for Music

You can search for an item in your Music library by using the Search feature.

1. With Music open, tap the Search button at the bottom of the screen (see **Figure 18-6**). The Search screen appears showing Recent Searches and Trending Searches, along with a Search field at the top of the screen. Tap either the Your Library tab to search for songs stored on your iPhone, or tap Apple Music to search the Apple Music library. You may search for items in Apple Music, but you must be subscribed to the service to play selections from it.

2. Enter a search term in the Search field. Results are displayed, narrowing as you type, as shown in **Figure 18-7.**

3. Tap an item to play it.

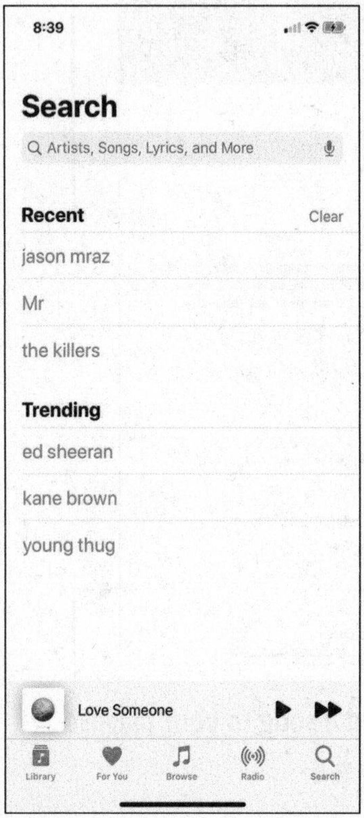

FIGURE 18-6

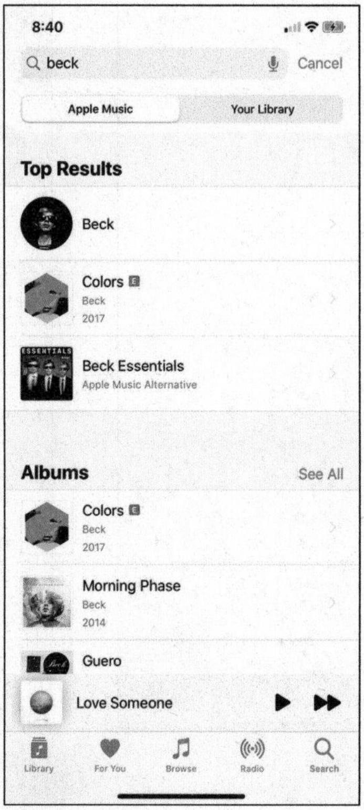

FIGURE 18-7

You can enter an artist's name, a lyricist's or a composer's name, a word from the item's title, or even lyrics in the Search field to find what you're looking for.

Play Music

Now that you know how to find your music, let's have some real fun by playing it!

You can use Siri to play music hands free. Just press and hold the Home button (or the Side button for iPhone X and newer models), and when Siri appears, say something like "play 'L.A. Woman'" or "play 'Fields of Gold.'"

To play music on your iPhone, follow these steps:

1. Locate the music that you want by using the methods described in previous tasks in this chapter.

2. Tap the item you want to play. If you're displaying the Songs category, you don't have to tap an album to open a song; you need only tap a song to play it. If you're using any other categories, you have to tap items such as albums (or multiple songs from one artist) to find the song you want to hear.

Home Sharing is a feature of iTunes that you can use to share music among up to five devices that have Home Sharing turned on. After Home Sharing is set up via iTunes, any of your devices can stream music and videos to other devices, and you can even click and drag content between devices using iTunes. For more about Home Sharing, visit this site: https://support.apple.com/en-us/ HT202190.

3. Tap the item you want to play from the list that appears; it begins to play (see **Figure 18-8**).

4. Tap the currently playing song title near the bottom of the screen to open it displaying playback controls. Use the Previous and Next buttons at the bottom of the screen shown in **Figure 18-9** to navigate the audio file that's playing:

   • The Previous button takes you back to the beginning of the item that's playing if you tap it, or rewinds the song if you press-and-hold it.

   • The Next button takes you to the next item if you tap it, or fast-forwards the song if you press-and-hold it.

Use the Volume slider on the bottom of the screen (or the Volume buttons on the side of your iPhone) to increase or decrease the volume.

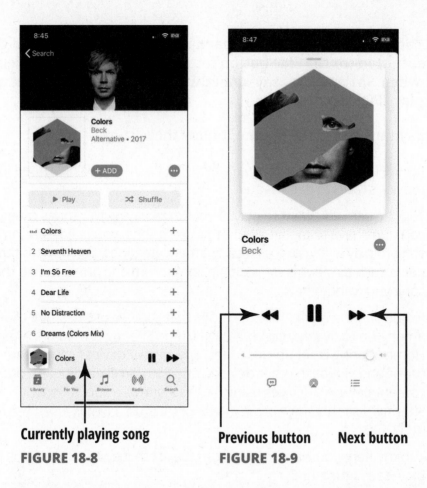

Currently playing song

FIGURE 18-8

Previous button   **Next button**

FIGURE 18-9

5. Tap the Pause button to pause playback. Tap the button again to resume playing.

You can also use music controls for music that's playing from the lock screen.

6. Tap and drag the red line (it appears gray until you touch it) near the middle of the screen (underneath the album art) that indicates the current playback location. Drag the line to the left or right to "scrub" to another location in the song.

7. Do you like to sing along but sometimes flub the words? Tap the Lyrics button in the lower-left (looks like a speech box with a quotation mark in it), and if the song is from the Apple Music library, the lyrics will scroll up the screen in sync with the song, as shown in **Figure 18-10.** You can swipe through the lyrics, or if you tap a lyric Music will jump to that point in the song.

FIGURE 18-10

8. If you don't like what's playing, here's how to make another selection: Drag down from the top of the playback controls screen to view other selections in the album that's playing.

TIP

Family Sharing allows up to six members of your family to share purchased content even if they don't share the same iTunes account. You can set up Family Sharing under iCloud in Settings. See Chapter 16 for more about Family Sharing.

Shuffle Music

If you want to play a random selection of the music in an album on your iPhone, you can use the Shuffle feature.

1. Tap the name of the currently playing song at the bottom of the screen.

2. Tap the Menu button in the lower-right (it looks like three dots and three lines stacked).

3. Tap the Shuffle button, located to the right of Up Next, which looks like two lines crossing to form an X (see **Figure 18-11**). Your content plays in random order.

4. Tap the Repeat button (refer to **Figure 18-11**) to play the songs over again continuously.

Repeat button
Shuffle button

FIGURE 18-11

Listen with Your Earbuds

If you're playing music and have set the Volume slider as high as it goes and you're still having trouble hearing, consider using the earbuds that came with your iPhone. These cut out extraneous noises and improve the sound quality of what you're listening to.

For iPhone models older than the iPhone 7 and 7 Plus, use 3.5 mm stereo earbuds; insert them in the headphone jack at the bottom of your iPhone. If you have an iPhone 7, 7 Plus, or a newer model, you'll need earbuds that use a Lightning connector, or you can use a Lightning-to-3.5mm adaptor with standard 3.5mm headphones.

You might also look into purchasing Bluetooth earbuds, which allow you to listen wirelessly. For a top-of-the-line wireless experience, try out Apple's AirPods (go to www.apple.com/airpods for more info); they're a little pricey but getting rave reviews, and for very good reason.

Use AirPlay

AirPlay streaming technology is built into the iPhone, iPod touch, Macs and PCs running iTunes, and iPad. Streaming technology allows you to send media files from one device that supports AirPlay to be played on another. For example, you can send a movie that you've purchased on your iPhone or a slideshow of your photos to be played on your Apple TV, and then control the TV playback from your iPhone. You can also send music to be played over compatible speakers, such as Apple's HomePod. (Go to www.apple.com/homepod for more information.) Check out the Apple TV Remote app in the App Store, which you can use to control your Apple TV from your iPhone.

To stream music via AirPlay on your iPhone with another AirPlay-enabled device on your network or in close proximity, tap the AirPlay button (looks like a pyramid with sound waves emanating from it) at the bottom center of the playback control screen while listening to a song. Then select the AirPlay device to stream the content to (see **Figure 18-12**), or choose your iPhone to move the playback back to it.

FIGURE 18-12

TIP

One of the beauties of AirPlay is that you can still use your iPhone to check email, browse photos or the Internet, or check your calendar while the media file is playing on the other device.

Play Music with Radio

You can access Radio by tapping the Radio button at the bottom of the Music screen, as shown in **Figure 18-13**.

Swipe from left to right and you'll find lots of music categories to listen to, or swipe all the way to the bottom and tap Radio Stations, and then swipe down to see the entire gamut of Radio's offerings by Genre (see **Figure 18-14**).

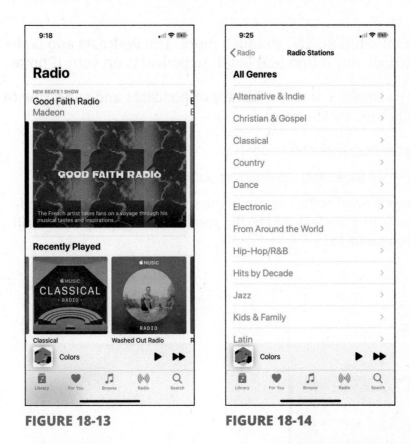

FIGURE 18-13

FIGURE 18-14

TECHNICAL STUFF

At one time, the Radio feature was free in the Music app, but now it's tied into Apple's Music service, which is subscription-based. So if you want to listen to stations in Radio, you'll have to become a member of Apple Music, or you can listen to Apple's flagship radio station, Beats 1, for free. To learn more about Apple Music (which is a great service), visit `www.apple.com/music`. Apple offers a free three-month trial to new subscribers, so you can get a feel for the service before deciding if you want to pay for it.

Find and Subscribe to Podcasts

First, what the heck is a podcast? A podcast is sort of like a radio show that you can listen to at any time. You'll find podcasts covering just about any subject imaginable, including news, sports, comedy, education, religion, and so much more. The Podcasts app is the vehicle by which you'll find and listen to podcasts on your iPhone.

To search Apple's massive library of podcasts and subscribe to them (which is free, by the way):

1. Tap the Podcasts icon to open it.

2. There are three ways to discover podcasts:

   - Tap Browse at the bottom of the screen; there you'll find podcasts that are featured by the good folks at Apple, as shown in **Figure 18-15.**

FIGURE 18-15

   - Tap Browse at the bottom of the screen, swipe down to Top Shows or Top Episodes; tap See All and you'll be greeted with lists of the most popular podcasts. Tap the All Categories button in the upper-right corner to sift through the podcasts based on the category (such as Arts, Health, or Music).

- Tap Search and then tap the Search field at the top of the screen. When the keyboard appears, type the name or subject of a podcast to see a list of results.

3. When you find a podcast that intrigues you, tap its name to see its information page, which will be similar to the one in **Figure 18-16**.

4. Tap the Subscribe button (refer to **Figure 18-16**). The podcast will appear in the Library section of the app, and the newest episode will be downloaded to your iPhone.

5. Tap Library in the toolbar at the bottom of the screen and then tap the name of the podcast you subscribed to and view its information screen.

Subscribe button

FIGURE 18-16

6. Tap the More button (looks like a circle containing three dots) and then tap Settings to see the settings for the podcast. From here (see **Figure 18-17**), you can customize how the podcast downloads and organizes episodes. Tap Done in the upper-right corner when you're finished with the Settings options.

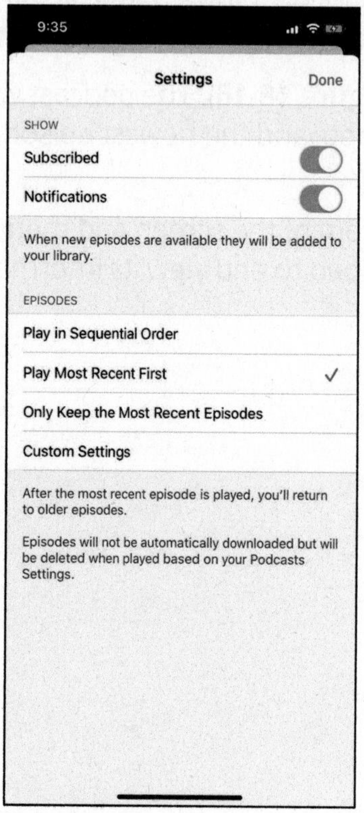

FIGURE 18-17

Play Podcasts

Playing podcasts is a breeze, and works very much like playing audio files in the Music app.

1. Open the Podcasts app and tap Library at the bottom of the screen.

2. Tap the name of the podcast you'd like to listen to.

3. Tap the episode you want to play. The episode begins playing; you can see the currently playing episode near the bottom of the screen, just above the toolbar.

4. Tap the currently playing episode to open the playback controls, shown in **Figure 18-18.**

FIGURE 18-18

5. Drag the line in the middle of the screen to scrub to a different part of the episode, or tap the Rewind or Fast Forward buttons to the left and right of the Pause/Play button, respectively.

6. Adjust the playback speed by tapping the 1x icon in the lower-left of the Play controls. Each tap increases or decreases playback speed.

7. Adjust the volume by dragging the Volume slider near the bottom of the screen, or using the Volume buttons on the side of your iPhone.

Tap the Listen Now button in the toolbar at the bottom-left of the app's screen to see a list of the newest episodes that have been automatically downloaded to your iPhone.

IN THIS CHAPTER

» **Take pictures with your iPhone**

» **Save photos from the web**

» **View albums and single photos**

» **Edit and organize photos**

» **View photos by time and place**

» **Share and delete photos**

Chapter **19**

Taking and Sharing Photos

With its gorgeous screen, the iPhone is a natural for taking and viewing photos. It supports most common photo formats, such as JPEG, TIFF, and PNG. You can shoot your photos by using the built-in cameras in iPhone with built-in square or panorama modes. With recent iPhone models, you can edit your images using smart adjustment filters. You can also sync photos from your computer, save images that you find online to your iPhone, or receive them by email, MMS, or iMessage.

The Photo Sharing feature lets you share groups of photos with people using iCloud on an iOS device or on a Mac or Windows computer with iCloud access. Your iCloud Photo Library makes all this storage and sharing easy.

When you have taken or downloaded photos to play with, the Photos app lets you organize photos and view photos in albums, one by one, or in a slideshow. You can also view photos by the years in which they were taken, with images divided into collections by the location or time you took them. With iOS 13, videos and live photos will play as you browse through Photos, making it a more dynamic and interesting experience. You can also AirDrop (iPhone 5 and later), email, message, or tweet a photo to a friend, print it, share it via AirPlay, or post it to Facebook. Finally, you can create time-lapse videos with the Camera app, allowing you to record a sequence in time, such as a flower opening as the sun warms it or your grandchild stirring from sleep. You can read about all these features in this chapter.

Take Pictures with the iPhone Cameras

The cameras in the iPhone are just begging to be used, so no matter which phone model you have, get started!

TIP

For all iPhone models other than iPhone X models and newer, to open the camera with the lock screen displayed, swipe up from the bottom of the screen and tap the Camera app icon in Control Center to go directly to the Camera app. If you have an iPhone X model or newer, swipe down from the right corner of your screen to open Control Center and tap the Camera app icon. You can also swipe down from the top of the screen to open Notification Center (with the iPhone unlocked) and then swipe from right to left to access Camera.

1. Tap the Camera app icon on the Home screen to open the app.

2. If the camera type at the bottom or side of the screen (see **Figure 19-1**), depending on how you're holding your iPhone, is set to Video or something other than Photo, swipe to choose Photo (the still camera).

TIP

iPhone's front- and rear-facing cameras allow you to capture photos and video (see Chapter 20 for more about the video features) and share them with family and friends. Newer models offer incredible cameras with such features as

- Autofocus with Focus Pixels
- Automatic image stabilization to avoid fuzzy moving targets
- True Tone Flash, a sensor that tells iPhone when a flash is needed

Swipe to Photo

FIGURE 19-1

The following are options for taking pictures after you've opened the Camera app:

» You can set the Portrait, Pano (for panorama), and Square options using the slider control above or next to the Capture button. These controls let you create flattering portraits or square images like those you see on the popular Instagram site. With Pano selected, tap to begin to take a picture and pan across a view and then tap Done to capture a panoramic display.

» Tap the Flash button (looks like a lightning bolt) in the top-left corner of the screen when using the rear camera and then select a flash option:

  • On, if your lighting is dim enough to require a flash

  • Off, if you don't want iPhone to use a flash

  • Auto, if you want to let iPhone decide for you

» To use the High Dynamic Range or HDR feature, tap the HDR setting at the top of the screen and tap to turn it on. This feature uses several images, some underexposed and some overexposed, and combines the best ones into one image, sometimes providing a more finely detailed picture.

HDR is enabled by default for iPhone XS, XS Max, XR, 11, and 11 Pro; the feature is called Smart HDR on those models. Since it's already on, you won't see the HDR option on the screen when using the Camera app. You can disable the feature by going to System ⇨ Camera and toggling the Smart HDR switch to Off (white). Now the feature will appear as an option in the Camera screen, where you can enable it manually when needed, as opposed to it being automatically used.

HDR pictures can be very large in file size, meaning they'll take up more of your iPhone's memory than standard pictures.

» If you want a time delay before the camera snaps the picture, tap the Time Delay button at the top of the screen, and then tap either 3s or 10s for a 3- or 10-second delay, respectively.

» Tap the Live button (looks like concentric circles) to take Live Photos. As opposed to freezing a single moment in time, Live Photos lets you capture 3-second moving images, which can create some truly beautiful photos. Be sure to hold your iPhone still for at least 3 seconds so that you don't move too soon and cause part of your Live Photo to show the movement of your iPhone as you get into position for the picture.

» Tap the Filters button in the upper-right if you'd like to apply color filters to your photos before taking them. Swipe through the filter options above the Capture button to find one that suits you.

» Move the camera around until you find a pleasing image. You can do a couple of things at this point to help you take your photo:

- Tap the area of the grid where you want the camera to autofocus.

- Place two fingers apart from each other on the screen and then pinch them together (still touching the screen) to display a digital zoom control. Drag the circle in the zoom bar to the right or left to zoom in or out on the image.

» Tap the Capture button at the bottom center of the screen (the big, white button). You've just taken a picture, and it's stored in the Photos app gallery automatically.

TIP

You can also use a Volume button (located on the left side of your iPhone) to capture a picture or start or stop video camera recording.

» Tap the Switch Camera button in the lower-right corner to switch between the front camera and rear camera. You can then take selfies (pictures of yourself), so go ahead and tap the Capture button to take another picture.

» To view the last photo taken, tap the thumbnail of the latest image in the bottom-left corner of the screen; the Photos app opens and displays the photo.

» Tap the Share button (it's the box with an arrow coming out of it, located in the bottom-left corner of the screen) to display a menu that allows you to AirDrop, email, or instant message the photo, assign it to a contact, use it as iPhone wallpaper, tweet it, post it to Facebook, share via iCloud Photo Sharing or Flickr, or print it (see **Figure 19-2**).

» You can tap images to select more than one.

» To delete the image, have it displayed and tap the Trash button in the bottom-right corner of the screen. Tap Delete Photo in the confirmation menu that appears.

TIP

You can use the iCloud Photo Sharing feature to automatically sync your photos across various devices. Turn on iCloud Photo Sharing by tapping Settings on the Home screen, tapping Photos, and then toggling the iCloud Photos switch to On (green).

FIGURE 19-2

Save Photos from the Web

The web offers a wealth of images that you can download to your Photo Library. To save an image from the web, follow these steps:

1. Open Safari and navigate to the web page containing the image you want, as seen in Figure 19-3.

TIP

For more about how to use Safari to navigate to or search for web content, see Chapter 12.

2. Press and hold the image. A menu appears on the screen, as shown in **Figure 19-4.**

3. Tap Add to Photos. The image is saved to your Camera Roll album in the Photos app.

FIGURE 19-3

FIGURE 19-4

If you want to capture your iPhone screen as a photo, the process is simple. Press the Sleep/Wake button and Home button simultaneously (press the Side and Volume Up buttons for iPhone X models and newer); the screen flashes white, and the screen capture is complete. The capture is saved in PNG format to your Recently Added album.

To save a picture sent as an email attachment in Mail, tap the attachment icon and the picture opens. Press the screen until a menu appears and then tap Save.

View an Album

The Photos app organizes your pictures into albums, using such criteria as the folder or album on your computer from which you synced the photos or photos captured using the iPhone camera (saved in the Camera Roll album). You may also have albums for images that you synced from other devices through iTunes or shared via Photos.

1. To view your albums, start by tapping the Photos app icon on the Home screen.

2. Tap the Albums button at the bottom of the screen to display your albums, as shown in **Figure 19-5.**

3. Tap an album. The photos in it are displayed.

Albums button

FIGURE 19-5

TIP You can associate photos with faces and events. When you do, additional tabs appear at the bottom of the screen when you display an album containing that type of photo.

View Individual Photos

You can view photos individually by opening them from within an album.

1. Tap the Photos app icon on the Home screen.

2. Tap Albums (refer to **Figure 19-5**).

3. Tap an album to open it; then, to view a photo, tap it. The picture expands, as shown in **Figure 19-6.**

FIGURE 19-6

4. Flick your finger to the left or right to scroll through the album to look at the individual photos in it.

5. You can tap the Back button in the upper-left corner (looks like a left-pointing arrow) and then the Albums button to return to the Album view.

You can place a photo on a person's information record in Contacts. For more about how to do this, see Chapter 7.

TIP

Edit Photos

iPhone Photos isn't Photoshop, but it does provide some tools for editing photos.

1. Tap the Photos app on the Home screen to open it.

2. Using methods previously described in this chapter, locate and display a photo you want to edit.

3. Tap the Edit button in the upper-right corner of the screen; the Edit Photo screen appears. The one shown in **Figure 19-7** is for a photo shot in Portrait mode.

4. At this point, you can take several possible actions with these tools (the screen location of these options depends on whether you're holding your iPhone in landscape or portrait mode):

   • **Crop:** To crop the photo to a portion of its original area, tap the Crop button. You can then tap any corner of the image and drag inward or outward to remove areas of the photo. Tap Crop and then Save to apply your changes.

   • **Filters:** Apply any of nine filters (such as Vivid, Mono, or Noir) to change the look of your image. These effects adjust the brightness of your image or apply a black-and-white tone to your color photos. Tap the Filters button in the middle of the tools at the bottom of the screen and scroll to view available filters. Tap one and then tap Apply to apply the effect to your image.

   • **Adjustments:** Swipe the options just above the Depth slider and immediately below the photo to see adjustment options such as

Light, Color, or B&W. There are a slew of other tools that you can use to tweak contrast, color intensity, shadows, and more.

- **Auto-enhance:** The icon for this feature looks like a magic wand, and it pretty much works like one. Tapping the wand allows your iPhone to apply automatic adjustments to your photo's exposure, saturation, contract, and so on.

- **Depth:** With this slider, you can control the depth of field of the any photo shot in Portrait mode. A lower value, like $f1.8$, gives you more background blur. A higher number, like $f16$, reveals a more detailed background.

Adjustments **Crop** **Depth**

Auto-enhance **Filters**

FIGURE 19-7

5. If you're pleased with your edits, tap the Done button. A copy of the edited photo is saved.

Each of the editing features has a Cancel button. If you don't like the changes you made, tap this button to stop making changes before you save the image.

Organize Photos

You'll probably want to organize your photos to make it simpler to find what you're looking for.

1. If you want to create your own album, open the Camera Roll album.

2. Tap the Select button in the top-right corner and then tap individual photos to select them. Small check marks appear on the selected photos (see **Figure 19-8**).

3. Tap the Share button in the lower-left corner, tap Add To Album, and then tap the New Album option button at the bottom of the screen and then tap New Album.

If you've already created albums, you can choose to add the photo to an existing album at this point.

4. Enter a name for a new album and then tap Save. If you create a new album, it appears in the Photos main screen with the other albums that are displayed.

You can also choose several other Share options or Delete when you've selected photos in Step 2 of this task. This allows you to share or delete multiple photos at a time.

Checkmarks show selected items

FIGURE 19-8

Share Photos with Mail, Twitter, or Facebook

You can easily share photos stored on your iPhone by sending them as email attachments, as a text message, by posting them to Facebook, sharing them via iCloud Photo Sharing or Flickr, or as tweets on Twitter. (You have to go to Chapter 14 to learn how to set up accounts for Facebook or Twitter before you can use this feature.)

1. Tap the Photos app icon on the Home screen.

2. Tap the Photos or Albums button and locate the photo you want to share.

3. Tap the photo to select it and then tap the Share button. (It looks like a box with an arrow jumping out of it.) The menu shown in **Figure 19-9** appears. Tap to select additional photos, if you want them.

FIGURE 19-9

4. Tap the Mail, Message, Twitter, iCloud Photo Sharing, Facebook, Flickr, or any other option you'd like to use.

5. In the message form that appears, make any modifications that apply in the To, Cc/Bcc, or Subject fields and then type a message for email, or enter your Facebook posting or Twitter tweet.

6. Tap the Send or Post button, and the message and photo are sent or posted.

TIP

You can also copy and paste a photo into documents, such as those created in the Pages word-processor app. To do this, tap a photo in Photos and tap Share. Tap the Copy command. In the destination app, press and hold the screen and tap Paste.

Share a Photo Using AirDrop

AirDrop, available to users of iPhone 5 and later, provides a way to share content, such as photos with others who are nearby and who have an AirDrop-enabled device (more recent Macs that can run macOS 10.10 or later).

Follow the steps in the previous task to locate a photo you want to share.

1. Tap the Share button.

2. If an AirDrop-enabled device is in your immediate vicinity (such as within 30 feet or so), you see the device listed (see **Figure 19-10**). Tap the device name and your photo is sent to the other device.

TIP

Other iOS devices (iPhones or iPads) must have AirDrop enabled to use this feature. To enable AirDrop, open Control Center (swipe up from the bottom of any screen, or down from the upper-right corner for iPhone X models and newer, as well as iPads) and tap AirDrop. If you don't see AirDrop as an option, press-and-hold the Communications area in Control Center. The Communications area houses Wi-Fi and other options; the options will expand and you'll see AirDrop there, as illustrated in **Figure 19-11.** Choose Contacts Only or Everyone to specify whom you can use AirDrop with.

AirDrop-enabled devices nearby

FIGURE 19-10

Tap AirDrop

FIGURE 19-11

Share Photos Using iCloud Photo Sharing

iCloud Photo Sharing allows you to automatically share photos using your iCloud account.

1. Select a photo or photos you would like to share, and tap the Share button in the lower-left.

2. In the Share screen that opens, tap Add to Shared Album.

3. Enter a comment if you like, tap Shared Album to choose the album you want to use, tap iCloud to go back, and then tap Post. The photos or moment are posted to your iCloud Photo Library.

Delete Photos

You might find that it's time to get rid of some of those old photos of the family reunion or the latest community center project. If the photos weren't transferred from your computer, but instead were taken, downloaded, or captured as screenshots on the iPhone, you can delete them.

1. Tap the Photos app icon on the Home screen.

2. Tap the Albums tab and then tap an album to open it.

3. Locate and tap on a photo that you want to delete, and then tap the Trash icon. In the confirming dialog that appears, tap the Delete Photo button to finish the deletion.

WARNING

If you delete a photo in Photo Sharing, it is deleted on all devices that you shared it with.

TIP

If you'd like to recover a photo you've deleted, tap the Albums tab, swipe to the bottom of the page, and tap Recently Deleted. Tap the photo you want to retrieve, tap the Recover button in the lower-right corner, and then tap the Recover Photo button when prompted.

» Play movies or TV shows

» Turn on closed-captioning

» Delete a video from the iPhone

Chapter **20**

Creating and Watching Videos

U sing the TV app (formerly known as Videos), you can watch downloaded movies or TV shows, as well as media that you've synced from iCloud on your Mac or PC, and even media that's provided from other content providers, such as cable and streaming video services. The TV app aims to be your one-stop shop for your viewing pleasure.

In addition, newer iPhone models sport both a front and rear video camera that you can use to capture your own videos, which iOS now allows you to edit in the same way you can edit photos: You can apply adjustments, and filters as well as crop your videos. Speaking of editing, you can also download the iMovie app for iPhone (a more limited version of the longtime mainstay on Mac computers) that allows you to do an editing deep-dive with the ability to add titles, music, transitions, and much more.

In this chapter, I explain all about shooting and watching video content from a variety of sources. For practice, you might want to refer to Chapter 16 first to find out how to purchase or download one of many available TV shows or movies from the iTunes Store.

Capture Your Own Videos with the Built-In Cameras

The camera lens that comes on newer iPhones has perks for photographers, including a large aperture and highly accurate sensor, which make for better images all around. In addition, auto image stabilization makes up for any shakiness in the hands holding the phone, and autofocus has sped up thanks to the fast processors being used. For videographers, you'll appreciate a fast frames-per-second capability as well as a slow-motion feature.

1. To capture a video, tap the Camera app on the Home screen. In iPhone, two video cameras are available for capturing video, one from the front and one from the back of the device. (See more about this topic in the next task.)

2. The Camera app opens (see **Figure 20-1**). Tap and slide the camera-type options above or next to the red Record button (depending on how you're holding your iPhone) until Video rests above or next to the button; this is how you switch from the still camera to the video camera.

3. If you want to switch between the front and back cameras, tap the Switch Camera button in the top-right corner of the screen (refer to **Figure 20-1**).

4. Tap the red Record button to begin recording the video. (The red dot in the middle of this button turns into a red square when the camera is recording.) When you're finished, tap the Record button again to stop recording. Your new video is now displayed in the bottom-left corner of the screen. Tap the video to play, share, or delete it. In the future, you can find and play the video in your Camera Roll when you open the Photos app.

TIP

Before you start recording, remember where the camera lens is — while holding the iPhone and panning, you can easily put your fingers directly over the lens! Also, you can't pause your recording; when you stop, your video is saved, and when you start recording, you're creating a new video file.

Switch Camera button

Record button

Camera-type options

FIGURE 20-1

Edit Videos

iPhone Photos (where your videos are stored) isn't Final Cut Pro, but it does provide a few handy tools for editing videos.

1. Tap the Photos app on the Home screen, locate your video, and tap to open it.

2. Tap the Edit button in the upper-right corner of the screen; the Edit screen appears. The one shown in **Figure 20-2** is for a video shot in Landscape mode.

3. At this point, you can take several possible actions with the tools provided:

- **Crop:** To crop the video to a portion of its original area, tap the Crop button. You can then tap any corner of the image and drag inward or outward to remove areas of the video. Tap Crop and then Save to apply your changes.

- **Filters:** Apply any of nine filters (such as Vivid, Mono, or Noir) to change the look of your video images. These effects adjust the brightness of your video or apply a black-and-white tone to your color videos. Tap the Filters button on the left side of the screen and then scroll through the list on the right side to view available filters. Tap one to apply the effect to your video.

FIGURE 20-2

- **Adjustments:** Tap Light, Color, or B&W to access a slew of tools that you can use to tweak contrast, color intensity, shadows, and more.

- **Auto-enhance:** The icon for this feature looks like a magic wand, and it pretty much works like one. Tapping the wand allows your iPad to apply automatic adjustments to your video's exposure, saturation, contrast, and so on.

- **Trim:** Use the trim tool to remove parts of your video you no longer want to view.

4. If you're pleased with your edits, tap the Done button. A copy of the edited video is saved.

TIP

Each of the editing features has a Cancel button. If you don't like the changes you made, tap this button (in the upper-left corner) to stop making changes before you save the image. How about if you make changes you later regret? Just open the video, tap Edit, and then tap the red Revert button in the upper-right to discard changes to the original.

Play Movies or TV Shows with TV

Open the TV app for the first time and you'll be greeted with a Welcome screen; tap Get Started. You'll be asked to sign in to your television provider, if you've not done so already.

Signing in will allow you to use the TV app to access content in other apps (like ESPN or Disney), if such services are supported by your TV provider. This way, you only need to use the TV app to access content and sign in, as opposed to having multiple apps to juggle and sign in to.

TIP

Should you decide to skip signing in to your TV provider and worry about it later (or if you've already opened the TV app and cruised right past this part), you can access the same options by going to Settings ⇨ TV Provider (as shown in **Figure 20-3**), tapping the name of your provider, and then entering your account information. If you're not sure of your account information, you'll need to contact your provider for assistance.

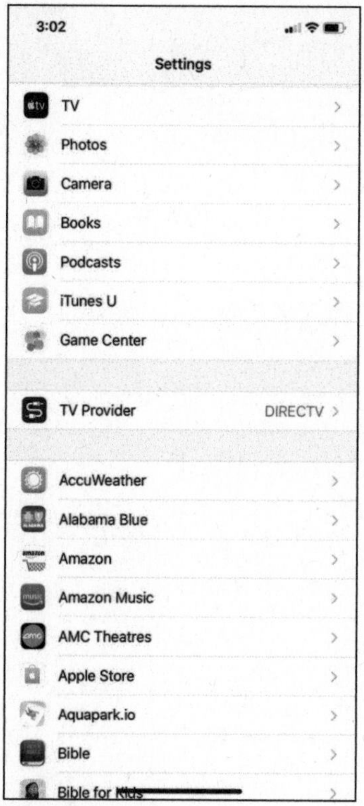

3:02		
	Settings	
TV		>
Photos		>
Camera		>
Books		>
Podcasts		>
iTunes U		>
Game Center		>
TV Provider	DIRECTV	>
AccuWeather		>
Alabama Blue		>
Amazon		>
Amazon Music		>
AMC Theatres		>
Apple Store		>
Aquapark.io		>
Bible		>
Bible for Kids		>

FIGURE 20-3

The TV app offers a couple of ways to view movies and TV shows: via third-party providers or items you've purchased or rented from the iTunes Store.

Content from third-party providers

To access content from third-party providers like NBC, ABC, PBS, and more, tap the Watch Now button in the bottom-left of your screen (**Figure 20-4**). Swipe to see hit shows and browse by genres like Comedy, Action, and others.

Watch Now button

FIGURE 20-4

Tap on a show that interests you and then tap an episode to see a description, like I've done in **Figure 20-5**. Tap Play Episode. If you have the app that supports the video, the video will open automatically in the correct app. You may be prompted to connect apps from providers like PBS and ABC to the TV app so you can watch their videos in TV; if you want to do so, tap Connect, but if not just tap Not Now. If you don't have the app installed that you need to watch the video, you'll be asked if you'd like to download and install it, as shown in **Figure 20-6**.

FIGURE 20-5　　　　　　**FIGURE 20-6**

TIP

If your iPhone is on the same Wi-Fi network as your computer and both are running iTunes, with the iPhone and iTunes set to use the same Home Sharing account, you see the Shared List. With this setup, you can stream videos from iTunes on your computer to your iPhone.

Content from iTunes

To access video you've purchased or rented from the iTunes Store, follow these steps:

1. Tap the TV app icon on the Home screen to open the application, and then tap Library at the bottom of the screen.

2. On a screen like the one in **Figure 20-7**, tap the appropriate category at the top of the screen (TV Shows or Movies, depending on the content you've downloaded), and then tap the video you want to watch.

   Information about the movie or TV show episodes appears.

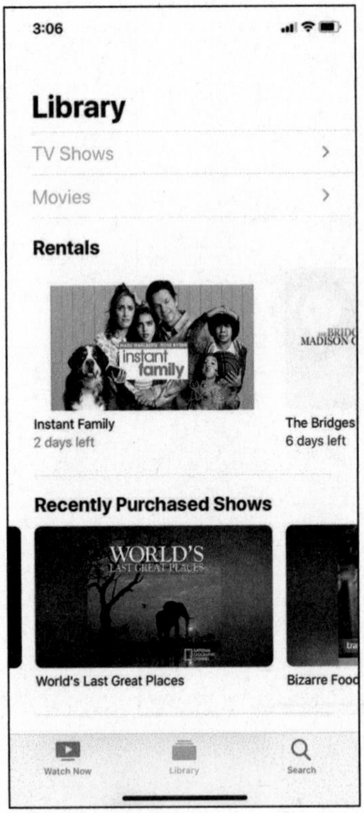

FIGURE 20-7

3. For TV Shows, tap the episode that you'd like to play; for Movies, the Play button appears on the description screen. Tap the Play button and the movie or TV show begins playing. (If you see a small,

cloud-shaped icon instead of a Play button, tap it and the content is downloaded from iCloud.)

4. With the playback tools displayed (as shown in **Figure 20-8**), take any of these actions:

- Tap the Pause button to pause playback.

- Tap either Go to Previous Chapter or Go to Next Chapter to move to a different location in the video playback.

  If a video has chapter support, another button called Scenes appears here for displaying all chapters so that you can move more easily from one to another.

- Tap the circular button on the Volume slider and drag the button left or right to decrease or increase the volume, respectively.

TIP If your controls disappear during playback, just tap the screen and they'll reappear.

FIGURE 20-8

5. To stop the video and return to the information screen, tap the Done button to the left of the Progress bar.

Turn On Closed-Captioning

iTunes and iPhone offer support for closed–captioning and subtitles. Look for the CC logo on media that you download to use this feature.

Video that you record won't have this capability.

If a movie has either closed-captioning or subtitles, you can turn on the feature in iPhone.

1. Begin by tapping the Settings icon on the Home screen.

2. Tap Accessibility, scroll down, and tap Subtitles & Captioning.

3. On the menu that displays, tap the Closed Captions + SDH switch to turn on the feature (green). Now when you play a movie with closed-captioning, you can tap the Audio and Subtitles button to the left of the playback controls to manage these features.

Delete a Video from the iPhone

You can buy videos directly from your iPhone, or you can sync via iCloud or iTunes to place content you've bought or created on another device on your iPhone.

When you want to get rid of video content on your iPhone because it's a memory hog, you can delete it:

1. Open the TV app and then go to the TV show or movie you want to delete.

2. Tap the Downloaded button (looks like a rectangle containing a check mark).

3. Tap Remove Download in the options that appear. The downloaded video will be deleted from your iPhone.

If you buy a video using iTunes and sync to download it to your iPhone, and subsequently delete it from your iPhone, it's still saved in your iTunes Library. You can sync your computer and iPhone again to download the video. Remember, however, that rented movies, when deleted, are gone with the wind. Also, video doesn't sync to iCloud as photos and music do.

- » **Change views and zoom**

- » **Go to other locations or favorites**

- » **Drop markers and find directions**

- » **Get turn-by-turn navigation help**

Chapter **21**

Navigating with Maps

The redesigned Maps app has lots of useful functions. You can find directions with alternative routes from one location to another. You can bookmark locations to return to them again. And the Maps app delivers information about locations, such as phone numbers and web links to businesses. You can even add a location to your Contacts list or share a location link with your buddy using Mail, Messages, Twitter, or Facebook. The Nearby feature helps you explore local attractions and businesses, and the Transit view lets you see public transit maps for select cities around the world. Maps also includes other great features, such as lane guidance (helps you get in the correct lane for upcoming turns), speed limit indicators for many roads, and maps of such indoor locations as shopping centers and airports. And we can't forget about the awesome new Look Around feature, new to iOS 13!

You're about to have some fun exploring Maps in this chapter. Just don't do it while driving!

Go to Your Current Location

iPhone can figure out where you are at any time and display your current location.

1. From the Home screen, tap the Maps icon. Tap the Current Location button (the small arrow in the upper-right corner; see **Figure 21-1**). A map is displayed with your current location indicated (also shown in **Figure 21-1**).

TECHNICAL STUFF

Depending on your connection, Wi-Fi or cellular, a pulsating circle may appear around the marker, indicating the area surrounding your location is based on cell tower triangulation. Your exact location can be anywhere within the area of the circle, and the location service is likely to be less accurate using a Wi-Fi connection than your phone's cellular connection.

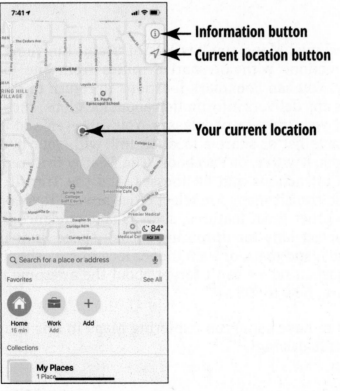

FIGURE 21-1

2. Double-tap the screen to zoom in on your location. (Additional methods of zooming in and out are covered in the "Zoom In and Out" section in this chapter.)

As mentioned previously, if you access maps via a Wi-Fi connection, your current location is a rough estimate based on a triangulation method. Your iPhone can more accurately pinpoint where you are by using your cellular data connection, your iPhone's global positioning system (GPS), and Bluetooth. But you can get pretty accurate results with just a Wi-Fi–connected iPhone if you type a starting location and an ending location to get directions.

Change Views

The Maps app offers three primary views: Map, Transit, and Satellite. iPhone displays the Map view (refer to **Figure 21-1**) by default the first time you open Maps.

1. To change views, with Maps open, tap the Information button in the upper right of the screen (refer to **Figure 21-1**) to reveal the Maps Settings dialog, shown in **Figure 21-2.**

In the Maps Settings dialog, you can also access a Traffic overlay feature. If you live in a large metropolitan area (this feature doesn't really work in small towns or rural settings), turn on this feature by toggling the Traffic switch to On (green).

2. Tap the Transit button, and then tap the Close button (looks like an X within a gray circle) in the upper right of the Maps Settings dialog. In Transit view, if you have a major city for which Transit information is available, you'll see data about public transit.

3. Tap the Information button again in the upper right, tap the Satellite button, and then tap the Close button. The Satellite view (shown in **Figure 21-3**) appears.

You can also toggle the Labels switches in the Maps Settings dialog to see street names superimposed on maps while in Satellite view. This is a huge help if navigating with Satellite view!

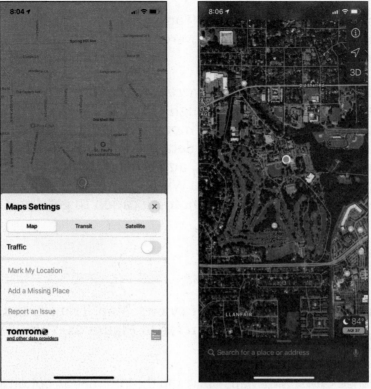

FIGURE 21-2   **FIGURE 21-3**

4. You can display a 3D effect (seen in **Figure 21-4**) on any view by
   tapping the 3D map option in the Maps menu. Tap 2D to revert to
   two-dimensional imaging.

TIP

Maps displays a weather icon in the lower-right corner of a map
to indicate the weather conditions in the area.

FIGURE 21-4

Zoom In and Out

You'll appreciate the Zoom feature because it gives you the capability to zoom in and out to see more or less detailed maps and to move around a displayed map.

1. With a map displayed, double-tap with a single finger to zoom in (see **Figure 21-5**; the image on the left shows the map before zooming in, and the image on the right shows the map after zooming).

2. Double-tap with two fingers to zoom out, revealing less detail.

3. Place two fingers positioned together on the screen and move them apart to zoom in.

4. Place two fingers apart on the screen and then pinch them together to zoom out.

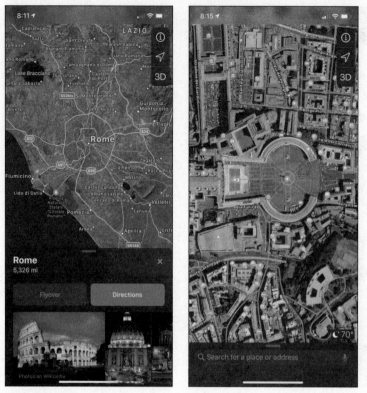

FIGURE 21-5

5. An option called one-handed zoom allows you to zoom in and out with just one finger. To start it, double-tap on the screen, but on the second tap hold your finger on the screen. Now, drag your finger up or down the screen to zoom in or out.

6. Press your finger to the screen and drag the map in any direction to move to an adjacent area.

TIP

It can take a few moments for the map to redraw itself when you enlarge, reduce, or move around it, so be patient. Areas that are being redrawn look like blank grids but are filled in eventually. Also, if you're in Satellite view, zooming in may take some time; wait it out. The blurred image resolves itself and looks quite nice, even tightly zoomed.

Go to Another Location or a Favorite

1. With Maps open, tap in the Search field (see **Figure 21-6**). The keyboard opens.

Search field

FIGURE 21-6

2. Type a location, using either a street address with city and state, a stored contact name, or a destination (such as Empire State Building or Lincoln Memorial). Maps may make suggestions as you type if it finds any logical matches. Tap the result you prefer. The location appears with a marker on it (the marker depends on which kind of establishment the location is, such as restaurant or landmark) and an information dialog with the location name and a Directions button (see **Figure 21-7**). Swipe up on the information dialog and more

information is displayed, such as pictures of the location, address and phone information, and more.

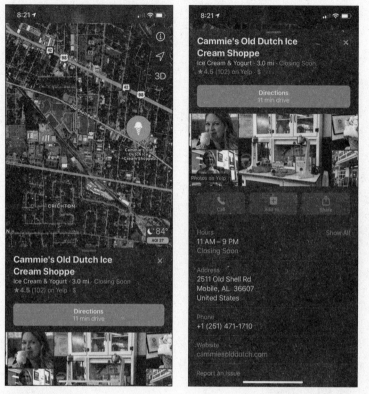

FIGURE 21-7

3. Swipe down on the information dialog. You move back to the map, where you can tap the screen and drag in any direction to move to a nearby location.

Drop a Marker (or Pin)

Markers and pins are the same thing, but the iOS 13 version of Maps leans toward using markers as the default term. I felt that this part of the chapter was the best place to explain that difference, in case you've used iOS devices in the past and have always referred to marked locations as pins and were wondering what this marker business was all about.

1. Display a map that contains a spot where you want to drop a marker to help you find directions to or from that site.

2. If you need to, you can zoom in to a more detailed map to see a better view of the location you want to mark.

3. Press and hold your finger on the screen at the location where you want to place the marker. The marker appears, together with an information dialog (refer to **Figure 21-7**).

4. Swipe up on the information dialog to display details about the marker location (see **Figure 21-8**).

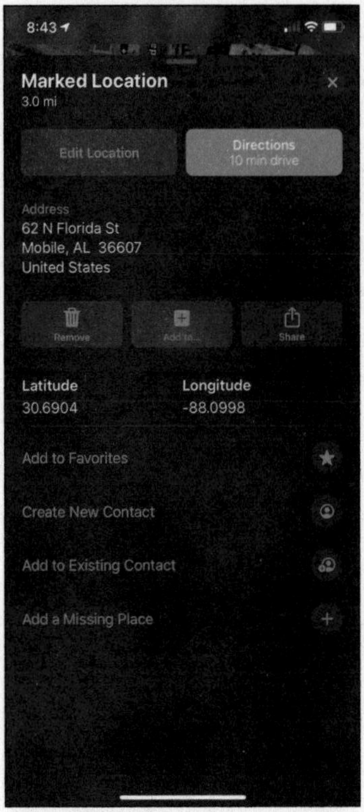

FIGURE 21-8

TIP

If a location has associated reviews on sites, such as the restaurant and travel review site Yelp (www.yelp.com), you can display details about the location and scroll down to read the reviews.

Find Directions

You can get directions in a couple of different ways.

1. Tap a marker on your map and then tap the Directions button in the information dialog. A blue line appears, showing the route between your current location and the chosen marker (see **Figure 21-9**). Sometimes alternate routes will display as well (in a lighter shade of blue), allowing you to select which you'd rather take; just tap the alternate route if you deem it's best for you. Tap the Close button to return to the Maps main screen.

Alternate route

Preferred route

FIGURE 21-9

2. You can enter two locations to get directions from one to the other. Tap the Search field to open the keyboard and type the location you'd like to get to, and then select the location from the list. In the information dialog that appears, you see the destination at the top and From just below it (shown in **Figure 21-10**).

3. My Location is the default, but if you want to change it to a different location, just tap My Location, type in the new starting point, and then tap Route in the upper-right corner (see **Figure 21-11**).

TIP

At the bottom of the directions dialog you have buttons called Walk, Transit, and Ride (along with the default Drive). Tap one of them to see directions that are optimized for that particular mode of transportation.

4. Tap the green Go button when you're ready to start on your route.

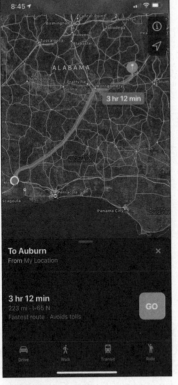

FIGURE 21-10

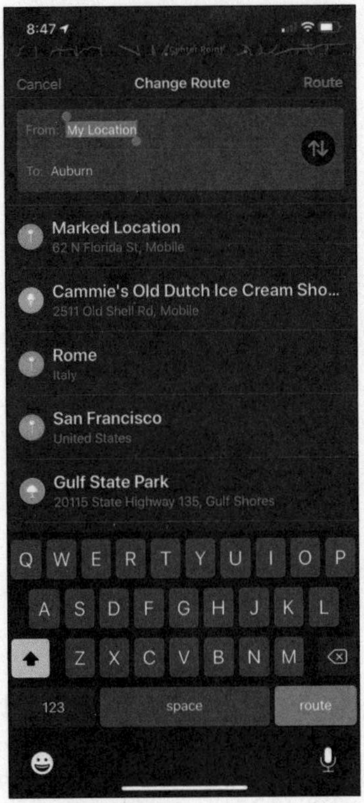

FIGURE 21-11

Get Turn-by-Turn Navigation Help

1. After you've found directions, tap the green Go button to get started.

The narration begins and text instructions are displayed at the top of the screen, as you can see in **Figure 21-12.** Estimated arrival time and distance are shown at the bottom of the screen in the collapsed information dialog. Continue on your way according to the route until the next instruction is spoken.

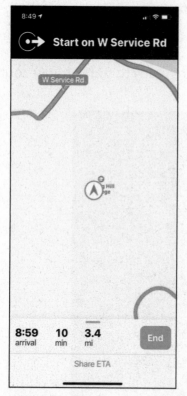

FIGURE 21-12

2. To share an ETA to your destination with others (as shown in **Figure 21-13**) at any time, swipe up on the information dialog, and then tap the Share ETA button that appears in the lower-left corner. Select a contact from the list of your favorites, or tap Contacts to search for the one you want to share with, and then go along your merry way. You will see at the bottom of the screen that you're sharing your ETA with the contact you've selected. To stop sharing, swipe up on the information dialog and tap the contact (also shown in **Figure 21-13**). Then swipe down to return to your directions.

Tap a contact to share ETA   **Tap to stop sharing your ETA**

FIGURE 21-13

3. To see the details of your route (seen in **Figure 21-14**), swipe up on the information dialog, and then tap the Details button. Tap Done when you're ready to resume turn-by-turn navigation.

FIGURE 21-14

4. To adjust the volume of the spoken navigation aid, swipe up on the information dialog, and then tap the Audio button. Adjust the audio settings to either No Voice, Low Volume, Normal Volume, or Loud Volume (as seen in **Figure 21-15**). Toggle the Pause Spoken Audio switch to On if you want to pause other audio that you may be listening to when Maps needs to give you directions. Tap Done to get back to your route.

5. Maps will end the route automatically after you arrive. You may also end the route manually by tapping the End button and then confirming by tapping the End Route button, shown in **Figure 21-16** (tap Resume to continue along your merry way).

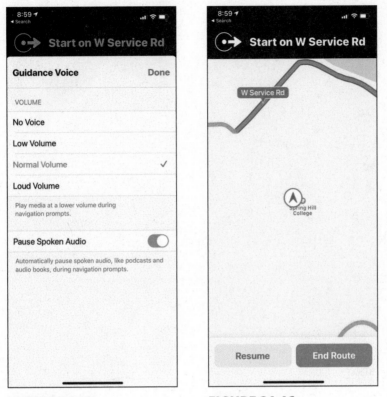

FIGURE 21-15   **FIGURE 21-16**

TIP

It's no problem if you need to perform another task while in the middle of getting directions. Press the Home button or swipe up from the bottom of the screen (iPhone X and newer models) to get out of Maps, and you'll notice a blue bar appearing at the top of your screen. Simply tap that blue bar to get back to your navigation in Maps after the other task is complete.

5

Living with Your iPhone

Chapter **22**

Keeping on Schedule with Calendar and Clock

Whether you're retired or still working, you have a busy life full of activities (perhaps even busier if you're retired, for some unfathomable reason). You need a way to keep on top of all those activities and appointments. The Calendar app on your iPhone is a simple, elegant, electronic daybook that helps you do just that.

In addition to being able to enter events and view them in a list or by the day, week, or month, you can set up Calendar to send alerts to remind you of your obligations and search for events by keywords. You can even set up repeating events, such as birthdays, monthly get-togethers with friends, or weekly babysitting appointments with your grandchild. To help you coordinate calendars on multiple devices, you can also sync events with other calendar accounts. And by taking advantage of the Family Sharing feature, you can create a Family calendar that everybody in your family can view and add events to.

Another preinstalled app that can help you stay on schedule is Clock. Though simple to use, Clock helps you view the time in multiple locations, set alarms, check yourself with a stopwatch feature, and use a timer.

In this chapter, you master the simple procedures for getting around your calendar, creating a Family calendar, entering and editing events, setting up alerts, syncing, and searching. You also learn the straightforward ins and outs of using Clock.

View Your Calendar

Calendar offers several ways to view your schedule.

1. Start by tapping the Calendar app icon on the Home screen to open it. Depending on what you last had open and the orientation in which you're holding your iPhone, you may see today's calendar, List view, the year, the month, the week, an open event, or the Search screen with search results displayed.

If you're lucky enough to own one of the iPhone models with wider screens (iPhone 11, for example), when you hold them horizontally and you're in the Calendar app, you see more information on the screen than you see on other iPhone models. For example, in Monthly view, you see the entire month on the left and detailed information on events for the selected day.

2. Tap the Today button at the bottom of the screen to display Today's view (if it isn't already displayed), and then tap the List View button to see all scheduled events for that day. The List view, shown in **Figure 22-1,** displays your daily appointments for every day in a list, with times listed on the left. Tap an event in the list to get more event details, or tap the Add button (the + symbol in the upper-right corner) to add an event.

If you'd like to display events only from a particular calendar, such as the Birthday or US Holidays calendars, tap the Calendars button at the bottom of the List view and select a calendar to view by tapping the circle(s) to the left of the listed calendar(s).

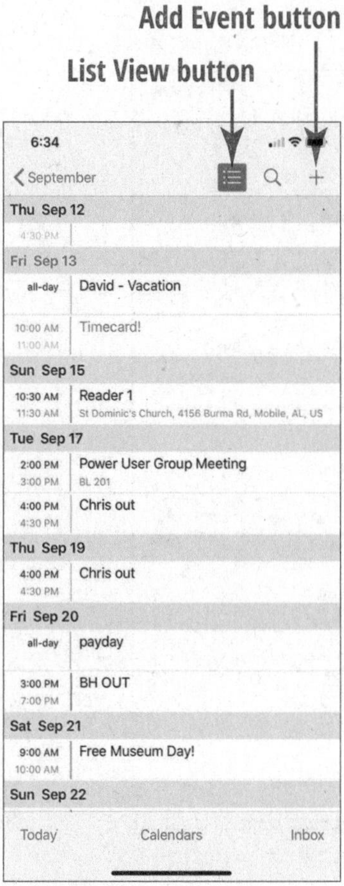

Add Event button

List View button

6:34

‹ September

Thu Sep 12
4:30 PM

Fri Sep 13
all-day   David - Vacation

10:00 AM   Timecard!
11:00 AM

Sun Sep 15
10:30 AM   Reader 1
11:30 AM   St Dominic's Church, 4156 Burma Rd, Mobile, AL, US

Tue Sep 17
2:00 PM   Power User Group Meeting
3:00 PM   BL 201

4:00 PM   Chris out
4:30 PM

Thu Sep 19
4:00 PM   Chris out
4:30 PM

Fri Sep 20
all-day   payday

3:00 PM   BH OUT
7:00 PM

Sat Sep 21
9:00 AM   Free Museum Day!
10:00 AM

Sun Sep 22

Today   Calendars   Inbox

FIGURE 22-1

3. Tap the current month in the upper-left corner to display months; in the Month view, the List View button changes to a Combined View button. Tap this to show the month calendar at the top and a scrollable list of events at the bottom, as shown in **Figure 22-2**. Tap the button again to return to the Month view.

4. Tap a date in the Month calendar and you'll see that week at the top and the selected day's events below.

   The Week view can't display combined lists.

5. In the Month view, note the year displayed at the top left of the screen. Tap the arrow to its left to get a yearly display (see **Figure 22-3**), and then tap another month to display it. In the Year view, you see the calendar for the entire year with a red circle around the current day.

Combine View button

FIGURE 22-2   FIGURE 22-3

6. To move from one month to the next in Month view, you can also scroll up or down the screen with your finger.

7. To jump back to today, tap the Today button in the bottom-left corner of the screen. The month containing the current day is displayed.

TIP

To view any invitation that you accepted, which placed an event on your calendar, tap Inbox in the lower-right corner and a list of invitations is displayed. You can use text within emails (such as a date, flight number, or phone number) to add an event to Calendar. Tap Done to return to the calendar.

Add Calendar Events

1. With any view displayed, tap the Add button (which looks like a plus symbol) in the upper-right corner of the screen to add an event (refer to **Figure 22-3**). The New Event dialog appears.

2. Enter a title for the event and, if you want, a location.

3. Tap the All-day switch to turn it on for an all-day event, or tap the Starts and Ends fields to set start and end times for the event. As shown in **Figure 22-4,** the scrolling setting for day, hour, and minute appears.

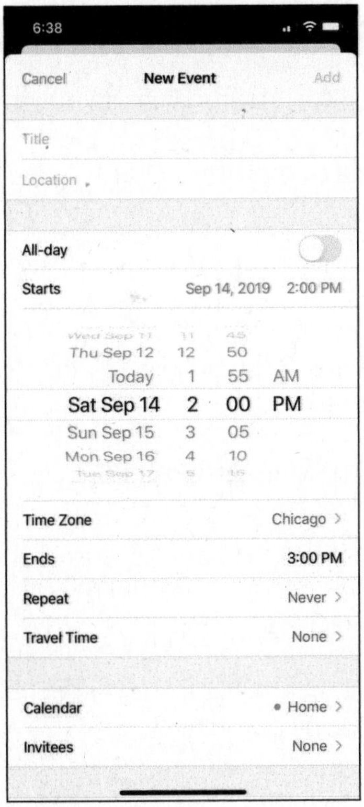

FIGURE 22-4

4. Place your finger on the date, hour, minute, or AM/PM column and move your finger to scroll up or down.

5. If you want to add notes, use your finger to scroll down in the New Event dialog and tap in the Notes field. Type your note and then tap the Add button to save the event.

TIP

You can edit any event at any time by simply tapping it in any view of your calendar and, when the details are displayed, tap Edit in the upper-left corner. The Edit Event dialog appears, offering the same settings as the New Event dialog. Tap the Done button to save your changes or Cancel to return to your calendar without saving any changes.

Add Events with Siri

Play around with this feature and the Calendar app; it's a lot of fun!

1. Press and hold the Home button (Side button for iPhone X and newer models) or say "Hey Siri."

2. Speak a command, such as "Hey Siri. Create a meeting on October 3 at 2:30 p.m."

3. When Siri asks you whether you're ready to schedule the event, say "Yes." The event is added to Calendar.

TIP

You can schedule an event with Siri in several ways:

» Say "Create event." Siri asks you first for a date and then for a time.

» Say "I have a meeting with John on April 1." Siri may respond by saying "I don't find a meeting with John on April 1; shall I create it?" You can say "Yes" to have Siri create it.

Create Repeating Events

If you want an event to repeat, such as a weekly or monthly appointment, you can set a repeating event.

1. With any view displayed, tap the Add button to add an event. The New Event dialog (refer to **Figure 22-4**) appears.

2. Enter a title and location for the event and set the start and end dates and times, as shown in the preceding task, "Add Calendar Events."

3. Scroll down the page if necessary and then tap the Repeat field; the Repeat dialog, shown in **Figure 22-5**, is displayed.

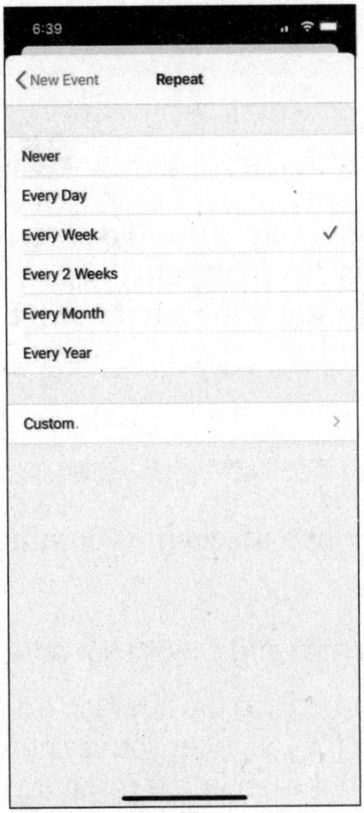

FIGURE 22-5

4. Tap a preset time interval: Every Day, Week, 2 Weeks, Month, or Year and you return to the New Event dialog. Tap Custom and make the appropriate settings if you want to set any other interval, such as every two months on the 6th of the month.

5. Should you like to set an expiration date for the repeated event, tap End Repeat and make the necessary settings.

6. Tap Done and you'll return to the Calendar.

TIP

Other calendar programs may give you more control over repeating events. For example, you might be able to make a setting to repeat an event the fourth Tuesday of every month. If you want a more robust calendar feature, you might consider setting up your appointments in an application such as the macOS version of Calendar, Outlook, or Google Calendar and syncing it to your iPhone. But if you want to create a simple repeating event in iPhone's Calendar app, simply add the first event on a Tuesday and make it repeat every week. Easy, huh?

View an Event

Tap a Calendar event anywhere — on a Day view, Week view, Month view, or List view — to see its details. To make changes to the event you're viewing, tap the Edit button in the upper-left corner.

Add Alerts

If you want your iPhone to alert you when an event is coming up, you can use the Alert feature.

1. Tap the Settings icon on the Home screen and choose Sounds.

2. Scroll down to Calendar Alerts and tap it; then tap any Alert Tone, which causes iPhone to play the tone for you. After you've chosen the alert tone you want, tap Sounds in the upper-left corner to return to Sounds settings. Press the Home button (or swipe up from the bottom of the screen for iPhone X and newer models) and then tap Calendar and create an event in your calendar or open an existing one for editing, as covered in earlier tasks in this chapter.

TIP

You can also set your iPhone to alert you of a Calendar event with a vibration for times when you have your sound muted and can't hear an alert (the vibrations can also act as a secondary alert to the alert tones). Tap the Settings icon on the Home screen, tap Sounds, tap Calendar Alerts, and then tap Vibration at the top of the screen. Select a vibration pattern from one in the list or create your own by tapping Create New Vibration. You can also disable vibrations for Calendar alerts by tapping None at the very bottom of the screen.

3. In the New Event (refer to **Figure 22-4**) or Edit Event dialog, tap the Alert field. The Event Alert dialog appears, as shown in **Figure 22-6.**

4. Tap any preset interval, from 5 Minutes to 2 Days Before or At Time of Event, and you'll return to the New Event or Edit Event dialog.

The Alert setting is shown in the New Event or Edit dialog (see **Figure 22-7**).

5. Tap Done in the Edit Event dialog or Add in the New Event dialog to save all settings.

Alert for an event

FIGURE 22-6

FIGURE 22-7

TIP

If you work for an organization that uses a Microsoft Exchange account, you can set up your iPhone to receive and respond to invitations from colleagues in your company. When somebody sends an invitation that you accept, it appears on your calendar. Check with your company network administrator (who will jump at the chance to get her hands on your iPhone) or the iPhone User Guide to set up this feature if it sounds useful to you.

TIP

iCloud offers individuals functionality similar to Microsoft Exchange.

Search for an Event

Can't remember what day next week you scheduled lunch with your brother Mike? You can do a search:

1. With Calendar open in any view, tap the Search button (looks like a magnifying glass) in the top-right corner.

2. Tap the Search field to display the onscreen keyboard, if it doesn't automatically open.

3. Type a word or words to search by and then tap the Search key. Using the example mentioned above, maybe search for "Mike" or "lunch." While you type, the Results dialog appears.

4. Tap any result to display the event details.

Delete an Event

When an upcoming luncheon or meeting is canceled, you should delete the appointment.

1. With Calendar open, tap an event (see **Figure 22-8**).

2. Tap Delete Event at the bottom of the screen.

3. If this is a repeating event, you have the option to delete this instance of the event or this and all future instances of the event (see **Figure 22-9**). Tap the button for the option you prefer. The event is deleted, and you return to Calendar view.

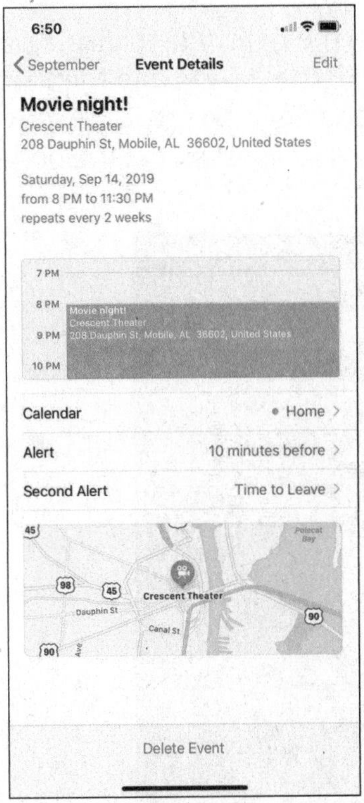

FIGURE 22-8

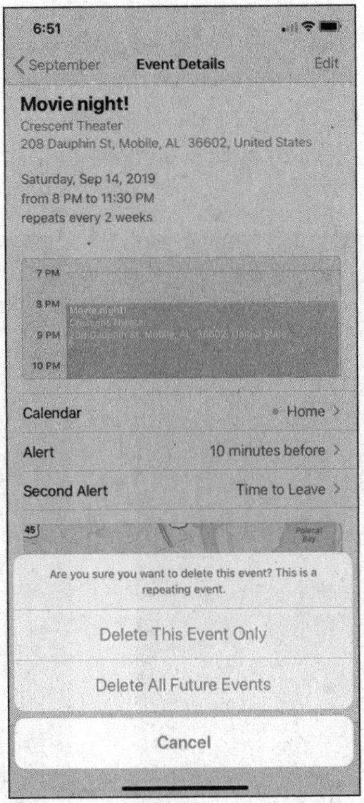

FIGURE 22-9

> **TIP**
> If an event is moved but not canceled, you don't have to delete the old one and create a new one. Simply edit the existing event to change the day and time in the Event dialog.

Display Clock

Clock is a preinstalled app that resides on the Home screen along with other preinstalled apps, such as Apple Books and Camera.

1. Tap the Clock app to open it. If this is the first time you've opened Clock, you'll see the World Clock tab (see **Figure 22-10**).

2. You can add a clock for many (but not all) locations around the world. With Clock displayed, tap the Add button (looks like a plus symbol) in the upper-right corner.

3. Tap a city on the list or tap a letter on the right side to display locations that begin with that letter (see **Figure 22-11**), and then tap a city. You can also tap in the Search field and begin to type a city name to find and tap a city. The clock appears in the last slot at the bottom.

FIGURE 22-10

FIGURE 22-11

Set an Alarm

It seems like nobody has a bedside alarm clock anymore; everyone uses his or her phone instead. Here's how you set an alarm:

1. With the Clock app displayed, tap the Alarm tab.

2. Tap the Add button, the + in the upper-right corner. In the Add Alarm dialog shown in **Figure 22-12,** take any of the following actions, tapping Back after you make each setting to return to the Add Alarm dialog:

   - Tap Repeat if you want the alarm to repeat at a regular interval, such as every Monday or every Sunday.

   - Tap Label if you want to name the alarm, such as "Take Pill" or "Call Glenn."

   - Tap Sound to choose the tune the alarm will play.

   - Tap the On/Off switch for Snooze if you want to use the Snooze feature.

3. Place your finger on any of the three columns of sliding numbers at the top of the dialog and scroll to set the time you want the alarm to occur (don't forget to verify AM or PM!); then tap Save. The alarm now appears in the Alarm tab.

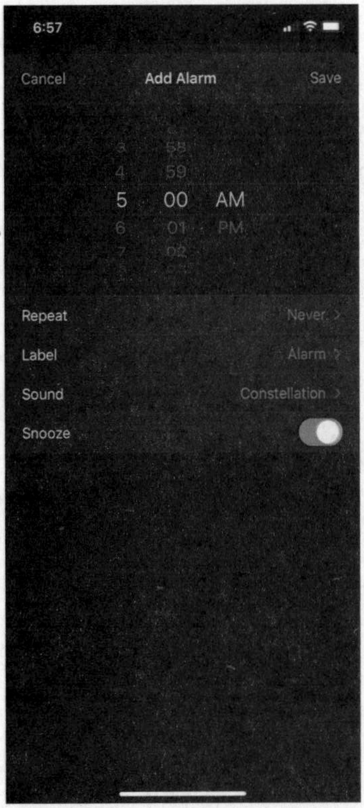

FIGURE 22-12

TIP

To delete an alarm, tap the Alarm tab and tap Edit. All alarms appear. Tap the red circle containing the minus sign, tap the Delete button, and the alarm is deleted. Be careful: When you tap the Delete button, the alarm is unretrievable and will need to be re-created from scratch if you mistakenly removed it.

Set Bedtime and Waking Alerts

The Clock can also help you develop better sleeping habits by allowing you to set bedtime and wake alerts and keeping track of your sleep habits.

1. Tap the Bedtime button at the bottom of the Clock app screen.

2. If this is your first time to open the Bedtime feature, tap Get Started and answer the questions you're asked to help configure the Bedtime settings.

3. When you've completed the initial configuration, you will see a screen displaying your bedtime and waking hours (see **Figure 22-13**).

4. You can manually change the bedtime by pressing the Bedtime button (looks like Z's) and dragging it around the clock face. You can do the same for the Wake Up time by pressing and dragging the button that looks like a bell. To keep the same amount of sleep time you can press and drag the orange band that connects the Bedtime and Wake Up buttons. You can also adjust the days the Bedtime feature is used.

5. Tap the Bedtime button in the upper-left, and then tap the Options button in the upper-left corner to configure optional settings for Bedtime (see **Figure 22-14**). You can adjust the reminder time, enable or disable the Do Not Disturb During Bedtime feature, set the Wake Up Sound, and adjust the volume for the Wake Up Sound. The other option in this screen is Track Time in Bed, which analyzes how many times you use your iPhone while in bed. Tap Done when finished (or Cancel if you don't want to make any changes).

6. Tap Bedtime, then tap the Bedtime Schedule toggle switch to Off to disable or On (green) to enable, and then tap the Bedtime button in the upper-left corner to return to the Bedtime screen.

FIGURE 22-13   **FIGURE 22-14**

TIP

On the Bedtime screen, tap the Show more in Health button to open the Health app (covered in Chapter 24) and see a history of your sleep patterns.

Use Stopwatch and Timer

Sometimes life seems like a countdown or a ticking clock counting the minutes you've spent on a certain activity. You can use the Timer and Stopwatch tabs of the Clock app to do a countdown to a specific time, such as the moment when your chocolate chip cookies are done cooking or to time an activity, such as a walk.

These two work very similarly: Tap the Stopwatch or Timer tab from Clock's screen, and then tap the Start button (see **Figure 22-15**). When you set the Timer, iPhone uses a sound to notify you when time's up. When you start the Stopwatch, you have to tap the Stop button when the activity is done.

FIGURE 22-15

TIP

Stopwatch allows you to log intermediate timings, such as a lap around a track or the periods of a timed game. With Stopwatch running, just tap the Lap button and the first interval of time is recorded. Tap Lap again to record a second interval, and so forth.

IN THIS CHAPTER

» **Make and edit reminders and lists**

» **Schedule a reminder**

» **Sync reminders and lists**

» **Complete or delete reminders**

» **Set notification types**

» **View notifications and use Notification Center**

» **Set up Do Not Disturb**

Chapter **23**

Working with Reminders and Notifications

The Reminders app and Notification Center features warm the hearts of those who need help remembering all the details of their lives.

Reminders is a kind of to-do list that lets you create tasks and set reminders so that you don't forget important commitments.

You can even be reminded to do things when you arrive at or leave a location, or receive a message from someone. For example, you can set a reminder so that, when your iPhone detects that you've left the location of your golf game, an alert reminds you to pick up your grandchildren, or when you arrive at your cabin, iPhone reminds you to turn on the water . . . you get the idea.

Notification Center allows you to review all the things you should be aware of in one place, such as mail messages, text messages, calendar appointments, and alerts.

If you occasionally need to escape all your obligations, try the Do Not Disturb feature. Turn this feature on, and you won't be bothered with alerts until you're ready to be.

In this chapter, you discover how to set up and view tasks in Reminders and how Notification Center can centralize all your alerts in one easy-to-find place.

Create a Reminder

Creating an event in Reminders is pretty darn simple:

1. Tap Reminders on the Home screen.

2. On the screen that appears, tap Reminders, and then tap the New Reminder button with a plus sign to the left of it in the lower-left corner to add a task (see **Figure 23-1**). The onscreen keyboard appears.

3. Enter a task name or description using the onscreen keyboard, and then tap Done in the upper-right corner.

TIP

The following task shows how to add more specifics about an event for which you've created a reminder.

Tap here to add tasks and reminders

FIGURE 23-1

Edit Reminder Details

TIP

1. Tap a reminder and then tap the Details button (an i in a circle) that appears to the right of it to open the Details dialog shown in **Figure 23-2.**

I deal with reminder settings in the following task.

2. Tap Notes and enter any notes about the event using the onscreen keyboard.

3. Toggle the Flagged switch to enable or disable a flag for the reminder.

4. Tap Priority and then tap None, Low (!), Medium (!!), or High (!!!) from the choices that appear. Tap Details in the upper-left to return to the Details screen.

TIP

With this version of the app, priority settings now display the associated number of exclamation points on a task in a list to remind you of its importance.

5. Tap List and then tap which list you want the reminder saved to, such as your calendar, iCloud, Exchange, or a category of reminders that you've created (see **Figure 23-3**). Tap Details in the upper-left to return to the Details screen.

6. Tap Done to save the task.

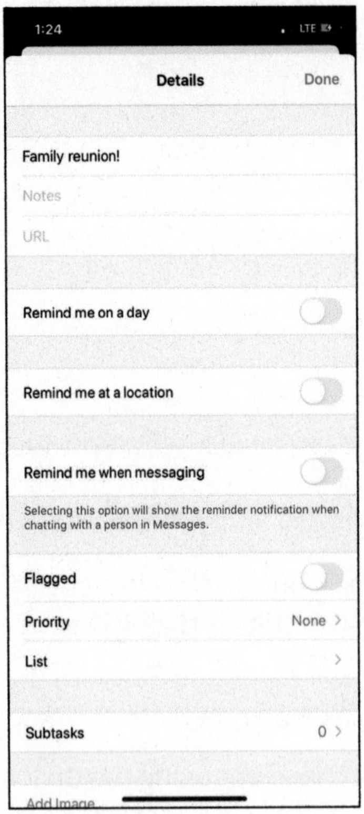

FIGURE 23-2

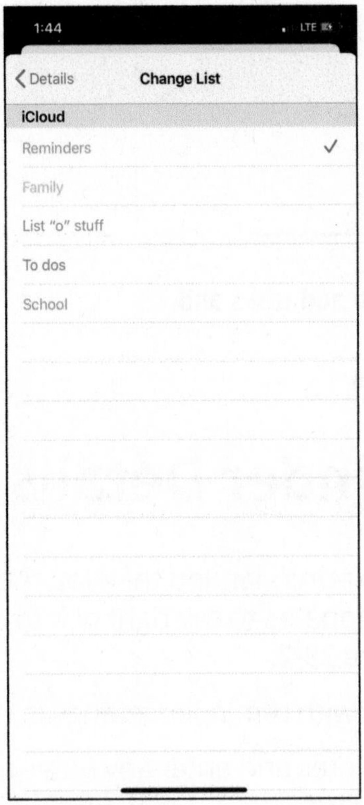

FIGURE 23-3

Reminders in iOS 13 includes a quick toolbar that appears just above the keyboard, which allows you to quickly add a time, location, flags, or images to the reminder you've tapped in a list. Just tap the icon for whichever item you want to activate and make the appropriate settings as prompted.

Schedule a Reminder by Time, Location, or When Messaging

One of the major purposes of Reminders is to remind you of upcoming tasks. To set options for a reminder, follow these steps:

1. Tap a task and then tap the Details button that appears to the right of the task.

2. In the dialog that appears (refer to **Figure 23-2**), toggle the Remind me on a day switch to turn the feature On (green).

3. Tap the Alarm field that appears below this setting (see **Figure 23-4**) to display date settings.

4. Tap and flick the month, day, and year fields to set the correct date.

5. Toggle the Remind me at a time switch to On (green).

6. Tap and flick the hour, minutes, and AM/PM fields to scroll to the correct time for the reminder. Tap Repeat and select an appropriate option if this is something you frequently need to be reminded of.

7. Toggle the Remind me at a location switch to On and then tap the Location field. If prompted, tap Allow to let Reminders use your current location.

You have to be in range of a GPS signal for the location reminder to work properly.

8. Use the field labeled Current Location to find your location or enter a location in the Search field. Tap Details in the upper-left corner to return to the task detail screen.

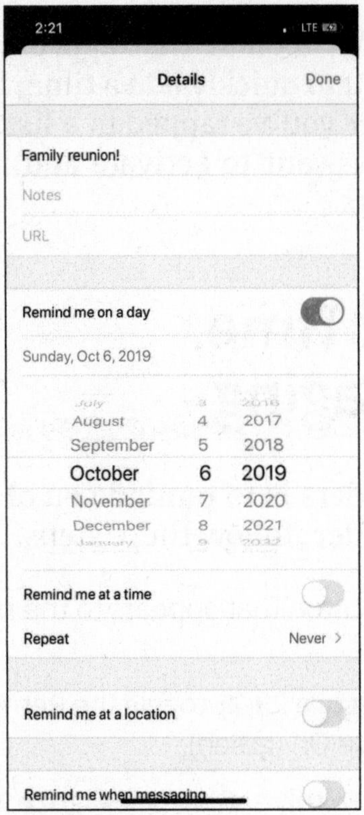

FIGURE 23-4

9. Toggle the Remind me when messaging switch to On and then tap Choose Person. Select a person or group from your Contacts. Using this option will cause you to be reminded of the item when you're engaged in messaging with the person or group selected.

10. Tap Done to save the settings for the reminder.

Create a List

You can create your own lists of tasks to help you keep different parts of your life organized and even edit the tasks on the list in List view.

1. Tap Reminders on the Home screen to open it. If a particular list is open, tap Lists in the upper-left corner to return to the List view.

2. Tap Add List in the lower-right corner to display the New List form shown in **Figure 23-5.**

FIGURE 23-5

3. Tap the text field and then enter a name for the list.

4. Tap a color; the list name will appear in that color in List view.

5. Tap an icon to customize the icon for the list. This feature helps you to better organize your lists by using icons for birthdays, medications, groceries, and whole host of other occasions and subjects (see in **Figure 23-6**).

6. Tap Done to save the list. Tap the New Reminder button to enter a task, or tap Lists in the upper-left to return to the List view.

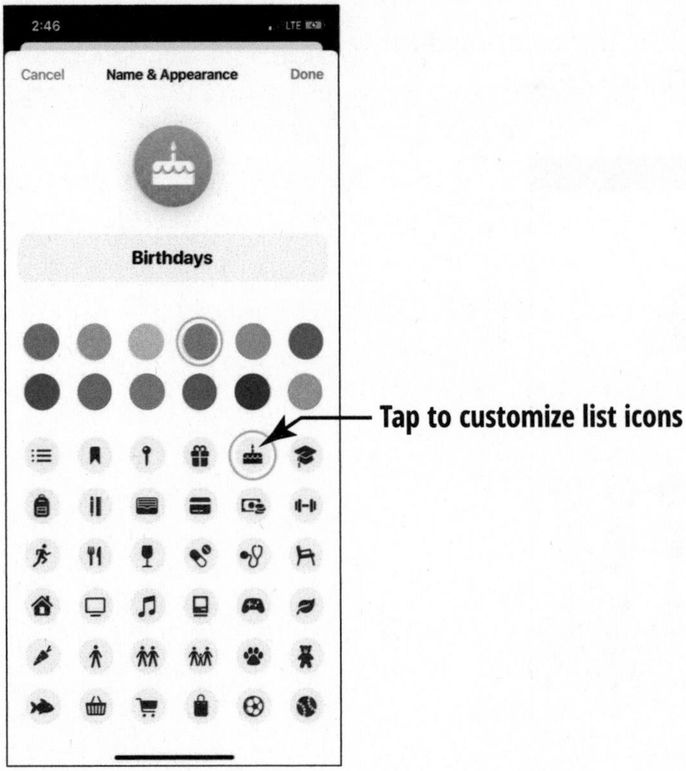

Tap to customize list icons

FIGURE 23-6

Sync with Other Devices and Calendars

To make all these settings work, you should set up your default Calendar in the Settings ➪ Calendar settings and set up your iCloud account to enable Reminders (Settings ➪ Apple ID [top of the screen] ➪ iCloud).

TIP Your default Calendar account is also your default Reminders account.

1. To determine which tasks are brought over from other calendars (such as Outlook), tap the Settings button on the Home screen.

2. Tap your Apple ID and then tap iCloud. In the dialog that appears, be sure that Reminders is set to On (green).

3. Tap Apple ID in the upper-left and then Settings in the upper-left to return to the main settings list, swipe up on the screen to scroll down a bit, and then tap Passwords & Accounts.

4. Tap the account you want to sync Reminders with and then toggle the Reminders switch to On, if available (shown in **Figure 23-7**).

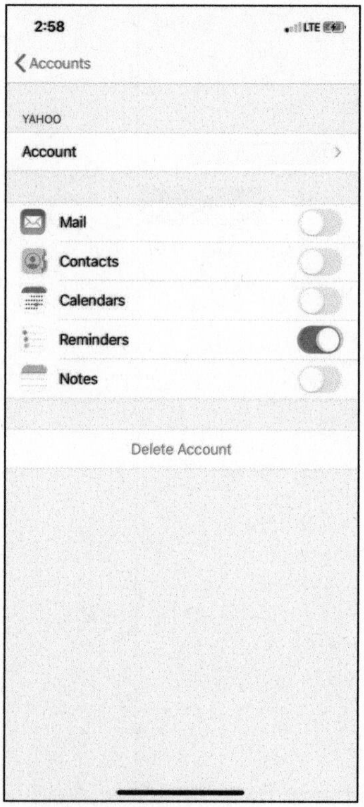

FIGURE 23-7

Mark as Complete or Delete a Reminder

You may want to mark a task as completed or just delete it entirely.

1. With Reminders open and a list of tasks displayed, tap the circle to the left of a task to mark it as complete. When you next open the list, the completed task will have been removed. To view completed tasks, tap the More button in the upper-right (looks like a gray circle containing three tiny dots) and tap Show Completed in the options

(seen in **Figure 23-8**). To hide completed tasks, just tap the More button and then tap Hide Completed.

2. To delete a single task, with the list of tasks displayed, swipe the task you want to delete to the left. Tap the red Delete button to the right of the task (see **Figure 23-9**) and it will disappear from your list.

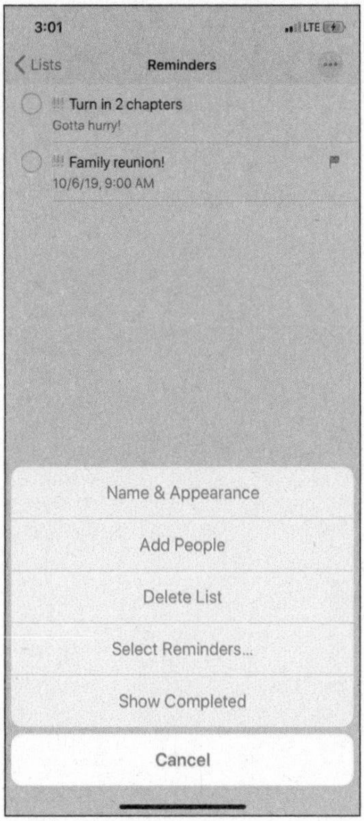

FIGURE 23-8

FIGURE 23-9

Be aware that if you delete a task, it's gone for good. There is no area in Reminders to retrieve deleted tasks. If you simply want to remove the item from the list without deleting it entirely, be sure to mark it as completed, as instructed in Step 1.

3. To delete more than one task, with the list of tasks displayed, tap the More button and tap Select Reminders in the options. In the screen shown in **Figure 23-10,** tap the circle to the left of the tasks you want to select, and then tap the Delete button in the lower-right corner.

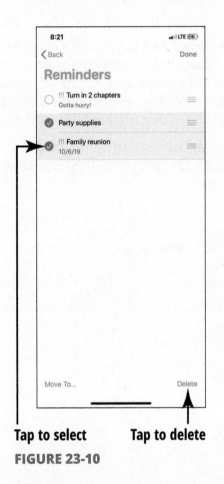

Tap to select   **Tap to delete**

FIGURE 23-10

Set Notification Types

Notification Center is a list of various alerts and scheduled events; it even provides information (such as stock quotes) that you can display by swiping down from the top of your iPhone screen. Notification Center is on by default, but you don't have to include every type of notification there if you don't want to. For example, you may never want to be notified of incoming messages but always want to have reminders listed here — it's up to you. Some Notification Center settings let you control what types of notifications are included:

1. Tap Settings and then tap Notifications.

2. In the settings that appear (see **Figure 23-11**), you see a list of items to be included in Notification Center. You can view the state of an item by reading it directly under the item's name. For example, under Accuweather in Figure 23-11, you read "Banners, Sounds, Badges," indicating the methods of notifications that are enabled for that app.

3. Tap any item. In the settings that appear, set an item's Allow Notifications switch (see **Figure 23-12**) to On or Off, to include or exclude it from Notification Center.

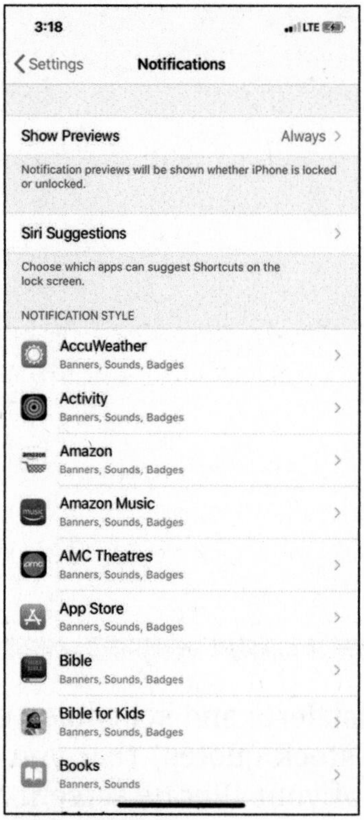

FIGURE 23-11 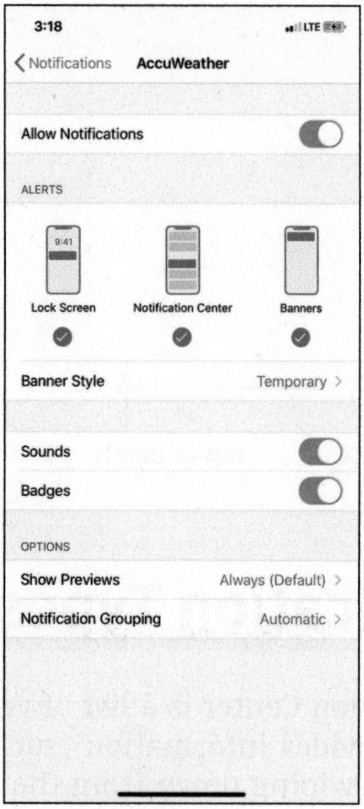   **FIGURE 23-12**

4. In the Alerts section, choose to display alerts on the lock screen, Notification Center, as Banners, or a combination of one or more. You may also decide to have no alerts appear when nothing is checked in the Alerts section.

TIP

If you enable Banners, choose a style by tapping the Banner Style option. Banners will appear and then disappear automatically if you tap the Temporary style. If you choose Persistent, you have to take an action to dismiss the alert when it appears (such as swiping it up to dismiss it or tapping to view it). Tap the Back button in the upper-left to return to the previous screen.

5. Toggle the Sounds and Badges switches On or Off to suit your taste.

6. Tap Show Previews to determine when or if previews of notifications should be shown on your iPhone's screen. Options include Always (which is default), When Unlocked (previews only appear when your iPhone is unlocked), or Never. Tap Back to go to the previous screen.

7. Select a Notification Grouping option. This feature allows you to group notifications if you like, which can keep things much cleaner, as opposed to seeing every single notification listed. Options include

- **Automatic:** Notifications are grouped according to their originating app, but they may also be sorted based on various criteria. For example, you may see more than one group for Mail if you receive multiple emails from an individual; those email notifications may merit their own grouping.

- **By App:** Notifications are grouped according to their originating app — period. You'll only see one grouping for the app, not multiple groups based on the varying criteria, as described for the Automatic setting.

- **Off:** All notifications for this app will be listed individually.

Tap the Back button to return to the previous screen.

8. Tap Notifications in the upper-left corner to return to the main Notifications settings screen. When you've finished making settings, press the Home button or swipe up from the bottom of the screen (iPhone X models and newer only).

View Notification Center

After you've made settings for what should appear in Notification Center, you'll regularly want to take a look at those alerts and reminders.

1. From any screen, tap and hold your finger at the top of the screen and drag down to display Notification Center (see **Figure 23-13**).

TIP

Swipe from left-to-right on the date at the top of the Notification Center to view other notifications such as weather, reminders, Siri app suggestions, and more. Swipe from right-to-left on the date at the top to return to app notifications.

2. To close Notification Center, swipe upward from the bottom of the screen.

FIGURE 23-13

To determine what is displayed in Notification Center, see the previous task.

There are two sections in Notification Center for you to play with: Notification Center and Today.

1. Swipe down from the top of the screen to open Notification Center. Notifications are displayed by default.

2. Swipe from left to right on the date/time at the top of Notification Center to access the Today tab to view information in widgets that pertain to today, such as Reminders, weather, stock prices, Calendar items, and other items you've selected to display in Notification Center (see the preceding task).

You select which widgets appear in the Today tab by tapping the Edit button at the bottom of the Today screen and then selecting the items you want to see. Tap Done to return to the Today screen.

3. Swipe from right to left on the date/time at the top of Today tab to go back to the Notifications section to see all notifications that you set up in the Settings app. You'll see only notifications that you haven't responded to, deleted in the Notifications section, or haven't viewed in their originating app.

Get Some Rest with Do Not Disturb

Do Not Disturb is a simple but useful setting you can use to stop any alerts, phone calls, text messages, and FaceTime calls from appearing or making a sound. You can make settings to allow calls from certain people or several repeat calls from the same person in a short time period to come through. (The assumption here is that such repeat calls may signal an emergency situation or urgent need to get through to you.)

1. Tap Settings and then tap Do Not Disturb.

2. Set the Do Not Disturb switch to On (green) to enable the feature.

3. In the other settings shown in **Figure 23-14,** do any of the following:

- Toggle the Scheduled switch to On (green) to allow alerts during a specified time period to appear.

- Tap Allow Calls From and then, from the next screen select Everyone, No One, Favorites, or Groups such as All Contacts.

- Toggle the Repeated Calls switch to On to allow a second call from the same person in a three-minute time period to come through.

- Choose to silence incoming calls and notifications Always or Only while iPhone is locked.

4. Press the Home button or swipe up from the bottom of the screen (iPhone X models and newer only) to return to the Home screen.

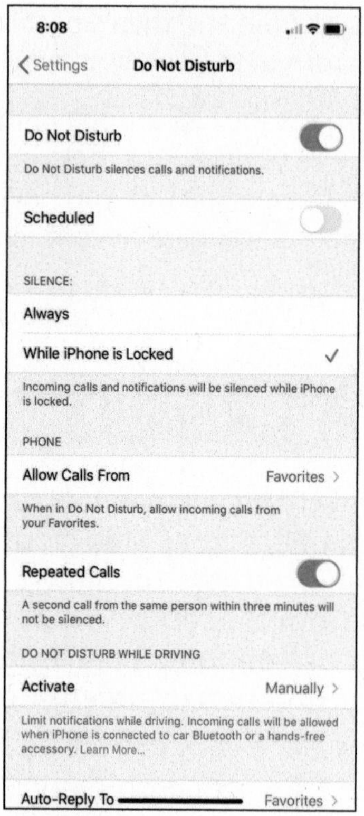

FIGURE 23-14

Chapter **24**

Keeping Tabs on Your Health

A pple has begun a major push into health and wellness, and the Health app is an important tool in the company's quest to help customers achieve a healthier life. Essentially, Health is an aggregator for health and fitness data, and it can be accessed from the first Home screen on your iPhone. You can input information about your height, weight, medications, nutrition, sleep quality, and more. You can then view exercise tracking based on that data in the dashboard view.

In this chapter, I provide an overview of the Health app and how to get information into and out of it. I also give you a glimpse at some of the possible apps and health equipment that are slated to interact with Health to make it even more useful in months and years to come.

Health App Overview

The Health app is meant to be a one-stop repository for your health information. It will not only allow you to manually input information, but it can also collect health data from other health-related apps and equipment that support working with the Health app (you'll need to check with the app's developer or the equipment's manufacturer for details on Health support).

The first time you open Health, you'll see screens informing you of what's new in iOS 13. As you progress through those screens, the last one will allow you to set up your Health Profile, shown in **Figure 24-1**. This is the most basic information about you, such as your date of birth, gender, height, and weight. Tap a field to enter the appropriate information and then tap the blue Done button when finished to be whisked into the Health app.

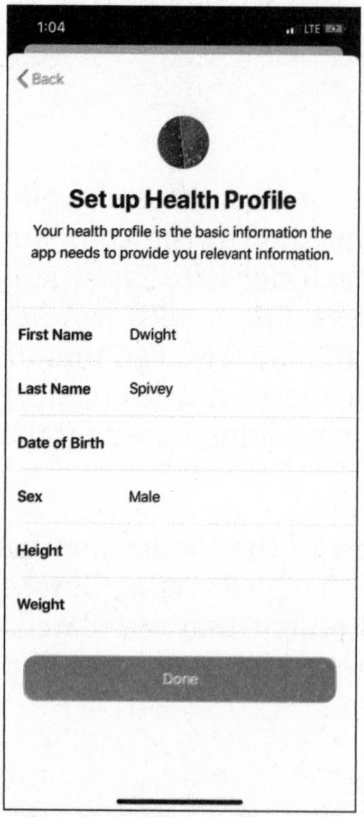

FIGURE 24-1

The first thing you're met with is the Summary screen, shown in **Figure 24-2**. Summary is a snapshot of health-related highlights and metrics that you've accumulated.

The Favorites section is a list of metrics that have been collected about your health through apps and devices. You can customize what metrics are viewed in this section:

1. Tap the blue Edit button in the upper-right corner.

2. Tap the star next to metrics you want to add (the star turns solid blue) or remove (the star turns white), shown in **Figure 24-3**.

3. Tap the Done button in the upper-right when finished. The Favorites section will now display your customized content.

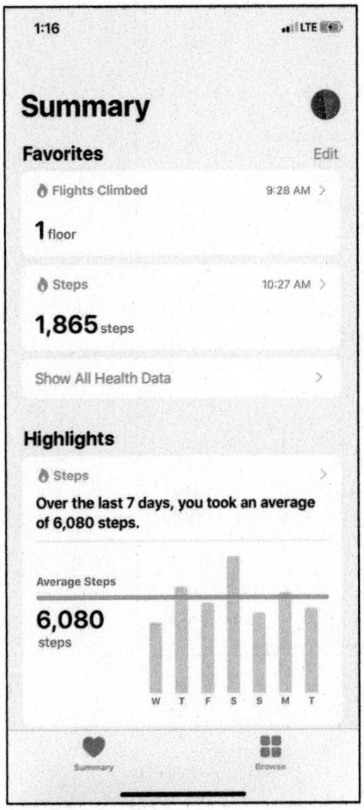

FIGURE 24-2

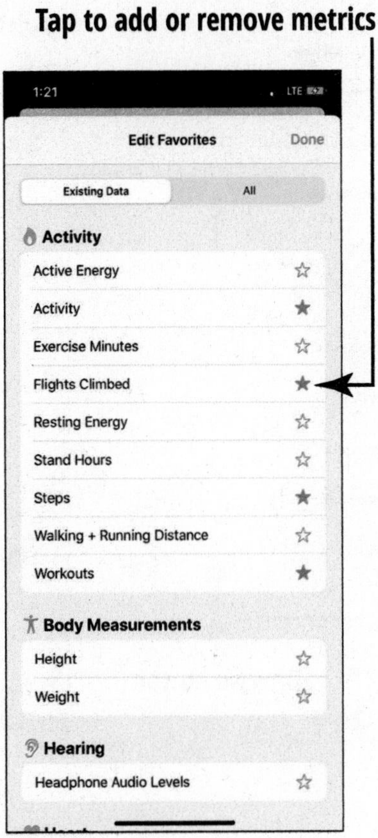

FIGURE 24-3

TIP

Tap on any of the metrics in the Favorites section to see a much more detailed breakdown of the item or activity.

Health is divided into such categories as Activity, Mindfulness, Nutrition, and Sleep. You see these categories when you tap the Browse button at the bottom of the Health screen (see **Figure 24-4**).

Each of these categories can have subtopics contained within it that you reach by tapping a main topic, such as Activity (shown in **Figure 24-5**).

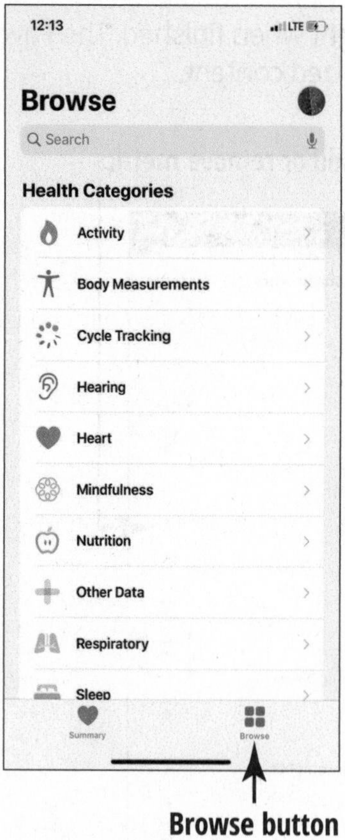

Browse button

FIGURE 24-4

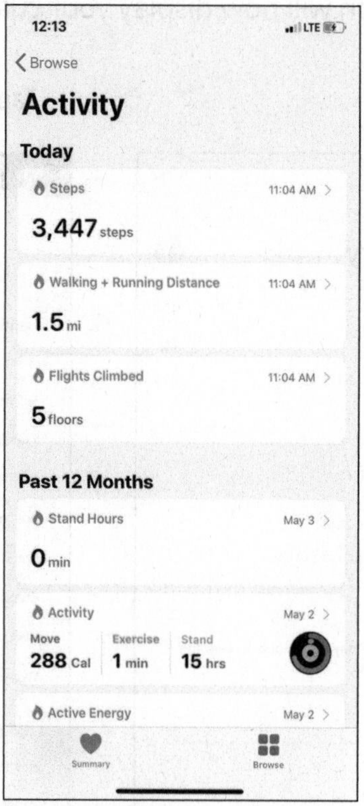

FIGURE 24-5

Categories include Activity, Body Measurements, Cycle Tracking, Hearing, Heart, Mindfulness, Nutrition, Other Data (such as blood glucose, number of times fallen, and more), Respiratory, Sleep, and Vitals.

The Health app also has a medical record feature called Medical ID, which is covered in the next task, as well as the capability to help you sign up to be an organ donor.

TECHNICAL STUFF

At some point during your use of the Health app, you may be asked to share your health and activity data with Apple. Whether you do so is, of course, entirely up to you, but be assured that if you elect to share that data with Apple, it will be done so completely anonymously and confidentially. None of your personal information will be shared as part of the health and activity data.

Apps that Health can collaborate with

Health is essentially an information aggregator, and it is continuing to grow in terms of available apps that are designed to interact with it to supply imported data, such as calories consumed and steps walked. Here are just a handful of the apps available today (there are many, many more!) that work with the Health app: Mayo Clinic, MyChart, Nike apps, Fitbit, CARROT Hunger, Human – Activity Tracker, and MyFitnessPal.

What equipment connects with Health

Health is designed to connect with a variety of equipment to wirelessly import data about your health and fitness, such as treadmills, cycling computers, indoor bike trainers, pulse oximeters, electronic toothbrushes, thermometers, glucose monitors, sleep monitors, posture trainers, smart jump ropes (no kidding!), scales, EKGs or ECGs (electrocardiograms), Apple Watch (www.apple.com/watch), blood-pressure monitors, and a very wide variety of more devices, with more on the way seemingly every day.

Create Your Medical ID

One of the simplest features is Medical ID, which allows you to store your vital statistics. This could be useful if you're in an accident and emergency medical personnel need to access such information as your blood type or allergies to medications.

1. In the Health app, tap the Apple ID button in the upper-right corner (refer to **Figure 24-2**), and then tap the Medical ID option.

2. Tap Get Started on the Set Up Your Medical ID screen.

3. Toggle the Show When Locked switch to On (seen in **Figure 24-6**) to allow your medical ID to be accessed from the lock screen. This is important to turn on so that emergency responders can see your medical information without needing you to allow them access.

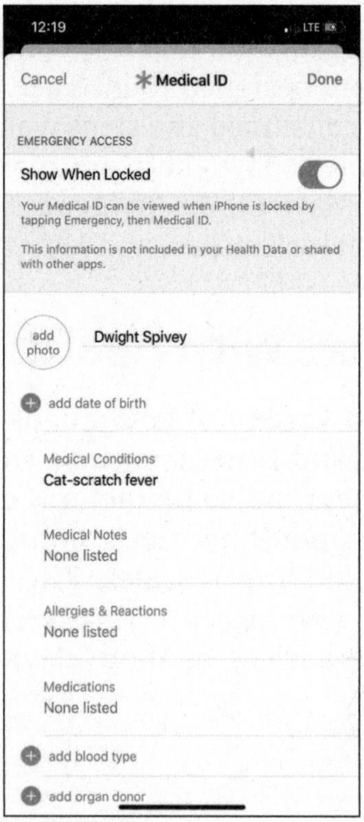

FIGURE 24-6

4. Scroll down and tap the + next to items on the screen (such as blood type) to add the particular information to your ID.

Be as specific as possible when entering your medical information! The more info healthcare providers have, the better.

TIP

5. Tap a field, such as Medical Conditions or Allergies & Reactions, to enter information using the onscreen keyboard that appears.

6. Tap Done in the upper-right corner to save your entries.

Become an Organ Donor

Apple is the first company to make it easy to sign up as an organ donor through its operating system (iOS, the software that controls your iPhone). To sign up to be an organ donor, follow these steps:

1. In the Health app, tap the Apple ID button in the upper-right corner (refer to **Figure 24-2**).

2. Tap the Organ Donation option.

3. Tap Learn More to find out more about this option, or tap Sign Up with Donate Life to become a donor. If you tap Sign Up with Donate Life, you'll be taken to the screen shown in **Figure 24-7**.

4. Enter your information as needed and then tap Continue at the bottom of the page.

5. On the next screen, you will be asked to confirm your registration with Donate Life. Tap the Complete Registration with Donate Life button at the bottom of the screen to confirm.

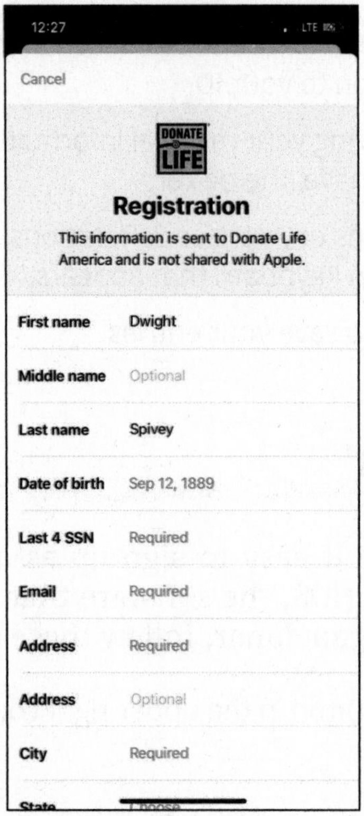

FIGURE 24-7

View Health App Data

Knowing where and how to view your health data in the Health app is important to getting the most from its features.

1. Tap the Browse button at the bottom of the Health app screen.

2. Tap a category, such as Activity.

3. Tap one of the subtopics listed, such as Steps, and you'll see a screen similar to **Figure 24-8.**

FIGURE 24-8

4. This screen can provide a wealth of information, graphically display-ing data about your activity on a daily, weekly, monthly, or yearly basis (tap D, W, M, or Y in the top bar, respectively). As you continue to scroll down, you'll see the activity data broken down into even more helpful categories. You'll find a description of exactly how this subtopic is monitored and why, and you'll see a list of apps related to the subtopic will also be listed (like that shown in **Figure 24-9).**

5. Scroll all the way down to the bottom of the screen and tap Data Sources & Access.

   If you have other health-related apps on your iPhone that can receive data from Health, they'll appear in the Apps Allowed to Read Data section. To enable or disable these apps, tap Edit in the upper-right corner, tap the app's name to enable (shown by a check mark) or dis-able it, and then tap Done in the upper-right.

6. Devices that report data to the Health app can be seen in the Data Sources section. Tap the device name to see the data it's reported to Health.

7. Tap Back in the upper-left corner of the screen to return to the previous screen, and then tap the name of the subtopic in the upper-left.

8. Tap Show All Data near the bottom of the screen (refer to **Figure 24-9**) to see a table of entries (as shown in **Figure 24-10**), including your most recent entry.

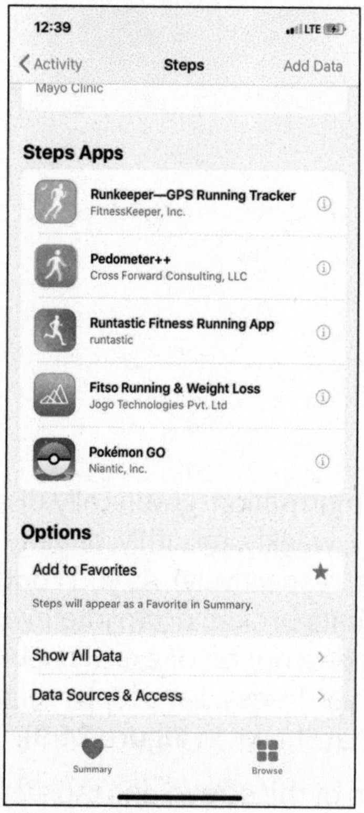

FIGURE 24-9

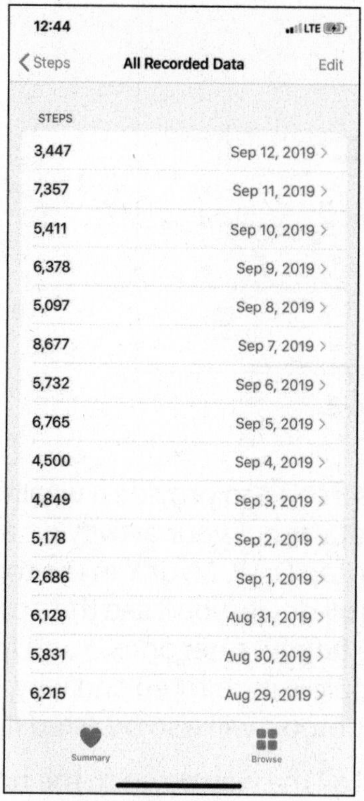

FIGURE 24-10

Import and Export Health Data

Some apps from which you can import data are MyFitnessPal, Strava: Run, Ride, Swim, and LifeSum. Different apps may send or receive data from Health using different interfaces and commands. But, in essence, here's how it works: When you use an app that supports Health, those apps will request permission to update data. For example, a pedometer or activity tracker app might be able to upload data to Health, saving you the drudgery of manual entry. Here's how you view supporting apps that you've downloaded and installed to your iPhone:

1. In the Health app, tap the Apple ID button in the upper-right corner.

2. Tap Apps in the Privacy section.

3. Tap each app to find out and modify what data it supplies to the Health app.

To find apps that work with Health, go to the App Store. Open Health & Fitness in the Categories list and scroll down until you find the Apps for Health section.

In addition, you can export data using such apps as the Mayo Clinic app so that you can keep your physician informed about your progress or challenges.

You can also export all of your Health data as a file that you can share with caregivers. Tap the Apple ID button in the upper-right, tap the Export All Health Data button at the bottom of the next screen, tap Export to confirm, and then select a method for sharing the information (text message, email, AirDrop, and more). This file may be large if you've saved a lot of information in Health, so saving it to and sharing it from the cloud using iCloud or another service like Google Drive or Dropbox may be preferred.

View Health Records

Apple's foray into healthcare is rapidly gaining momentum as patients, doctors, and other providers rely more heavily on the Apple ecosystem of devices and software. Today, hundreds of healthcare institutions (and that number is growing at a tremendous clip) are using the Health app to allow patients to view their health records right on their iPhone.

1. Contact your health provider and make sure they provide information through the Health app. Once you confirm that, ask them what account information you need to connect to their systems so that you can view your records. You'll use this information in Step 8 below.

2. Tap the Browse button on the bottom of the Health app screen.

3. Scroll down the screen until you reach the Health Records section.

4. Tap the type of record you're looking to view.

5. On the Access Your Records screen, tap Get Started.

6. Tap Allow While Using App or Allow Once to allow the Health app to access your location. This feature helps it locate providers in your area that currently provide health records through the Health app.

7. In the list that displays, locate and tap your provider, and then tap the Connect to Account button.

8. From this point, enter the account information you gathered from your provider in Step 1. Afterwards, you'll be able to view your health records from that provider in the Health app.

TIP

You can see the ever-growing list of healthcare providers using Health to allow patients to view their records by visiting Apple's Support site at https://support.apple.com/en-us/HT208647.

Chapter **25**

Troubleshooting and Maintaining Your iPhone

Phones don't grow on trees — they cost a pretty penny. That's why you should learn how to take care of your iPhone and troubleshoot any problems it might have so that you get the most out of it.

In this chapter, I provide some advice about the care and maintenance of your iPhone, as well as tips about how to solve common problems, update iPhone system software, and even reset the iPhone if something goes seriously wrong. In case you lose your iPhone, I even tell you about a feature that helps you find it, activate it remotely, or even disable it if it has fallen into the wrong hands. Finally, you get information about backing up your iPhone settings and content using iCloud.

Keep the iPhone Screen Clean

If you've been playing with your iPhone, you know (despite Apple's claim that the iPhone has a fingerprint-resistant screen) that it's a fingerprint magnet. Here are some tips for cleaning your iPhone screen:

» **Use a dry, soft cloth.** You can get most fingerprints off with a dry, soft cloth, such as the one you use to clean your eyeglasses or a cleaning tissue that's lint and chemical free. Or try products used to clean lenses in labs, such as Kimwipes (which you can get from several major retailers, such as Amazon, Walmart, and office supply stores).

» **Use a slightly dampened soft cloth.** This may sound counter-intuitive to the previous tip, but to get the surface even cleaner, very (and I stress, very) slightly dampen the soft cloth. Again, make sure that whatever cloth material you use is free of lint.

» **Remove the cables.** Turn off your iPhone and unplug any cables from it before cleaning the screen with a moistened cloth, even a very slightly moistened one.

» **Avoid too much moisture.** It's best to keep your phone dry. iPhone 7 and later models have some degree of water resistance, but you don't want to press your luck. So you don't have to freak out if you splash some water on your iPhone 11 Pro Max, but do be sure to wipe it dry right away, and it should be fine.

» **Don't use your fingers!** That's right, by using a stylus rather than your finger, you entirely avoid smearing oil from your skin or cheese from your pizza on the screen. There are a number of top-notch styluses out there; just search Amazon for "iPhone stylus" and you'll be greeted with a multitude of them (most are reasonably priced).

» **Never use household cleaners.** They can degrade the coating that keeps the iPhone screen from absorbing oil from your fingers. Plus, there's just simply no need to go that far since the screen cleans quite easily with little or no moisture at all.

TIP Don't use premoistened lens-cleaning tissues to clean your iPhone screen! Most brands of wipes contain alcohol, which can damage the screen's coating.

Protect Your Gadget with a Case

Your screen isn't the only element on the iPhone that can be damaged, so consider getting a case for it so that you can carry it around the house or travel with it safely. Besides providing a bit of padding if you drop the device, a case makes the iPhone less slippery in your hands, offering a better grip when working with it.

Several types of covers and cases are available, but be sure to get one that will fit your model of iPhone because their dimensions and button placements may differ, and some models have slightly different thicknesses. There are differences between covers and cases.

Extend Your iPhone's Battery Life

The much-touted battery life of the iPhone is a wonderful feature, but you can do some things to extend it even further. Here are a few tips to consider:

» **Keep tabs on remaining battery life.** You can estimate the amount of remaining battery life by looking at the Battery icon on the far-right end of the Status bar, at the top of your screen.

» **Use standard accessories to charge your iPhone most effectively.** When connected to a recent-model Mac or Windows computer for charging, the iPhone can slowly charge; however, the most effective way to charge your iPhone is to plug it into a wall outlet using the Lightning to USB Cable and the USB power adapter that come with your iPhone.

TIP

Third-party charging cables usually work just fine, but some are less reliable than others. If you use a third-party cable and notice that your iPhone is taking longer than usual to charge, it's a good idea to try another cable.

» **Use a case with an external battery pack.** These cases are very handy when you're traveling or unable to reach an electrical outlet easily. However, they're also a bit bulky and can be cumbersome in smaller hands.

» **The fastest way to charge iPhone is to turn it off while charging it.** If turning your iPhone completely off doesn't sound like the best idea for you, you can disable Wi-Fi or Bluetooth to facilitate a faster recharge.

TIP

Activate Airplane Mode to turn both Wi-Fi and Bluetooth off at the same time.

» **The Battery icon on the Status bar indicates when the charging is complete.**

WARNING

Be careful not to use your iPhone in ambient temperatures higher than 95-degrees Farenheit (35-degrees Celcius), as doing so may damage your battery. Damage of this kind may also not be covered under warranty. Charging in high temperatures may damage the battery even more.

TIP

If you notice that you're battery won't charge more than 80%, it could be getting too warm. Unplug the iPhone from the charger and try again after it's cooled down a bit.

Your iPhone battery is sealed in the unit, so you can't replace it yourself the way you can with many laptops or other cellphones. If the battery is out of warranty, you have to fork over about $79 to have Apple install a new one with AppleCare coverage.

Deal with a Nonresponsive iPhone

If your iPhone goes dead on you, it's most likely a power issue, so the first thing to do is to plug the Lightning to USB Cable into the USB power adapter, plug the USB power adapter into a wall outlet, plug the other end of the cable into your iPhone, and charge the battery.

Another thing to try — if you believe that an app is hanging up the iPhone — is to press the Sleep/Wake button for a couple of seconds, and then press and hold the Home button. For iPhone X and newer models, swipe up from the bottom of the screen, pause and hold your finger on the screen until the App Switcher opens, and then swipe up on the app that's causing issues. The problematic app should then close.

You can always use the tried-and-true reboot procedure: On the iPhone, you press the Sleep/Wake button on the right until the red slider appears. Drag the slider to the right to turn off your iPhone. After a few moments, press the Sleep/Wake button to boot up the little guy again.

If the situation seems drastic and none of these ideas works, try to force restart your iPhone. To do this, press the Sleep/Wake button and the Home button at the same time for at least ten seconds until the Apple logo appears onscreen. For iPhone X and newer models, press and hold the Side button until the Apple logo appears.

TIP

If your phone has this problem often, try closing out some active apps that may be running in the background and using up too much memory. To do this, press the Home button twice to open the App Switcher (swipe up from the bottom of the screen and pause for iPhone X and newer models), and then from the screen showing active apps, swipe an app upward. Also check to see that you haven't loaded up your iPhone with too much content, such as videos, which could be slowing down its performance.

Update the iOS Software

Apple occasionally updates the iPhone system software, known as iOS, to fix problems or offer enhanced features. You should occasionally check for an updated version (say, every month). You can check by connecting your iPhone to a recognized computer (that is, a computer that you've used to sign into your Apple account before) with iTunes installed, but it's even easier to just update from your iPhone Settings, though it's a tad slower:

1. Tap Settings from the Home screen.

2. Tap General and then tap Software Update (see **Figure 25-1**).

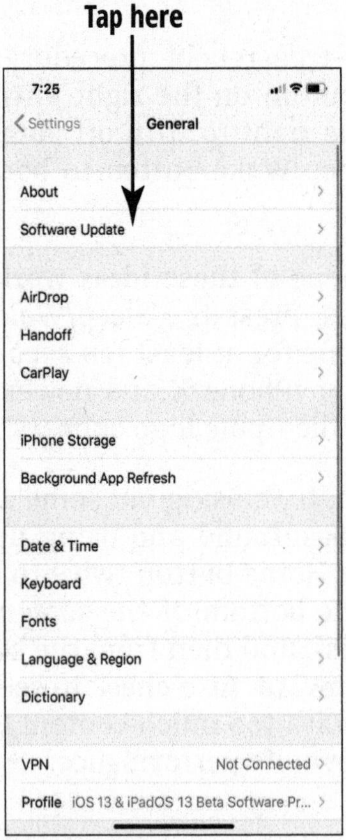

Tap here

FIGURE 25-1

3. A message tells you whether your software is up-to-date. If it's not, tap Download and Install and follow the prompts to update to the latest iOS version.

If you're having problems with your iPhone, you can use the Update feature to try to restore the current version of the software. Follow the preceding set of steps and then tap the Restore button instead of the Software Update button in Step 2.

Restore the Sound

My wife frequently has trouble with the sound on her iPhone, and subsequently we've learned quite a bit about troubleshooting sound issues, enabling us to pass our knowledge on to you. Make sure that:

» **You haven't touched the volume control buttons on the side of your iPhone.** They're on the left side of the phone.

Be sure not to touch the volume decrease button and inadvertently lower the sound to a point where you can't hear it. Pushing the volume buttons will have no effect if the iPhone is sleeping, so don't worry about this happening while the iPhone is just sitting in your pocket or purse.

» **You haven't flipped the Ringer/Silent switch.** Moving the switch located on the left side above the volume buttons mutes sound on the iPhone.

This switch can be moved if you drop your iPhone, so don't do that!

» **The speaker isn't covered up.** No, really — it may be covered in a way that muffles the sound.

» **A headset isn't plugged in.** Sound doesn't play over the speaker and the headset at the same time.

» **The volume limit is set to On.** You can set up the volume limit for the Music app to control how loudly your music can play (which is useful if you have teenagers around). Tap Settings on the Home screen and then, on the screen that displays, tap Music. Now tap Volume Limit under the Playback section if it is set to On. Use the slider that appears (see **Figure 25-2**) to set the volume limit. If the slider button is all the way to the left, you've set your volume limit too low (all the way down, as a matter of fact).

Slider button

FIGURE 25-2

TIP

When all else fails, reboot. This strategy worked for us. Just press the Sleep/Wake button until the red slider appears, and then drag the slider to the right. After the iPhone turns off, press the Sleep/Wake button again until the Apple logo appears, and you may find yourself back in business, sound-wise.

Find a Missing Apple Device

The Find My app can pinpoint the location of your Apple devices and your Apple-using friends. This app is extremely handy if you forget where you left your iPhone or someone steals it. Find My not only lets you track down the critter but also lets you wipe out the data contained in it if you have no way to get the iPhone (or other Apple device) back.

You must have an iCloud account to use Find My. If you don't have an iCloud account, see Chapter 4 to find out how to set one up.

If you're using Family Sharing, someone in your family can find your device and play a sound. This works even if the volume on the device is turned down.

Follow these steps to set up the Find My feature for your iPhone:

1. Tap Settings on the Home screen.

2. In Settings, tap your Apple ID at the top of the screen and then tap Find My.

3. In the Find My settings, tap Find My iPhone and then tap the On/Off switch for Find My iPhone to turn the feature on (see **Figure 25-3**).

You may also want to turn on the Enable Offline Finding option. This is a new option that allows Apple devices to be found using their built-in Bluetooth technology, even when not connected to Wi-Fi or a cellular network. When you mark your device as missing on www. icloud.com and another Apple user is close by the device, the two devices connect anonymously via Bluetooth and you're notified of its location. Pretty cool stuff, and completely private for all involved parties.

4. From now on, if your iPhone is lost or stolen, you can go to www. icloud.com from your computer, iPad, or another iPhone and enter your Apple ID and password.

5. In your computer's browser, the iCloud Launchpad screen appears. Click the Find iPhone button to display a map of your device's location and some helpful tools (see **Figure 25-4**).

Tap here

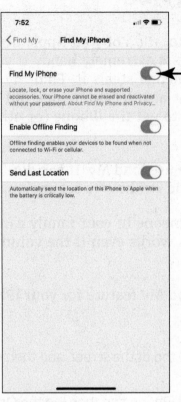

FIGURE 25-3

FIGURE 25-4

6. Click the All Devices option at the top of the window and click your iPhone in the list. In the window that appears, choose one of three options:

- To wipe information from the iPhone, click the Erase iPhone button.

- To lock the iPhone from access by others, click the Lost Mode button.

- Click Play Sound to have your iPhone play a "ping" sound that might help you locate it if you're in its vicinity.

The Erase iPhone option will delete all data from your iPhone, including contact information and content (such as music). However, even after you've erased your iPhone, it will display your phone number on the lock screen along with a message so that any Good Samaritan who finds it can contact you. If you've created an iTunes or iCloud backup, you can restore your iPhone's contents from those sources.

TIP

The Lost Mode feature allows you to send whomever has your iPhone a note saying how to return it to you.

Back Up to iCloud

You used to be able to back up your iPhone content using only iTunes, but since Apple's introduction of iCloud with iOS 5, you can back up via a Wi-Fi network to your iCloud storage. You get 5GB of storage for free or you can pay for increased storage (a total of 50GB for $0.99 per month, 200GB for $2.99 per month, or 2TB for $9.99 per month).

You must have an iCloud account to back up to iCloud. If you don't have an iCloud account, see Chapter 4 to find out more.

To perform a backup to iCloud:

1. Tap Settings from the Home screen and then tap your Apple ID at the top of the screen.

2. Tap iCloud and then tap iCloud Backup.

3. In the pane that appears, tap the iCloud Backup switch to enable automatic backups. To perform a manual backup, tap Back Up Now. A progress bar shows how your backup is moving along.

If you get your iPhone back after it wanders and you've erased it, just enter your Apple ID and password and you can reactivate it.

TIP

You can also back up your iPhone using iTunes. This method actually saves more types of content than an iCloud backup, and if you have encryption turned on in iTunes, it can save your passwords as well. However, this method does require that you connect to a computer to perform the backup. If you do back up and get a new iPhone down the line, you can restore all your data to the new phone easily.

Index

About the Author

Dwight Spivey has been a technical author and editor for over a decade, but he has been a bona fide technophile for more than three of them. He's the author of *iPhone For Seniors For Dummies*, 8th Edition (Wiley), *iPad For Seniors For Dummies*, 12th Edition (Wiley), *Idiot's Guide to Apple Watch* (Alpha), *Home Automation For Dummies* (Wiley), *How to Do Everything Pages, Keynote & Numbers* (McGraw-Hill), and many more books covering the tech gamut.

Dwight is also the Educational Technology Administrator at Spring Hill College. His technology experience is extensive, consisting of macOS, iOS, Android, Linux, and Windows operating systems in general, educational technology, desktop publishing software, laser printers and drivers, color and color management, and networking.

Dwight lives on the Gulf Coast of Alabama with his wife, Cindy, their four children, Victoria, Devyn, Emi, and Reid, and their pets, Rocky, Indy, and Rosie.

Dedication

To my nieces, Kelsey and Kelen.

I love you, ladies!

Author's Acknowledgments

Carole Jelen, agent extraordinaire, is always first to get my sincere thanks!

Next, the fantastic editors, designers, and other Wiley professionals are truly critical to completion of these books I'm so blessed to write. I hope every individual involved at every level knows how grateful I am for their dedication, hard work, and patience in putting together this book. Extra-special gratitude to Ashley Barth, Tim Gallan, and Tom Egan.

Publisher's Acknowledgments

Acquisitions Editor: Ashley Coffey

Project Editor: Tim Gallan

Production Editor: Mohammed Zafar Ali

Proofreader: Debbye Butler

Technical Reviewer: Thomas Egan

Cover Image: © pixelfit/Getty Image